Circumstances

David F. Bell

Circumstances:
Chance in the Literary Text

University of Nebraska Press Lincoln and London

Library of Congress
Cataloging-
in-Publication Data
Bell, David F.
Circumstances:
chance in the literary text
/David F. Bell. p. cm.
Includes bibliograph-
ical references and index.
ISBN 0-8032-1229-1 (cl)
1. French Fiction – 19th
century – History and
criticism.
2. Balzac, Honoré de,
1799–1850 – Criticism
and interpretation.
3. Stendhal, 1783–1842
Criticism and interpretation.
4. Realism in literature.
5. Chance in literature.
I. Title. PQ520.B37   1993
843'.70912–dc20
92-5568 CIP

For Dorian and Sophie

Contents

Acknowledgments

My thanks to the National Endowment for the Humanities for a generous grant during 1990–91, without which this project could not have been completed in such ideal conditions. The sabbatical accorded me by Duke University during the 1990–91 academic year was a mark of support for which I am extremely grateful. I would also like to express my deepest appreciation to the staff at the National Humanities Center for inviting me to spend ten months during 1990–91 at the Center and for providing me with the most congenial and stimulating working atmosphere imaginable. Thanks are also in order for Nancy Grey, who tirelessly compiled the bibliography and provided numerous wise editorial suggestions.

An early version of the first part of chapter 3 was published as "Balzac with Laplace: Remarks on the Status of Chance in Balzacian Narrative," in George Levine, ed., *One Culture: Essays in Science and Literature* (Madison: University of Wisconsin Press, 1987), pp. 180–99, © 1987 by the Board of Regents of the University of Wisconsin System. I thank the University of Wisconsin Press for permission to reproduce this material in revised form.

[Chance, a thousand fortuitous causes, a thousand unforeseen circumstances, accomplish what force and reason cannot accomplish or, rather, precisely because chance directs them, force is helpless. No matter what energy one gives dice when they leave the hand, they still do not come to rest any more easily on the desired number.]

Le hasard, mille causes fortuites, mille circonstances
imprévues font ce que la force et la raison ne sauraient
faire; ou plutôt, c'est précisément parce que le hasard les
dirige que la force n'y peut rien: comme les dés qui
partent de la main, quelque impulsion qu'on leur
donne, n'en amènent pas plus aisément le point qu'on
désire.—Rousseau

Introduction

The idea of studying chance, random, and disorderly phenomena in the context of the French realist novel must at first glance seem improbable, if not frankly paradoxical. Born in the first years of the nineteenth century, at essentially the same moment as the fledgling but rapidly developing discipline of historical analysis, the realist novel shared a set of presuppositions with the texts and the types of reasoning that the activity of historical study was beginning to produce. Not the least of these was a strong faith in the interpretative power of causal explanation, in the potential for using such explanation to decipher the significance of events by revealing hidden sequences of causes leading toward them. As Cornelius Castoriadis maintains, "It is certain that we cannot conceive of history without the category of causality, and it is perhaps even true, contrary to what idealist philosophers have affirmed, that history is the domain par excellence where causality has a meaning for us, since here cause assumes, at a preliminary level, the form of motivation, and thus we can understand a 'causal' chain, something we can never do in the case of natural phenomena."[1] The heating up of a flat surface that occurs when the sun shines on it, for example, signals a connection that, although imposed by a certain inductive necessity, will never be fully assimilated. It is a predictable phenomenon but one which is destined to remain to some extent incomprehensible, exterior to our innermost experience. Plunged into the midst of social and historical existence, however, we constantly explain our actions and relations in terms of motivations couched in causal reasoning and are truly at home within that method of rationalizing the world. Castoriadis continues:

There is causality in social and historical life because there is such a thing as "subjective rationality": the arrangement of the Carthaginian troops at Cannes (and their victory) is the result of Hannibal's rational plan. There is causality also because there is "objective rationality," because natural causal relations and purely logical necessities are constantly present in historical relations: under certain technological and economic conditions, the production of steel and the mining of coal are in a constant and quantifiable (more generally, functional) relation. And there is also "raw causality," which we recognize without being capable of reducing it to rational subjective or objective relations, correlations that are established of which we ignore the basis, regularities of behavior, both individual and social, which remain pure facts. (pp.60–61)

From the broadest down to the most minute, detailed perspective, causal reasoning appears to dominate analysis of historical and social developments.

The seduction exercised by the category of causality in the domain of history and of the novel derives from an additional source, moreover. The source is to be found in the significance attributed to historical developments *after the fact,* lending them an air of inevitability and coherence which the actors involved in those developments could never have grasped in the heat of events. For all intents and purposes, large-scale historical movements (the development of capitalism, for example) are the result of a myriad of processes and types of behavior that, taken individually, cannot reveal the overall structure being formulated during a given period. When combined, they produce an identifiable historical state or structure capable of being analyzed as an entity once it has been generated. History, continually in the process of revealing itself, seems to have a motor all its own which drives it, despite and beyond the individual participants. It thus appears eminently rational and explicable through causal reasoning (but only after the fact). What is at stake here is what Hegel termed the *ruse de la raison,* about which I shall have more to say in chapter 2. Suffice it to observe at present that Balzac, for example, was partially a contemporary of Hegel (slightly more than a generation younger than Hegel was) and that his view of the development of history bears much relation to Hegel's in the generalized attempt to reconstruct and rationalize the broad processes which propel large historical evolutions. One need only cite *Les Paysans* as an example demonstrating amply that Balzac was capable of visualizing history at a universal level, integrating individual actors whose own consciousness of the direction in which their particular and singular acts were leading them was necessarily incomplete. In the preface to *La Comédie humaine,* Balzac goes so far as to express theoretically the concerns that occupied him during the writing of his social fresco or, perhaps more correctly stated, to couch his writing in theoretical terms in hindsight. He reveals in a conscious reflection his own penchant for broad generalization, which a novel like *Les Paysans* illustrates: "Was it not necessary to study the reasons or reason behind these social effects, to discover the hidden meaning of this immense collection of figures, passions, and events. . . . Thus portrayed, Society must carry within itself the reason for its movement."[2] Several stylistic elements in this statement are characteristic of the attitude toward history I have been outlining. The word "reasons" (*raisons*), for example, quickly becomes singular, "reason" (*raison*), with the attendant implications in French—not just a reason (one of many), but Reason in a more Hegelian sense. In addition, "Society" (*la Société*) is capitalized and ultimately personified as a force above and beyond its individual members, with its own movement, its own set of laws of development. An even balder statement of Balzac's attitude toward the question of causal explanation occurs in *Le*

Cousin Pons: "In fact, everything is linked to everything else in the real world. Every movement corresponds to a cause, every cause is linked to the whole, and, consequently, the whole is represented in the smallest movement of the part" (7:587).[3]

The apparent ease with which historical events can be analyzed by means of causal reasoning succumbs, however, to an important restriction tied to the essential nature of human social structures.[4] The fact remains that the individual is capable of acting in atypical fashion, of behaving in a manner outside the norm and thus of introducing noise and disturbances into any generalized laws of social and historical development. But this alone is not sufficient reason to abandon a determinist and causal approach to historical and social analysis, at least at the global level. Even if such atypical behavior is in some sense aleatory, it is susceptible to calculation based on probabilities and can be incorporated into a broadly deterministic framework. What undoes a causal approach to history in a more fundamental sense is the behavior of individual historical actors, which is not simply unpredictable (if approached from a point of view focusing on the singular) but creative: "the noncausal . . . appears not simply as 'unpredictable,' but as creative (of individuals, of groups, of classes, or of entire societies); not simply as a divergence with respect to an existing type, but indeed as a *place* [*position*] for a new type of behavior, as the *institution* of a new social rule, as an *invention* of a new object or form, in short, as a coming into view or production which cannot be deduced from the preceding situation, a conclusion which surpasses the premises or which is the place of new premises."[5] Historical analysis—and the realist novel for which such analysis is an indispensable model and support—becomes the seat of conflicting tendencies. On the one hand, there is the desire to explain everything, to motivate everything; on the other hand, one realizes that society and history are also the domain in which creation and the new are possible, where chance and potential disorder inevitably appear and by their appearance provoke something original, both unexpected and radically different.

These issues are at the heart of the texts of Stendhal and Balzac with which I deal in the following chapters. Within works conceived to represent in some sense a series of historical and social developments and thus to explicate the logic of such developments in a rational and deterministic way—that is, in a manner largely dependent on causal reasoning—certain events, acts, and behaviors unsusceptible to such analyses always seem to surge forth at crucial moments. The same Balzac who expresses confidence in the possibility of discovering history's reason, as we saw above, is simultaneously fascinated by phenomena which cannot be explained in a straightforward causal fashion and makes an observation such as the following in his preface: "The Social State contains chance events [*des hasards*] that Nature does not permit" (1:9). By the same token, Stendhal will create a pair of main characters in *La Chartreuse de Parme* who are governed by something more subtle than simple causal strategies in their attempts to demonstrate their personal worth.

Illustrations of the tensions elucidated here can be found elsewhere in the cultural productions of the period. To prove my point, I shall turn for a moment to a book which appeared in 1832, that is, at essentially the same time that Balzac's and Stendhal's major works began appearing and that the two novelists were formulating their mature novelistic praxis. The book to which I am referring is Carl von Clausewitz's *On War*. As one of Clausewitz's commentators states: "Clausewitz views war as a rational instrument of national policy."[6] Far from representing the act of personal and national vengeance it has so often been in the past, war should become a calculated endeavor, just like any other decision of national principle. One of the first steps to take in order to rationalize war is to understand its parts, which can be divided at the broadest level, according to Clausewitz, into *tactic* and *strategy*: "[fighting] consists of a greater or lesser number of single *acts, each complete in itself,* which . . . are called "engagements" and which form new entities. This gives rise to the completely different activity of *planning and executing these engagements themselves,* and of coordinating each of them with the others in order to further the object of the war. One has been called *tactics,* the other *strategy*."[7] A version and interpretation of this division will be a central element in my discussion of Stendhal's *La Chartreuse de Parme* in chapters 1 and 2, for the issue at stake here involves a great deal more than simple nomenclature and categorization (as Clausewitz himself grasped well enough). I will argue that nothing less than the possibility of theory is at stake in such a dichotomy. For the present, I should like to outline very briefly how Clausewitz's distinction between strategy and tactic encounters, in a way not unlike what occurs in Stendhal's and Balzac's writings, the cleavage between the causal approach—always, at least at the surface, conceived as the expression of what is most rationalizable in any given situation—and chance phenomena, which introduce a certain amount of noise into neat causal diagrams. If indeed war should be an instrument of rational policy, then strategy must logically be of primary importance. Only at the level of the general direction of policy can one grasp the totality of political and military actions and thus keep to the right path over the long haul: "Everything in strategy is very simple, but that does not mean that everything is very easy. Once it has been determined, from the political conditions, what a war is meant to achieve and what it can achieve, it is easy to chart the course. But great strength of character, as well as great lucidity and firmness of mind, is required in order to follow through steadily, to carry out the plan, and not to be thrown off course by thousands of diversions" (p.178). Only someone who is possessed of unusual qualities will be capable not only of conceiving a strategy but of following it to the hilt. Clausewitz clearly valorizes strategy as the broader and more encompassing of the types of approaches and actions that make up the domain of war: "It takes more strength of will to make an important decision in strategy than in tactics" (p.178).

On the other hand, however, the domain of tactics contains the very element which at every moment risks overturning the plans that the strategist intends to implement, namely, the aleatory in the form of the chance event: "No other human activity is so continuously or universally bound up with chance" (p.85). And shortly thereafter, "Should theory leave us here, and cheerfully go on elaborating absolute conclusions and prescriptions? Then it would be no use at all in real life. No, it must also take the human factor into account. . . . It must always leave a margin for uncertainty" (p.86). The heat of combat is precisely the domain where situations arise which have not been and can never be calculated and which produce disturbances that can easily escalate and force the demise of any strategy. Like the novelist or the historian, Clausewitz is forced to walk a difficult line which represents an insoluble dilemma. How can war become a true instrument of rational policy when the aleatory occurrence of an event on the battlefield, in tactical combat, can always potentially destroy the general strategy in the name of which the war was launched in the first place? It is not enough to claim that intelligence and strength of character will grant a stability sufficient to overcome in time the many fortuitous circumstances arising in the course of a campaign. Any strategist who steadfastly pursues a preconceived plan is destined to fail. The aleatory events produced on the battlefield do more than make it difficult to follow through on a strategy; they *alter* strategy profoundly. The basic question remains unanswered despite all attempts to describe the interaction between strategy and tactic: what precisely is a strategy in war if one is to give the full measure of importance to aleatory phenomena? Which comes first and which should dominate? There is no easy answer to that question—any response is necessarily caught up in the dynamics of shifting perspectives and circumstances. Without pursuing the issue in detail as it is played out in Clausewitz's text, I will say that the problem he confronts is not unlike the one found at another level in the fictional texts of Balzac or Stendhal. I do not in the least wish to claim that either author knew of Clausewitz's work, but I think it not without interest to encounter another contemporary version of the same type of problem facing the novelist and historian of the period.

I would like to return for a moment to the statement quoted above from Balzac's preface, namely, "The Social State contains chance events [*des hasards*] that Nature does not permit" (1:9). There is a crucial distinction drawn here between natural phenomena and social phenomena. Balzac's observation comes on the heels of a short discussion in which he compares his project in *La Comédie humaine* to that of the biological and natural sciences in search of an explanation for the development of the countless animal and plant species. Balzac has undertaken in his own project to explain social development in a similar manner. There are differences, however: "Among animals there are few dramas, confusion hardly occurs; they simply clash with one another, period. Men also clash with one another, but the level of their intelligence makes the combat quite a bit more complicated" (1:9). We are not far here from the point Castoriadis makes when he claims that the potential for singular atypical behavior is also the potential for the new and creative. What I want to emphasize for the present, however, is the proximity between Balzac's project and the scientific models available to him. I shall argue in detail in chapter 3 that the deterministic framework given to science by the Laplacean synthesis of Newtonian physics was a tremendously influential scientific model at the time when both Stendhal and Balzac were producing their works. One may indeed counter that Laplace's demon was the image of an ideal which even Laplace knew was unattainable, but the demon nevertheless provided a neat and all-too-seductive figure for ambitions of total mastery in science during a good part of the nineteenth century—and it periodically resurfaces in scientific discussions even in the twentieth century. Laplace's demon illustrates in a striking, even poetic fashion a universe in which everything is determined and in which causal chains can be discovered leading up to and out from any given set of initial conditions.

My point is that the causal perspective on events in human society was furnished to the realist novelist by the science of the period as well as by the model produced by the fledgling discipline of historical analysis. And just as the novelist encounters tension between explanation based on a causal approach, on the one hand, and the occurrence of aleatory circumstances, on the other, so also do certain mathematicians and scientists immediately begin questioning Laplacean determinism both at the time of Laplace and beyond. In chapters 2 and 3, I will explore, for example, a series of parallels between the French mathematician Auguste Cournot's conceptions of chance and the typical realist device of chance encounters. Cournot's major texts that treat the question of chance were published shortly before and shortly after Balzac's death. As was true in the case of Clausewitz's book on war, I do not claim that Balzac actually read or knew of Cournot's work. I do maintain, however, that the problematic confronted by both (and by Stendhal as well) can be identified in a variety of places in the cultural production of the period.

At this point in my discussion, perhaps it would be useful to address the question of "influence," since indeed I have just indicated two possible directions outside of literature in which one might look in order to reflect on the formulation of the realist novelistic praxis. I put the term in quotation marks because it has come under some scrutiny in recent critical thought. Too often the problem of deciding what influence a given thinker or text exercised on a writer has been dealt with by an attempt to ascertain whether or not the writer in question read, either directly or indirectly, the work of the thinker or the particular text at stake in the discussion. To couch the question in these terms amounts to a reduction of the problem to an erudite exercise, which often makes for some rather fascinating footnotes but which also encourages a fragmentary view of the literary text. In his study of Emile Zola, Michel Serres faced this problem in a crucial way, since Zola left a large quantity of indications concerning the sources of his various theories on heredity, for example, in the copious notes he took in preparation for the actual composition of his novels. What, then, should one do when faced with the question of the place of science in Zola's text? Should one simply focus on the notes? Says Serres:

Example: recognize, in the story, the novel, or the play, scientific elements put there on purpose, imported from this or that shelf [in the library] into the text itself. That is, destroy the story as such and atomize it into preparatory notes. One can give oneself over to this destruction by means of the science of the erudite which hides a hatred. Talent is so detested that one analyzes its production with hairsplitting sharpness. The text no longer exists except in the form of scattered members found, from book to book, in the subset of reference.[8]

The quickest way to reduce the stature of any writer—and perhaps this is even more the case for the realist or naturalist writer than for any other—is to claim that he or she borrowed everything from other existing sources and subsequently to set out in search of those sources, whether they are in the scientific domain, in the works of his or her literary predecessors, or in any other cultural area. The only way to avoid such reductionism is to accept the text as a phenomenon which must be addressed on its own terms. As Serres puts it, "Do not destroy the text, leave it there, a phenomenon" (p.16). The literary work is not produced in a vacuum, but neither can it be reduced to a series of quotations, direct or indirect, borrowed from other sources. Only at the level of its specific structures does the work reveal its relation to the culture in which it was produced.

The problem is perhaps even more acute in instances when the critic refers to developments in the scientific domain in order to draw parallels with elements occurring in literary texts. The immediate reaction is too often the question of whether the writer actually knew anything about the science in question: had he read the work of a given scientist or theoretician? Apparently innocent, this inquiry in fact hides a major presupposition and prejudice, which is the following: nothing seriously scientific, or even philosophically important for that matter, can occur in a literary text. Anything scientific or truly philosophical in nature appearing in a literary text can only be borrowed, a secondary reflection of knowledge taken from another source. When I first presented part of my argument concerning Balzac, Laplace, and Cournot in chapter 3 to a colloquium audience early in the formulation of my project, one of the participants, on cue as it were, asked me if Balzac had read Cournot and indicated that my analysis would be more convincing if I could prove that fact. I did not respond in a particularly interesting way at the time, but I think that now I would simply turn the tables on the questioner. It seems to me impossible that Cournot could ever have developed his theoretical definition of chance (see chapters 2 and 3 for a detailed discussion of that definition) if he had not been a reader of the melodramatic and realist works which were part and parcel of the cultural context that formed him. I would thus be tempted to say that it was Cournot who needed to read Balzac rather than the reverse; in other words, in order for the scientific imagination to exorcise the seductive demon of Laplace, it had to look in many different cultural nooks and crannies for new ideas. Literature in its own rigor has its place in the formation of new scientific theories and research projects.

This is more often the case in science than many would like to admit. Since the eighteenth century, science has been ideologically presented to scientists and laymen alike as the foremost activity for curbing fuzzy, romantic, inexact thinking, for introducing a kind of rigorous reasoning that is duplicated nowhere else in human intellectual endeavors. Whatever one may respond to this rather narrow view of the meaning of science (the question is too vast to take up in this context), it is quite easy to discover immediately instances in which literary or visionary approaches to questions have inspired scientists and led to crucial breakthroughs.[9] One need look no further than recent developments in chaos theory. James Gleick, in a history of the development of the science of chaos, points out how important certain pseudoscientific works have been in setting directions for theories about chaotic phenomena: Goethe's essay on color, for example, or a book by one of Goethe's followers, Theodor Schwenk.[10] " 'Sensitive chaos'—*Das sensible Chaos*—was Schwenk's phrase for the relation between force and form. He used it for the title of a strange little book first published in 1965 and falling sporadically in and out of print thereafter. . . . Little pretense at science marred Schwenk's exposition, and none at mathematics.

Yet he observed flawlessly. He laid out a multitude of natural flowing shapes with an artist's eye. . . . He had an open-mindedness and a naïveté that would have made Goethe proud" (p.197). The capacity to grasp in an artistic and creative manner phenomena that otherwise have been ignored by the scientific establishment may sooner or later lead to breakthroughs inspired by the kind of overall and generalizing vision that is all too often missing in the technological approach to science prevailing in most research contexts.

The question of the relation between science and literature is indeed an important issue in parts of my analysis devoted to Balzac, but the problem of chance has been raised and analyzed in other sections of my work at other levels. The first two chapters, on Stendhal, are devoted more to the question of the limits of theory to be found in the vicinity of certain borderlines between order and disorder. Stendhal's *La Chartreuse de Parme* has often been described, and rightly so, in my opinion, as a sort of political treatise. Maneuvering within the political domain demands a requisite amount of guile in regions over which one never possesses perfect control or about which one's knowledge remains, of necessity, sketchy at best. I try to interpret Fabrice's and Gina's behavior in this light and assert that success for them depends on the capacity to realize the potential contained in unique moments when occasions for action occur. An analysis of *La Chartreuse de Parme* from the perspective I adopt inevitably confronts the problem of superstition as it is revealed in the novel, and this permits me to treat the relations between superstition and chance and between chance and interpretation, paying particular attention to how these relations are played out in one of the most ambitious of modern attempts at interpretation—Freudian psychoanalysis.

Ultimately, what interests me in both Balzac and Stendhal is the manifestation of yet another form of the interplay between chance and theory (or interpretation or explanation), which has accompanied the rise of both philosophical and scientific thought in the West. Marcel Détienne and Jean-Pierre Vernant have shown that from the beginning the development of Greek philosophy was accompanied by an interest in a kind of dirty praxis, the manifestations of which they have grouped under the heading of the goddess Metis.[11] The kinds of interventions Metis represents are tied to auspicious occasions, the right moment, unforeseen circumstances, and the like, when a certain kind of ruse is able to seize the opportunity to defeat the clairvoyance of the theoretician-master. Closer to us, it is a well-documented fact that the development of scientific and mathematical reasoning at the end of the Renaissance was accompanied by an interest in the question of probability and the problem of how to deal with chance within the broad context of the goal of the scientist, which is to discover and formulate regularities and general laws. The fascination with chance arose in the midst of an increasing interest in games of chance in early-seventeenth-century England and France, and I shall have more to say about the significance of chance in the game in chapter 4.[12] While interest in chance thus demonstrably accompanies developments in theory (often in the form of manifestations at the level of popular culture), the advance of theory has systematically been accomplished at the expense of chance phenomena. One of the most contemporary illustrations of the tendency is the ideal scientific experiment, which requires that noise be totally excluded. Inasmuch as this is impossible, the scientist is forced to ignore noise and to focus, rather, on what can be generalized in the experimental results in order to gain information from the experiment. But what if the noise is not simply interference? What if it is instead the manifestation of another kind of structure, one that is worthy of exploration in its own right? It turns out to be just a bit too easy to claim that chance disappears in the wake of theory's progress, to dismiss chance as nothing more than ignorance destined to be absorbed by increasing knowledge. The reader will progressively discover that I would grant a more essential role to chance phenomena.

The interplay between chance and order is one which became more and more acute as the nineteenth century progressed and which has now, in the latter part of the twentieth century, led toward a potential paradigm shift (in Thomas Kuhn's sense) in physics, chemistry, and biology. For this reason, I will conclude this book with a short analysis of a "noisy" debate which took place in France in 1980–81. The reader will see that a definitive interpretation of the relation between chance and order is still a crucial subject of discussion and is, perhaps, a part of the insoluble problem of the structure of the world which drives science and thought itself ever forward. We shall perhaps also be reminded, in the course of an analysis of these matters, that the separation between theory and practice under which we all too often operate is not only artificial but in many ways unfruitful.

[The immense difficulty of conquering and the dark uncertainty of the event.]

L'immensité de la difficulté à vaincre
et la noire incertitude de l'événement. —Stendhal

CHAPTER ONE

Tactics for Auspicious Occasions in *La Chartreuse de Parme*

Toward the end of the first part of *La Chartreuse de Parme,* the story's main character, Fabrice, increasingly unhappy with the ambivalent role of odd man out he is obliged to play between Gina, his aunt, and Mosca, Gina's lover, leaves Parma to visit his mother on the occasion of his sister's wedding and to make a surprise trip to Grianta to see his former mentor, Abbé Blanès. The journey undertaken is more than just an interlude for Fabrice, it is a veritable pilgrimage back to his sources in preparation for a symbolic break—from Gina, but, more important, from his own childhood. This episode will provide his final glimpse of Blanès and mark the last time he will go back to the château where he spent much of his youth. In the course of his return to Parma after the visit, an incident occurs that adds to the symbolic nature of the whole episode, because it later furnishes the occasion for a political lesson of no small import when Fabrice discusses the trip with Mosca and Gina following his reappearance in Parma.

I am referring to the theft of a horse by Fabrice on the road leading to the place where he is to meet the boat for his trip back across Lake Maggiore en route to Parma. The details of this incident merit consideration. The narrative segment begins when Fabrice takes refuge inside a hollow tree trunk after reflecting on the difficulties he might experience were he to encounter the Austrian border guards and customs officials (he is only a few miles from the Swiss-Austrian frontier). When he overhears a singing servant who is leading a horse down the road, Fabrice decides that the horse is the answer to his desire for a swift exit, and he steals it—or, rather, borrows it. Unwilling to harm the servant, he pays him instead of shooting him and even promises to send the horse back after he has finished with it—at the risk of being denounced and pursued. This choice of behavior immediately prompts self-criticism in anticipation of Mosca's commentary: " 'Ah! if only I reasoned like Mosca,' Fabrice said to himself, 'when he tells me repeatedly that the dangers a man faces are always the measure of his rights over his fellow man.' "[1] Mosca's reaction to the events will indeed be a variation on the same theme and will later be summed up by the following remark: "It's better to kill the devil than to be killed by him" (2:184).

But before we explore the meaning of the lesson itself and the reaction it provokes, it is important to emphasize several significant elements in the description of the event cited above, because together they furnish a structure that will have far-reaching repercussions in the course of the present analysis. First, this is one in a long and fascinating series of equestrian happenings in Stendhal's fiction. Fabrice himself was unceremoniously unhorsed by thieves during his Waterloo adventure at the beginning of the first part of *La Chartreuse de Parme*. Second, the chance nature of the meeting between Fabrice and the valet is of considerable importance. While reflecting on the perilous nature of his situation, Fabrice just happens to hear the valet's song and therefore discovers a solution to his dilemma. The previously dissimilar and distinct paths of the scene's two protagonists cross at a critical point where their unforeseen intersection provokes an event that becomes an occasion for action when Fabrice realizes its potential. The instant containing that occasion seems almost a suspension in time, graphically demonstrated when the valet is immobilized as Fabrice seizes the bridle of the horse, and underscored by the valet's utter silence: "The valet, stupefied, did not utter a word" (2:182). This suspension, however, far from marking the absence or insignificance of time, instead serves to emphasize the pregnant character of the instant at hand, its latent possibilities and importance. The valet's silence contrasts forcefully with the volubility of Fabrice, who proceeds to fill in the discursive blank with a fiction, a story he invents as he goes along and in which he plays the role of his brother plunged into the midst of an amorous intrigue: "With a peaceful air, Fabrice invented this tale as he went along" (2:182). One is obliged to conclude that the success of Fabrice's project is highly dependent on the veritable paralyzing effect his discourse exerts on the valet. Contemplating a murder only moments earlier, Fabrice now accomplishes that slaying discursively by mesmerizing his victim with a rather amusing story—"with a peaceful air." His narrative, filling the silence of the present, creates a nonexistent referent that replaces the very real scene of highway robbery with a reconstructed past (a bedroom scene) and a projected future (the flight to freedom). With his story, he seizes the moment, the encounter with the valet, because he discerns within it an occasion, the potential for his escape from a threatening predicament. Further, the whole incident takes place in a suggestive region: on a road, a space of passage, just a few miles from the border ("on the highway that goes from Lombardy into Switzerland" [2:181]). In other words, at stake here is a fairly undefined, uncertain domain, not only an interstice between political jurisdictions, but also, by definition, a domain of passage and instability where adventures and unusual phenomena can occur. One need only reflect on travel and roads as narrative devices motivating unsuspected encounters and singular events—this is a topos familiar to any reader of novels.

Finding himself in a place of passage, a kind of topological fold or irregularity, Fabrice spontaneously adopts a tactic to take advantage of a situation that presents itself by chance. He thereby succeeds in avoiding the arrest and imprisonment he fears. I would contend that despite the criticism of his course of action dispensed a few pages later by Mosca, Fabrice demonstrates in this instance a gift for maneuvering, which seems to be the mark of his lineage. This assertion becomes clearer in light of the conversation Fabrice has with Gina and Mosca following the escapade. As evidenced by the remark already quoted, Mosca believes Fabrice had every right to ensure his own safety by doing away with the valet in question on the spot. The Machiavellian traits in Mosca, his penchant for political expediency, are as manifest in this instance as they are anywhere else in *La Chartreuse de Parme*. The observation he makes— "It's better to kill the devil"—has a wider political implication, namely, that to rule effectively, one has to put aside certain inner moral convictions. Likewise, to save oneself in the face of grave personal danger, one has to accept the prospect of radical action— even murder.

The lesson hardly falls on deaf ears. On the contrary, it is clear that Fabrice had already anticipated it. To demonstrate his perception of the significance of what Mosca has said, Fabrice proceeds to relate the tale of an incident in the life of one of his ancestors, a portion of family history that has implications in the context of Mosca's preceding remarks and Fabrice's own narrow escape. Fabrice's tactical intervention on the road back to Parma possesses a certain correspondence with an episode already, perhaps unconsciously, a model for his action. We would do well to ponder the relationship between the two incidents. The subject of Fabrice's account is Vespasien del Dongo, the very forebear who built the château of Grianta, which was the object of Fabrice's impulsive voyage. Some detail is necessary to sketch out the narrative in question here, because it possesses a founding importance for Fabrice and contains a lesson destined to be repeated.[2]

Vespasien del Dongo is dispatched by the duke of Milan to visit and verify the state of one of the duke's fortresses on Lake Como. As he leaves, the duke calls him back to give him what is ostensibly a letter of greeting addressed to the commander of the fortress. During the journey on the lake, Vespasien unexpectedly remembers what Fabrice calls "an old Greek tale" (2:186; undoubtedly the story of Bellerophon), opens the letter, and discovers that far from being an introduction, it contains instead his own death sentence. Whereupon he proceeds to undo the duke's ruse: "Le Sforce [i.e., the duke], too absorbed by the act he was putting on for our ancestor, had left a blank space between the last line of the missive and the signature; Vespasien del Dongo wrote in it the order to recognize him as general governor of all the forts on the lake and destroyed the top portion of the letter" (2:186). On a preliminary level, the similarities between Vespasien's experience and Fabrice's are patent. In both cases there is danger. Just like Fabrice, who found himself at the moment of the theft exposed to the possible violence of a thorough and pitiless police force, Vespasien undertakes a military outing of sorts. No matter what the auspices might be, here supposedly to inspect fortifications and greet an ally, he is nonetheless engaged in an activity demanding supreme care and diplomacy. It is no easy task to represent authority and command obedience, and the Swiss are threatening an invasion that will put the fortress in question to the test. Both protagonists are engaged in a journey, moreover, and find themselves in a liminal region of passage: Fabrice on the road next to a frontier, Vespasien in the middle of a body of water, which is the very epitome of a space of shifting topology. No matter what political or military boundaries might be drawn through the lake, when one has embarked upon the water the preciseness of terrestrial circumscriptions no longer quite obtains.

Within the space described above, a chance event occurs. For Vespasien, it is a memory, long forgotten and now resurfacing in particularly insistent form. What is the significance of the intrusion of memory at such a critical moment? It would seem at first glance that the duke of Milan has played his role perfectly, to the hilt. The theatrical nature of the scene during which he transmits his charge to Vespasien is manifest. He appears to think of everything. The letter itself is casually presented as an afterthought, a trifle without consequence, and the act of sealing it as a gesture of politeness. Nothing in the duke's behavior suggests that a moment of crisis is being lived. The duke seems to hold all the cards. He is the one who rules not only over Vespasien but over the commander of the fortress in question as well. He also knows infinitely more than Vespasien—in particular, he knows the true contents of the letter. Knowledge of those contents is the manifestation of an all-seeing gaze, which the duke possesses exclusively in his role as sovereign. The very fortress Vespasien is sent out to visit is an outpost of the duke's watchful gaze. Vespasien appears consequently to be in a position of overwhelming weakness. And yet he will succeed in turning the tables through a chance encounter with a hidden memory. How does he accomplish this quasi-miraculous feat?

A reply to that question will require some theoretical reflection, which may begin with a distinction made by Michel de Certeau. In *L'Invention du quotidien,* de Certeau differentiates between two categories of action: strategic and tactical.[3] "I call 'strategy' the calculation (or the manipulation) of power relations that becomes possible as soon as a subject of will or of power . . . becomes isolatable. Strategy postulates *a place* that can be circumscribed as one's own [*un propre*] and can be the base from which one can organize relations with *an exteriority* of targets or threats."[4] De Certeau's definition of its structural complement, the tactic, which is "calculated action determined by the absence of one's own place [*un propre*]" (p.86), will help us clarify the meaning of the term "strategy." In the case of a tactic, "no limit marking what is exterior furnishes the condition of autonomy. The tactic has as its site of intervention a place belonging to the other. Thus it must devise its moves on a terrain imposed on it and organized by the law of an outside force" (p.86). A strategy is an action that is possible only after certain limits have been set, after a domain has been staked out allowing the strategist to define what is exterior, what is other. The domain that has been appropriated belongs to the actor or actors in question (it is their *propre*) and can then serve as a base for creating a set of relationships with whichever outside forces may alternately endanger or complement the organization within the defined region. De Certeau maintains that a strategy always represents a victory of place or space over time. It implies a stability that only an autonomous domain can provide, autonomous because it is independent—up to a point—of varying conditions arising over time. Strategy also implies control within the domain that has been appropriated in the form of what de Certeau calls, after Foucault, a panoptical practice. Strategists are astute observers capable of encountering elements that belong to what is outside the scope of their power and transforming them into things that are measurable and can be assimilated into their exercise of power.

Tacticians, on the other hand, are relegated to something other than strategic action precisely because they do not occupy a clearly defined, autonomous space of their own. They are forced to maneuver within the space of the power against which they desire to act. They do not possess sufficient means to mass their forces at a safe distance, in a position of retreat, and to apply them unilaterally in one swift confrontation. Instead, they are reduced to action on a much more immediate basis with whatever means they can assemble at any given instant. Whereas the domain of strategists is a spatial locus, that of tacticians is time—they must wait for the proper time and seize the moment as soon as it presents itself: "This non-place," de Certeau maintains, "doubtless gives [tacticians] the mobility—resulting from an attitude of readiness toward the aleatory events brought by time—to seize the possibilities offered by the moment. [They] must attentively use particular combinations of circumstances that open fault lines within the vigilance of the occupying power [*pouvoir propriétaire*]" (p.87). Time, the instant, conjunctures, circumstances—these define the domain of the tactician. They are hardly what one would term offensive weapons, for it is clear that tacticians must especially know how to wait, how to bide their time in inaction. Destined to remain constantly beyond their control are a whole series of unpredictable elements. Only the potential force of an unexpected combination of circumstances will allow tacticians to turn a situation to their advantage and thus to reverse a previously irremediable predicament. Tacticians are forced to maneuver, to delay; they must have a flair for circumstances which, if they occur at the proper moment and in a favorable conjuncture, can undo whatever organization strategists have installed. Baltasar Gracián saw that "the vast scope of time must be crossed in order to arrive at the center of the occasion. Reasonable temporizing ripens secrets and resolutions. The crutch of time accomplishes more than the iron club of Hercules." Gracián and his Italian counterpart, Machiavelli, knew full well that without an eye for the *kairos,* the occasional fleeting but decisive instant, people cast around aimlessly for solutions and rush lightly into failure: "There is a point of maturity even in the fruits of understanding, and it is important to know this point to profit from it."[5]

Strategists and tacticians are thus clearly distinguished by certain characteristics apparent in their respective situations. Strategists have outlined a domain that they organize by setting it apart from what is other or outside. Their attempts could well be interpreted as a bid to suppress the aleatory, to set up a system of rules allowing them to introduce certain regulatory features into their existence. What they reveal in their strategy is their belief that there can be and are rules or laws governing what exists. The real must necessarily seem to them characterized by a certain ordered structure which is the origin and underpinning of the world. From the perspective of strategy, there is a *nature* of some kind determined by a series of immutable laws. Tacticians, on the other hand, do not have it so easy. Deprived of the very ground on which they stand, they can defer to no reassuring foundations, only to the shifting sands of circumstance. At the heart of their experience is chance—not any ordered nature. Their outlook is hence fundamentally different from that of strategists. At stake in the confrontation of these two roles is the perspective to be adopted on the nature of the world. Is the real to be viewed as primarily ordered or as primarily disordered, a well-adjusted machine or a chaotically assembled series of chance occasions? Clément Rosset puts the choice this way:

The problem is to know whether or not, within the set of "things that exist," there exists not necessarily *a* nature, but at least certain groups of beings to which the expression "natures" could be applied. The required condition for the recognition of such natures is that the power of chance . . . would stop at the border of "something" which, prior to the possibility of such interventions, exists. Thus human, plant, or animal natures require, in order to exist, that something be contained within them that transcends all circumstance.[6]

If they are indeed thinkers of chance, tacticians must believe that everything which exists is the work of circumstance, not of any law of nature. Without a domain of their own carefully staked out and defined, they are at the mercy of circumstance. But perhaps this fact should not be expressed in a manner that insists too heavily on its negative aspect. While tacticians must wait in expectation of what the occasion brings, the occasion is also the source of their success. Because they do not believe that the domain organized by strategists represents the permanent structure of the world, they are open to difference, to propitious combinations of encounters that only time and chance can bring and that will reveal potentialities to which strategists are blind.

Such an approach to the position of tacticians requires the introduction of some nuances into de Certeau's description, especially when he suggests that tactic "must devise its moves on a terrain imposed on it and organized by the law of an outside force." We must not become too enamored of the idea of the law in this instance. I would be tempted to say that what tactic does is not simply to put into question this or that particular law but to challenge radically the hypothesis according to which there is a law at all, that is, a set of principles destined to remain constant indefinitely. Tactic posits not that one law can be replaced by another but that before the law, beyond the law, the reality of the world is composed of circumstance and chance. This is the source of potential force that tacticians are able to tap. Only a drastic hypothesis of this sort can explain the unforeseen and extreme reversal tacticians sometimes accomplish. If it were simply a question of pitting one law against another, the surprise, the fundamentally unexpected nature of the reversal that occurs, would be difficult to understand—and its true quality lost. The transposition resulting when tacticians seize the potential offered by a circumstance is so extreme it is literally inconceivable—and most of all for strategists.

Vespasien del Dongo's counterploy as he sails on Lake Como, then, can be approached fruitfully from the perspective of de Certeau's distinction. That this is the case becomes all the more evident when one considers the very place where Vespasien has his moment of insight. Proceeding on the inevitably aleatory trajectory imposed by travel on water, he finds himself in a space the duke could never completely plot, circumscribe, or reduce to a stable network, namely, the sea. Having defined strategists by insisting on their attachment to space and their attempt to organize space panoptically, we immediately encounter, in Vespasien's situation, a kind of space which cannot be to the liking of strategists. Although the duke nominally controls Lake Como, the nature of this territory is not as straightforward as dry land. The Greeks underlined the problem quite well when they described the sea as the most characteristic example of a space devoid of charted ways and passages: "The sea is the endless reign of pure movement, the most mobile space, the most polymorphous one, the one where every path disappears as soon as it is traced, transforming all navigation into an ever-renewed exploration that is dangerous and uncertain."[7] Were one to object that Lake Como could hardly be considered such a dangerous body of water, we shall have occasion shortly to observe that in Stendhal's text its waters can rage as furiously and perilously as those of any sea. Whoever ventures out on the water, then, must be a navigator, one who is capable of finding an exit (*poros*), a passage, a route, where none is to be found. Each time navigators initiate a voyage on the water, they must discover a new itinerary, because the polymorphous oscillation encountered there prevents any path from remaining immutably traced. Navigation is not a science of fixed laws; it is something else, something like the flair necessary to meet difference provoked by chance encounters and to choose correctly at the right moment. Navigators are, of necessity, tacticians forced to maneuver within a space forever beyond the total embrace of concept. Navigation (the tactic) is thus not for the faint-hearted. It is only for those who are prepared to set out even though there is no explored route to follow, for those who can recognize the solution to the aporia if it happens to cross their path: "Perhaps if we go forward in the search, we may stumble upon the thing we are looking for; but if we stay where we are, nothing will come to light."[8]

At the supremely charged moment when he is navigating on the water, Vespasien stumbles on something that crosses his path: time manifests itself and inscribes the sign of an exit out of the trap which has been laid in the duke's domain—memory intervenes. What the duke has not calculated, what he cannot calculate, is the full range of human experience and relations of force, chaotic and multitudinous—the reductive spatial approach of the strategist can never circumscribe them completely. Stochastic complexities infallibly reappear from within at crucial conjunctures. No matter how many details the duke takes into account, no matter how well he has mastered the scene he played with Vespasien, a moment arrives that undoes what has preceded. The unpredictably chance nature of the instant in question (a memory welling up from a cultural past) is not just a minor detail, it is, on the contrary, that instant's formative principle and an indication of the existence of an intricacy, an existential undulation beyond strategic reckoning. The chaotic, disordered nature of memory contrasts markedly with the measured act of rationalization and calculation represented by the attempt to formulate a superior strategy. Its appearance and function clearly oppose it to strategy, thereby emphasizing the hidden but ever-present partiality (in the two senses of the word) of strategy, its vulnerability to what unexpectedly intrudes on its domain. There must be no misunderstanding here concerning the origin of such an intrusion—it is produced not from *without* but from *within,* and it thereby threatens to expose the whole elaborate structure of the strategist's domain as an ephemeral fiction. In this particular instance, the duke fails to take into account a fact of which he is unaware, namely, that his scheme against Vespasien is at one level a cultural repetition. It is already immersed in a temporal series undermining the apparently autonomous, suprahistorical law he has promulgated. Quite simply put, it already exists in the form of a cultural memory belonging to Vespasien, the story of Bellerophon.[9]

That this particular story would occur to Vespasien in the context of his journey already possesses some importance with respect to a certain number of issues in the plot of *La Chartreuse de Parme*. It suggests, for example, that there may be a hidden rivalry involved in Vespasien's relationship with the duke, since in the Greek story Bellerophon was sent away with his death sentence by Proetus when Proetus suspected that Bellerophon had designs on his wife, Anteia. Let me recall a suggestive parallel developed earlier. When Fabrice takes the horse during his escape, he turns the scene into a comedy by inventing a story for the valet in which he assumes the role of Ascanio del Dongo (his own brother) and claims to be involved in an amorous intrigue. The ultimate cause of Fabrice's peril within his own country is the rivalry for family power which originally prompted his brother to turn against him. Suggestions of a comparable antagonism between Vespasien and the duke are distinctly implied in the family chronicle Fabrice recounts. Be that as it may, there is a more pressing, symbolic reason why the story of Bellerophon would emerge in the context at hand. In order to accomplish the death sentence sent with Bellerophon when Proetus dispatched him on his journey, Proetus's father-in-law, Iobates, orders Bellerophon to kill the Chimaera (believing, of course, that Bellerophon will fail and die). But Bellerophon succeeds and thus becomes the slayer of a mythological beast, a monster particularly intriguing from the perspective of the present analysis. The Chimaera is an inextricably jumbled collection of dissociated parts, monstrous in its very lack of order and relation. It is surely a representation of a chance assembling of aleatory elements, the very sign, in other words, of fortuitous conventions. Small wonder that the reminiscence of Bellerophon and the Chimaera occurs at the moment when Vespasien is navigating on water.

Because it is composed of such disparate elements, the Chimaera exposes a series of rifts or faults, visible borders where unsuspected juxtapositions occur. It represents and thus reproduces the liminal, borderlike spaces we already noticed in the valet incident when Fabrice was on the road back to Parma. In one such space of uncertain limits, on the water of the lake itself, Vespasien encounters the fault, the tear in the fabric of the duke's own strategy, a strange element in the form of a memory, which cannot be incorporated into the formula devised to destroy him, cannot, in other words, be neutralized within what appears otherwise to be a smooth and homogeneous whole (emphasized by the duke's near-seamless performance before the trip began). The faults visible on the surface of the Chimaera underline the fault in the duke's calculations. One must bear in mind an additional detail. Because of the Chimaera's changing, protean nature, Bellerophon can overcome it not by means of a direct confrontation but, rather, only by ruse. He is forced to cast about in search of a series of tactics in order to triumph [10] The beast at stake in the story suggestively reproduces the encircling nature of the duke's hold on Vespasien, the necessity for maneuvering within a space autonomously organized by the concepts of an adversary, and the search for some unsuspected, circumstantial ploy to circumvent what appear to be overwhelming odds. The complex symbol of the Chimaera seems to represent both sides of the same coin: on the one hand, the presence of chance and therefore of the rift that will provide a space for maneuver allowing a successful counterploy, but, on the other hand, the all-encompassing strength of the strategist, namely, the duke, who possesses the advantage of a well-outlined domain within which Vespasien, an adversary dispossessed of his own territory, must struggle. This convergence of significant mythological elements precipitates Vespasien's chance remembering of a pertinent cultural parallel, which in turn gives rise to a propitious and fortunate occasion for decisive action. In the flash of an instant, he is presented with the means required to loosen the knot that has been drawn tightly around him.

Perhaps the most telling element in the scene is that the space of maneuver encountered by Vespasien is figured in the missive itself. My discussion of this incident began with the following quotation: "Le Sforce, too absorbed by the act he was putting on for our ancestor, *had left a blank space between the last line of the missive and the signature*" (my emphasis). The aleatory structure of a certain liminality revealed and deployed in the preceding discussion had from the beginning made its way into the duke's writing in the guise of a blank space of indeterminacy not crisscrossed by his discourse, ripe for a transformation to be accomplished by anyone who gained control of it. The text indicates, furthermore, that the unoccupied (almost in the military sense) space is the effect of *too much* attention; it is the result of an overly confident strategy incapable of conceptualizing the other or of representing fortuitous events which can traverse its field of force and unfasten its hold: "too absorbed by the act he was putting on." The duke's mind is too clear, too focused on a preconceived design to retain the malleability and receptiveness required to meet the aleatory and incorporate it into his plan. Not only does Vespasien have the advantage of the past to bring against the duke (his memory of the Bellerophon story) but also of the future. Although it is not within the purview of mere mortals to foresee what is to come, Vespasien nonetheless seizes on the oversight of the duke and immediately transforms it into a project (in other words, he pro-jects it—what has befallen him is thrown forward).[11] His encounter with the fortuitous does much more than simply save him from the clutches of the duke, it is converted by an act of will into a founding event: "Vespasien del Dongo wrote in it the order to recognize him as general governor of all the forts on the lake and destroyed the top portion of the letter" (2:186). A more significant decapitation could hardly be imagined. Fabrice's ancestor instantly turns himself into a political and military rival of the duke by filling the space of potentiality left by accident with his own discourse—all this in a manner clearly related to Fabrice's own act of capturing the silence of his confrontation with the valet by means of a fiction. Just like Fabrice, who created a nonexistent referent effectively turning the valet's attention away from the theft, Vespasien now creates another nonexistent referent, which will divert the fortress governor's attention away from the usurpation he is accomplishing. The duke's signature, left hanging, will now be put to use otherwise and will ultimately be replaced by one of comparable force, Vespasien's.

The governor of the fortress, tricked by the letter, finds himself immediately thrown into a well or deep hole (or dungeon—I am uncertain of the exact translation to give here): Vespasien "threw the commanding officer in a hole" (2:186). Distracted by what he sees in front of his nose (the letter), the governor fails to see what is at his feet (the abyss): "Like Thales who did not see what was in front of his feet, the philosopher, lacking experience, falls into a well or into any other aporetic situation (*paisan aporian*)," as Sarah Kofman describes the famous incident involving the Greek philosopher.[12] The governor, a representative of the duke's supposedly panoptical gaze, may think he sees everything, but in fact, lacking the patience and patiently acquired experience of the tactician, he misses the essential and finds himself plunged into an aporia. He and Vespasien have effectively exchanged places, not only physically but symbolically as well, for it was Vespasien who lacked a way out only a short time before, trapped as he was without a fixed itinerary in the aporia of the undulating water, at the nexus of the confusing proliferation of paths. This detail of the story reveals yet another link between it and the episode lived by Fabrice. As mentioned earlier, just before the theft, Fabrice takes refuge in a hollow tree trunk, a veritable well without exit in its own right. Only the most unexpected incident will allow a solution to appear—provided, of course, that Fabrice knows how to exploit it. And we have seen that he does so without hesitation.

As a result of his coup, Vespasien appears to have made the transition from tactician to strategist, for, thanks to his ruse, he succeeds in staking out a space now his own—the fortress in question. The only way the duke will be able to recoup his losses is to pay him a generous ransom in the form of the land on which the château of Grianta will eventually be built, to give Vespasien yet another space which becomes Vespasien's own territory. More than one paradox is immediately apparent here. Earlier I termed Vespasien's act a founding event. But what might the act of founding a dynasty by usurpation really signify? This is surely a curious basis on which to construct the legitimacy of a family. In a sense, we could say instead that the family is actually without foundation. Rather, it is the stuff of an illusion all the more illusory, since the supposed act of founding was not only usurpatory but immersed as well in the domain of the fictitious: that act was a discursive trick and not a heroic military confrontation at all. Vespasien literally rewrote his own history by filling in the blank of the duke's letter. In a telling respect Fabrice spontaneously ("without having yet decided on anything, Fabrice jumped out" [2:182]) adopts the tactic of his ancestor when he fictionalizes on the road to Parma and succeeds in procuring a horse without physical violence. He constructs his own story and mesmerizes the valet. Jumping onto the road, he jumps over generations to regain the ground (but what ground? the shifting water?) of his forebear Vespasien. One could and must further ask in what way the success of Vespasien does not mark the definitive rallying of the del Dongo clan to the ranks of the strategists. After all, Vespasien does secure a château for his trouble, that is, a reinforced and circumscribed space, which is none other than a strategic property *(propriété)*. The behavior of Fabrice's father during the French occupation of Milan as *La Chartreuse de Parme* opens suggests that at least part of the family has forgone the lesson contained in the coup perpetrated by Vespasien: Fabrice's father's only rejoinder to the invasion of the Napoleonic troops is to withdraw behind the walls of the château of Grianta. Thereafter, despite short periods of time when he lives in Milan, the senior del Dongo chooses to make the château his permanent base of operations from which he ventures out only occasionally. The ascendancy of Ascanio over Fabrice is expressed by the fact that Ascanio will inherit the domain, will, in other words, become the new master of the château and thus the worthy successor of his embattled, encircled father. Fabrice, on the other hand, cavorts with the servants and village friends outside the château, then spends the first significant portion of his life going to school in Milan, away from Grianta altogether. Later, when his father, worried by Gina's influence over Fabrice, recalls him to the château, the events of the One Hundred Days, the ill-fated return of Napoleon in 1815, will soon prompt him to leave in search of the emperor. Fabrice thereupon becomes a constant wanderer in foreign territories, whether it be in Italy or elsewhere. Gina's decision to establish residence in Parma and then to invite Fabrice to come there himself puts the two protagonists squarely in the tactician's position—they are forced to maneuver within a domain marked out and dominated by someone else, namely, the prince of Parma. In one sense, then, Gina and Fabrice make a conscious choice to avoid a life circumscribed by a territory appropriated and ruled by them. It is not surprising, therefore, to discover that the portion of family history Fabrice recalls in a moment of crucial importance for his political education is none other than the occasion when his ancestor formulated his most brilliant tactical move—and one that we have now come to see in its close relationship with Fabrice's own actions on the road back to Parma after his visit to Grianta.

Besides, Fabrice has always been a navigator, as the text of the novel assures us in no uncertain terms:

Two or three times a year, Fabrice, fearless and impassioned in his pleasures, was on the verge of drowning in the lake [Como]. He was the leader of all the grand expeditions of the peasant children from Grianta. . . . The ultimate goal of these nocturnal expeditions . . . was to get to all of the unmanned fishing lines laid out on the lake before the fishermen heard the small bells ring. Stormy moments were chosen, and, for these hazardous outings, they set out in the morning an hour before dawn. (2:39)

Fabrice's greatest childhood pastime was braving storms on Lake Como, organizing expeditions that put his ingenuity to the test. By definition, each storm on a body of water is totally uncharted, differs from the preceding one, and requires original solutions. The outings organized by Fabrice are hazardous [*hasardeuses*] in the two senses of the French term: both dangerous and given over to the forces of chance, the chaos of the storm. Moreover, the rehearsal for the confrontation with chance takes place before the beginning of every outing in the travestied ceremony of the *Ave Maria*: "Now, it often happened that at the moment of departure, and in the instant following the *Ave Maria,* Fabrice was struck by an omen. . . . According to his young imagination, this omen announced success or failure with certainty" (2:40). The chance passage of a bird or some other natural sign is instantly interpreted by Fabrice and causes him either to go forward or to call off the adventure. I would argue, and I shall have occasion to return to this point, that Fabrice's superstition, well-documented in the novel, far from being a primitive or enslaving quality, is instead a sign of his fundamental link with the fleeting moment of the occasion, or *kairos.* In the meantime, let us insist that storms on Lake Como are not to be taken lightly: "they are terrible and unexpected on this beautiful lake" (2:46). Indeed, only a heroic presence of mind permits Fabrice to avoid a disaster some years later when he has gotten into the habit of going out on the lake with Gina and his mother and sister. He saves Gina from drowning when she falls into the water during one of the dangerous storms apparently common in the region. Not only is Fabrice drawn toward the side of Vespasien in the incident he lives while on the road to Parma, but it seems this has always been the case, even in the moments of his youthful exuberance at Grianta.

Our discussion began with the story of Fabrice's encounter with the peasant on the road and then his own narration of this event linked to the exemplary tale of his ancestor Vespasien. We must now turn our attention to Mosca's rejoinder to Fabrice's narration, a complex remark suggesting further commentary on the notions explored up to now, one which therefore merits our close scrutiny: " 'You speak like an academician,' exclaimed the count, laughing, 'this is quite a headstrong act you just described. But one has the amusing *occasion* to do such striking things *only every ten years.* A half stupid being, but one who is attentive, one who is prudent *every day, very often* tastes the pleasure of triumphing over men of imagination' " (2:186, my emphasis). Mosca's political conception of time as expressed here vividly underscores the differences in approach between strategists and tacticians. Strategists are forced to live within the confines of the present, of the everyday, of a constant attention to the minute, quotidian monotony of repetitive events. Tacticians, on the other hand, are attentive to difference, to the changes that time brings, to the occasion, rare by definition, but saturated with the potential to be transmuted into an elegantly effective act. The date of that occasion, its precise site within time, and the potential it will provide cannot be calculated in advance— too much depends on a fortuitous combination of circumstances that no mere prudence could foresee. But there is more than a question of time at stake in this passage. Mosca, after having heard Fabrice's story, proceeds immediately to draw a lesson from it. His preemptive intervention is in itself curious and significant. Fabrice has just finished a story meant to prove that the political penetration demanded by Mosca belongs to him (Fabrice) as a member of a lineage which illustrated such discernment from its beginning. Mosca's reluctance to grant Fabrice's point pierces immediately, however, when he commandeers the narrative himself and furnishes the moral of the story—in the place of the author. He steals the story from Fabrice just as Fabrice himself stole the horse and Vespasien the fortress. We would do well not to assign Fabrice and Mosca to opposing camps definitively, despite Gina's belief that Mosca could never be a true member of the del Dongo family. The moral itself, however, significantly worded and constructed, betrays the caution characterizing Mosca and setting him apart from Fabrice: " 'A half stupid being, but one who is attentive, one who is prudent *every day, very often* tastes the pleasure of triumphing over men of imagination' " (my emphasis). The victorious prudence of the stupid being applies every day, but the step from every day to always remains unaccomplished—the person in question does not *always* triumph, only *very often*. The moral falls short of the status of a law applicable in every instance, *toujours*. It applies only in most instances. "We are not in the domain of the apodeitic and of essences, but in that of empirical frequencies governed by the probable" as Louis Marin concludes with respect to the structure of a related occasion found in the memoirs of Cardinal de Retz.[13] In other words, we are in the domain of tactical acts, which function as exceptions to calculations and which strategists can only probably eliminate, not certainly eliminate. The probability of the strategists' triumph is high but never absolute. The comfort of the very often is precisely what prevents strategists from preparing for the moment that will become the occasion for tacticians to turn the tables. Strategists take for law what cannot be formulated as a law, because it belongs to chance, to the fleeting, to the decision of the propitious instant. The stupid being is the speculative philosopher who desires the universal, who wishes to eliminate duration from a totality in which every point is transparently *present* to every other. But duration is destined to return as a *kairos* which places the speculator face to face with time in the form of his own finitude.

More can be said in this context concerning the idea of repetition that is implicit in the expressions "every day" and "very often." The concept of repetition is a tricky one. From a traditionally understood point of view, it is the strategists who live in a world marked by repetition. The domain they have staked out, the structure they have created across their territory, results in a continuum that reduces every difference to an exact reproduction of the same. Every occurrence within the territory is filtered through an established law and transformed into an example of what has occurred previously. Strategists, in other words, are locked into a cycle of similitude. This does not mean, however, that the position of tacticians, or thinkers of chance, is the opposite in any simple way, that they are totally unfamiliar with repetition. Their situation involves a certain repetition as well, but of a different kind, what Clément Rosset, in *Logique du pire,* calls "differential repetition" (p.65). Tacticians view the world as a series of fortuitous combinations of circumstance; there are, in a rigorous sense, no events. An event is something which, as Rosset puts it, "stands out *in relief* against a background of being" (p.43). Since in a world in which chance

is the governing principle there is no essence or being, only becoming, there is logically no event: if everything is the product of
chance, then nothing stands out against a background of being, everything is "a natural addition to a nature which is the same: *chance
added to chance*" (p.43). And yet the seemingly monotonous and repetitive flux of the aleatory is simultaneously the source of difference, of modifications such that nothing is ever repeated in exactly
the same circumstances but always with certain differential singularities. The tacticians' domain is defined by such singularities. This
is why they escape the strategists, who live by and for the idea that
everything is interpretable, reducible to certain generalizable essences or laws. "The absence of reference points from which to
measure [singularity] makes it silent and blind" (p.69). The panoptical view of strategists cannot perceive singularities hidden within
the folds of the moment; they remain silent because they cannot be
interpreted. Those propitious instants are destined to undo their
efforts sooner or later.

The space of passage, the instant of the circumstance, the blank
whiteness on the page: these elements work together to make of
Fabrice's genealogical narrative something more general and representative than the isolated incident it might seem at first to be. The
parallels between his actions just prior to the scene during which he
narrates these events, on the one hand, and the actions of his ancestor, on the other, certainly motivate at one level the appearance of
his story. For the perspicacious reader, however, the suggestive
structure of the tale is clearly linked to other crucial moments in *La
Chartreuse de Parme,* which we must now explore. Take, for instance, the incipit of the novel, the justly famous description of the
eruption of the French army into the society of Milan. The "effemi-
nate mores" (2:25) of the Milanese are suddenly exposed to the
caustic wit and masculine bravura of the French, for whom nothing
is sacred and who sweep aside everything that the Austrians had
considered sacrosanct. The event signaling the change in Milan
with the arrival of the French occurs on the second page of *La*

Chartreuse de Parme and, as we shall see, is related in several characteristic ways to the story of Vespasien del Dongo:

In May of 1796, three days after the entrance of the French, a slightly crazy young painter of miniatures named Gros, . . . on hearing the story of the exploits of the archduke (who was, in addition, enormous) recounted in the spacious Servi café (which was in vogue at the time), picked up the ice cream menu printed on a sheet of poor-quality yellow paper. On the back of the sheet, he drew the fat archduke. A French soldier was plunging his bayonet into the archduke's stomach, and, instead of blood, an incredible quantity of wheat was flowing out. (2:26)

The inaugural symbolic gesture marking the new supremacy of the French in Milan turns out to be the act of taking possession of a space of play, a site of indeterminacy. In the chance interval of a café conversation (gossiping is a perfect example of the kind of sphere that cannot be fully dominated within an otherwise controlled political domain), the focal point of a successful tactic for exposing the corruption of a whole political system presents itself. On the surface of the most mundane and apparently neutral document, a café menu, Gros seizes control of an unoccupied space, which he proceeds to turn into a scathing indictment of Austrian control. Just like Vespasien, who used the blank in the duke's letter to neutralize his power, Gros uses the back of the menu to neutralize, at least symbolically, that of the Austrians. At stake here is an interval of play at the frontier of the rules of discourse instituted by the Austrians, a space they have not been able to blanket completely. The moment it falls into the hands of someone who knows how to grasp its potential at the right instant, it suddenly becomes the center of a highly charged political and ideological confrontation.

The significance of Gros's gesture becomes even more unmistakable in light of the description of the conduct of the Milanese before the arrival of the French. Cut off from any possibility for critical appraisal of their own situation, that is, surrounded by the strategic pervasiveness of the Austrians, they were reduced to the frivolous and thus powerless use of spaces such as the one commandeered by Gros: "Ever since they had become *faithful subjects,* their main activity had been to print sonnets on small handkerchiefs of pink taffeta when it was time to marry off a young lady belonging to some rich and noble family" (2:25). Love poems, not political indictments, occupy everyone's attention and camouflage Austrian oppression. The strategy of the Austrians has been to occupy their territory to such an extent no countervoice can be heard; they are the ones who fill the discursive interstices of public places, using, for example, an unscrupulous newspaper whose dirty paper recalls the yellowed café menu Gros seizes upon: "Only eight days before the arrival of the French, the Milanese still saw them only as a bunch of outlaws, always fleeing before the troops of His Royal and Imperial Highness; at least that is what a little newspaper hardly bigger than a hand and printed on dirty paper repeated to them three times a week" (2:25). Their propaganda insinuates itself everywhere via a thoroughly controlled network of official distribution. In an instant, however, Gros and the French transform the pompous, propagandistic style of discourse in the public domain into one whose iconoclastic thrust is as destructive as their military prowess has proven to be, and they bring down the whole house of cards: "What is called jesting or caricature was not known in this country of wary despotism" (2:26). The reversal Gros accomplishes originally in one very particular and specific place, on the back of a café menu, immediately invades the whole ideological network, heretofore utterly dominated by the Austrians, for the caricature is quickly distributed as widely as the newspaper which only a few days before was castigating the French forces: "An engraving was made during the night, and the next day twenty thousand copies were sold" (2:27).

In this episode, the reader again encounters a tactician at work, someone who has an eye for the chance occasion presented to him and immediately grasps how to incorporate it into a superior and successful move. As mentioned parenthetically above, it is significant to note that Gros's act is accomplished in a café. In a different and yet structurally parallel way, the café, like the road on which

Fabrice found himself or the lake upon which Vespasien journeyed, figures a space characterized by a certain relaxation of the structures of order (from the point of view of the authorities), a context in which there is room to maneuver against a strategic master. No matter what panoptical ideological control is exercised throughout the Austrian territory, no coercion can interrupt the exchange of information provided by intimate conversation in such a setting— that setting is very much the archetype of convivial, if not to say conspiratorial, exchange.[14] And there is yet another element that further draws the Gros incident toward the structure we have been developing: it takes place in the uncertainty of a moment of passing of powers from the Austrians to the French. Like Fabrice, who found himself on the road very near a frontier, Gros profits from a power vacuum that creates an interstice, momentarily empty but soon to be filled by the occupational government the French will establish. Tacticians thrive in such instants of mobile boundaries when they can be assured that responsibilities will be extremely difficult to determine and when their unexpected coup can thus be accomplished with maximum efficiency. The passing of conventions and their transformation into new configurations reveals not only the aleatory nature of what underlies them, as I have been arguing all along, but exposes as well potential openings for actions otherwise obscured and, more important, beyond calculation.

Not only is the historical moment described as one of uncertainty and floating rules, but the principal figure of the episode developed here, Gros himself, is to a large extent presented as a marginalized figure. "Slightly crazy," says the text, and situated in a problematic relation with respect to the French troops. He is apparently not a soldier by profession, rather, a hanger-on during the French campaign and thus ideally placed from the outset to test the limits of the law. The caricature itself, moreover, in its very structure, both content and form, reveals its link to the problematic we have been pursuing. In the first place, it represents a space of incongruity in an almost geometric sense of the word. The sword tearing into the body of the archduke does not reveal the normal corporeal continuity and homogeneousness one would expect (blood and guts), but instead provokes a change in registers—from the corporeal to the economic (wheat). The rift in the body juxtaposes previously unrelated elements: there is something of the Chimaera present in the very subject of the caricature. Caricature as a genre is itself in a complex and marginal relationship with both drawing and art on one side and discourse on the other side. A caricature is not conceived, for instance, to stand on its own without reference to a political or historical situation. On the contrary, to grasp fully its signification (usually highly polemical) requires a discursive reconstruction of the context in which it was produced. Unless the viewer can refer to the history surrounding the caricature, solve the enigma, and explain it, the caricature is a failure. Thus the very genre adopted by Gros partakes of the liminality in which it is created and which it produces.

We have, then, two incidents containing clearly parallel structures at two crucial moments in *La Chartreuse de Parme*. Just when Fabrice is preparing his break from Gina, he steals a horse, receives a political lesson, and recalls the founding incident of his family history in the form of an act symbolic of what we can now see as the del Dongo flair. But the gesture of Vespasien is insufficient in itself as a founding act for Fabrice's life and performance. As Stendhal critics have repeatedly pointed out, the novel carefully establishes that Fabrice's genealogy consists of an inextricable interconnection between the Italian side and an allusive French side represented by Lieutenant Robert and the invading Napoleonic forces to which Gros belongs. The triumph of the French summed up in Gros's caricature, therefore, possesses an equally inaugural status for Fabrice—and for *La Chartreuse de Parme* as a novel as well. The symbolic importance of the opening scene of the novel—certainly not something critics have overlooked in the context of other arguments—becomes all the more manifest when one can demonstrate the parallels between it and the story of Vespasien del Dongo.

These two incidents (Fabrice/Vespasien and Gros) are closely related to a third, which occurs in the second part of *La Chartreuse de*

Parme and is a variation on the same theme with some subtle differences. I have in mind the scene during which Gina goes to the prince of Parma and reveals her intention to leave the city as a result of the announcement that Fabrice has been found guilty in absentia of Giletti's murder.[15] It would be useful to point out the nature of the relationship between the two protagonists in question before outlining the episode on which I shall concentrate subsequently. Although Gina's arrival in the prince's state marks a new era of interest and excitement for the bored society gathered around the prince, the positive aspect of that notable event also has its negative side effects from the prince's point of view. With Gina, he inherits a subject who, in reality, is far from being a subject. Gina has no fundamental attachment to Parma, she is utterly mobile. In an instant she can decide to leave the state never to return, and the prince soon realizes that there is little he can do to modify the situation. His evaluation of the bind in which Gina has put him prompts him to make it his sole goal to tame her, somehow to limit her space of maneuver and to tie her down definitively to his state so that she will be at his mercy (the whole of this plan being, in addition, embedded in a dream of sexual conquest). The guilty verdict returned against Fabrice is nothing more than another ploy in this continuing struggle, for its effect will supposedly be to keep Gina forcibly in Parma in order to seek Fabrice's exoneration. Once again we may see how the strategist, within the territory he dominates, strives for a kind of panoptical control which attempts to remove any shadow of contestation or uncertainty and to assimilate whatever appears to be other within his domain. The structure the duchess creates for herself, socially indispensable and yet able to leave at any time, illustrates the tactician at work to maintain a certain freedom of movement until a decisive occasion for effective action appears.

Within the context of this ongoing masked conflict, Gina, despite Fabrice's now dangerous situation, decides in a fit of pique that she will indeed desert the state of Parma and announces her decision to the prince. On the spur of the moment, then, she chooses the most radical solution to the problem she has faced from the beginning—she elects to withdraw and thereby to put an end to her condition of inferiority within the prince's domain. Almost without realizing it, she undoes the whole scheme conceived by the prince, for he has no effective parry against such an act. In a flash, she unexpectedly goes to the heart of the matter and threatens to reverse the roles the two protagonists have been playing. Consequently, she will find herself suddenly projected into an unanticipated position of strength: "The prince had remained there as if he had been struck by lightning. . . . With these words the prince finally understood. He turned pale: in all the world he was the man who suffered the most when he saw his plans disrupted" (2:249–50).[16] Having incorrectly calculated his adversary because he did not foresee the completely different approach she would take, he now finds himself unarmed before her. Presented with an occasion to triumph, Gina, like Fabrice, Vespasien, and Gros before her, immediately attempts to convert her momentary advantage into a lasting victory by means of a now-familiar tactic: she requests a written statement from the prince denouncing the unfair sentence and promising no further harmful actions against Fabrice. Just like what occurred in the episodes we read earlier, the decisive moment turns out to be a discursive one, an instant in which an opening in the form of a blank space is exploited by the artful tactician who previously seemed definitively confined to inaction. Gina presents the prince with a blank sheet of paper (figuratively) and dictates its contents: "His Highness would write me a gracious letter, as only he knows how to write them. He would tell me that since he is not convinced of the guilt of Fabrice del Dongo, first grand vicar of the archbishop, he will absolutely not sign the sentence that will be presented to him, and that this unjust procedure will have no consequences in the future" (2:254). Her space for maneuver would appear even larger than any we have encountered in our reading thus far, for she is at first completely free to fill in a potentially rich blank as she wishes.

To pursue this point, we must first devote careful attention to the temporal sequence the passage constructs, or reconstructs, for we have seen the importance of the element of time in the course of the argument. Gina seizes on the fortuitous opening, the present instant, the occasion which has been presented to her, and immediately transforms it into a project replete with implications for the *future*. The prince must not only pledge to cease and desist from *future* machinations against Fabrice, he must, in addition, also condemn what has occurred in the *past,* "this unjust procedure." As we have seen, the tactician, given the fortuitous circumstances required, interjects time into the fortress of the strategist, makes him acknowledge that the allegedly timeless stasis within his circumscribed domain is only an illusory and temporary state. The tactician, here Gina, takes advantage of the fortunate circumstance patiently awaited and now at hand in order to transform the significance of the series of events leading up to it and unfolding from it. She will fail in this instance because her opponent succeeds in wresting time back from her. Unhappily, there is an intermediary between her and the prince in the dictation process, Mosca, who, consummate bureaucrat and strategist, intercepts Gina's discourse and deforms it at the crucial point, the phrase "this unjust procedure." He effaces the phrase with the tacit and silent consent of the prince, because he is torn between two loyalties and ultimately opts, at least in this scene, for the prince. Control over what has happened prior to the interview thus slips definitively from Gina's grasp. With the phrase in question eliminated, the prince has in no way taken a stand concerning the decision made beforehand by his judges and therefore maintains his independence with respect to the past. It is as if the discursive space Gina was preparing to invade and occupy abruptly closed, eliminating the occasion offered to her. Moreover, the prince, this time without Mosca's aid, bests Gina in the struggle for domination of what is to come by disfiguring as well the unfolding future temporal sequence sealed by the document he now signs: "The count noticed that his master was correcting the date and was putting in tomorrow's date. He looked at the clock, which read midnight. The minister saw in this corrected date only the pedantic desire to demonstrate exactness and good government" (2:255). In one quick stroke, the prince lays his hands on the future in addition to the past and thus renders Gina's provisions null and void, for he already possesses Fabrice's death sentence dated *from the preceding day,* that is, prior to the now-post-dated letter. What applied to the future if the true date had been respected has been thrown back into the past, and Gina has allowed the decisive moment to lapse. The temporal manipulation at stake in the scene confirms the importance of the element of time in confrontations between the strategist and the tactician.

Gina's failure is crucial for her—it is one of the few times in her life when she commits a clear tactical error, and it will be the most costly one. All hope for any "normal" life in Parma in the company of Fabrice ends for all practical purposes at this point. The potential contained within the fortuitous decisive moment is always at a maximum, and to forfeit the moment is to encounter a correspondingly profound reversal: defeat can be measured only by the extreme possibilities presented and missed.

We have now had the opportunity to explore in some detail a series of three related scenes in *La Chartreuse de Parme.* Not only must their similarities be emphasized but also their occurrence at such critical points in the narrative. The scene involving Gina and the prince marks the ultimate bifurcation of the novel toward Clélia and an impossible dream. And we have already had occasion to see the extent to which two other scenes play an inaugural role in the story of Fabrice. Before building further on the elements set forth in the above analysis, I would like to take a temporary detour into *Lucien Leuwen* in order to demonstrate, by means of an ultimate rehearsal, just how fundamental the structure revealed by the preceding readings is for Stendhal.

The reader will perhaps remember that after the military interlude at Nancy, which forms the first part of *Lucien Leuwen,* Lucien settles down to learn the ropes of the Parisian political bureaucracy of the Ministry of the Interior as personal secretary to the minister himself, M. de Vaize. An important episode in his education is the one during which Lucien attempts to salvage the election at Caen by preventing a ministerial adversary from being elected to the Chamber of Deputies. On that occasion, he meets and collaborates with a loyal and honest army general named Fari. Fari is destined to return in the novel and to be saved by Lucien in a manner that is structurally linked very closely to the scenes in *La Chartreuse de Parme* analyzed earlier. Things begin by chance once again—Lucien happens to see a report which crosses his desk at the ministry: "He had just seen a monthly police report sent by the minister of the interior to the minister of war indicating that General Fari had engaged in propaganda activities at Sercey, where he had been sent by the minister of war eight or ten days before the elections in ——, in order to calm the beginnings of liberal agitation" (1:1295). More than any of the protagonists we have studied, Lucien is placed in an interstice. Working for de Vaize without believing in him, with no illusions concerning him, Lucien is both within and without the sphere of influence of the power he serves and therefore able to maneuver at the boundaries, at the very place where he can learn what he is not always supposed to know. What better post than that of secretary in an administrative network circumscribing and invading the totality of French territory, namely, the Ministry of the Interior? In the course of his daily routine, access to a myriad of affairs is afforded him. While the police report in question is not originally a central concern of his, it nonetheless finds its way to his desk. He is therefore presented by chance with the possibility of intervening to save a friend by countering the wishes of his minister.

How does Lucien go about devising a method of intercession in this case? His first reaction is to confront de Vaize directly. As we might expect, his political force is far too inferior to that of de Vaize to hope seriously for success in this direction. After meeting with a rebuff, he sets out to maneuver in the back hallways, as it were. There, the help of idle gossip—the very type of discourse which, by definition, escapes the regulation imposed by the controlling political strategists—is enlisted, just as gossip of the same sort provided Gros with the subject of his famous caricature in Milan. Information upon which Lucien happens within his own space of maneuver (in his office) will lead to further information garnered within other comparable spaces (hidden halls, back staircases, and the like). Lucien consults one of de Vaize's former secretaries and ultimately discovers the truth: "The minister believed at one time that the general was courting his wife" (1:1296). Armed with this intelligence, Lucien must invent a tactic to forestall the disgrace of Fari. It should come as no surprise to discover that his mediation will focus on the written report condemning Fari. If it has been read, nothing can be done; but if not, there may still be an effective parry. Lucien hurries to the office that is the report's destination and fabricates a pretext to get the letter back. He pretends that a rough draft page was left in the report by accident:

"The Minister of the Interior sent me as quickly as he could—a page of the rough draft corrected by the minister was inserted in the last letter."

"Here is the letter," said the person in charge. "I have not yet read it. Take it back if you wish, but give it back to me before my working day begins tomorrow at ten o'clock."

"If it's only the middle page, I prefer to remove it here," said Lucien. (1:1297)

First success: no one has yet seen the contents of the report in question. Response by Lucien: immediate intervention in this fleeting, but absolutely propitious moment of floating uncertainty. Clearly at stake in this scene is another of the rifts permitting slippage and maneuver that we have encountered before. The letter is still in circulation between sender and receiver, vulnerable to an intervention in this ill-defined interval during which it belongs to no one. Evident also is the fact that the rift in question is directly related to the problem of time. The moment for action is embedded unstably between the past and the future, the composition of the letter and its reception by a reader. We are most certainly not in the stasis of presence sought by the strategist here, but in an undulating, uncertainly mobile instant which has not yet been seized by anyone. The resemblance to Vespasien's situation is striking indeed. Instead of a blank, we now have a three-page document signed on the final page by de Vaize. But doesn't this amount to the same thing? Nothing can prevent Lucien from sliding the second page out and substituting a different document in its place—which he proceeds to do forthwith. The critical passage for Fari's case is, by a stroke of luck (but isn't that what we have been talking about all along?), to be found on the second page: "He recopied the middle page. . . . The sentence relating to General Fari was the next to the last one on the back at the right" (1:1298). Lucien is able to modify the effects of his minister's signature by inserting a substituted discourse into the space preceding the endorsement. The crucial interval is represented in this instance by the material slippage of the sheet itself, as well as by the manner in which Lucien recasts the discursive space within the writing on the very surface of the replacement sheet: "Lucien was careful not to write his words and lines too closely together and succeeded so well that he eliminated the seven lines relating to General Fari without making the changes apparent" (1:1298). In this twist to the structure we have been reconstituting, Lucien is the one who creates a blank (he slips out the middle sheet and cuts out seven lines pertaining to Fari), but he is also the one who occupies it instantly. He recopies the second sheet and expands his writing in order to close up what could otherwise be detected by the potential future reader as empty lines.

No, a letter does not always reach its destination, as Lacan would have us believe.[17] And when it doesn't in this case, the blame falls squarely on chance. The axiom has now been verified four times between the texts of *La Chartreuse de Parme* and *Lucien Leuwen*. Although the structural similarities among the passages scrutinized have now become more visible, it remains for us to draw some general conclusions by summarizing at a more abstract level the factors that go into the construction of the propitious moments encountered. Having done this, we shall be better able to come back to the question of the characteristics and importance of the protagonists who must face the critical moments at stake in each instance. In the first place, the moments that have drawn our attention are in themselves apparently insignificant, neutral, like the countless other incidents occurring in the course of daily existence: a memory, a traveler who happens along a road, a café conversation, for instance. We have also noted, however, that they occur in topographically as well as temporally significant regions. There is, in other words, a curious combination of insignificance and potentiality attached to the spaces of marginality and indeterminacy we have encountered that makes of them points where something can occur, something which, although of no apparent import, offers the possibility of a rupture within preexistent structures both temporally and topographically ripe for reorganization. Simultaneously, however, there can be no passage to a new organization, to a new type of system without the presence of the potential to project those moments, in other words, to incorporate them into a structure that is elicited by them, to make of them occasions opening onto the new.

One must exercise caution when using the word "design" and its synonyms here. Whatever design there might be is formulated only when the provocation of the auspicious occasion triggers its necessity. Any prefabricated plan would be incapable of leading toward a difference, because its conception, inevitably tied too closely to what has come before, would be a mere repetition poorly adapted to unprecedented and fluctuating circumstances. The tactician is precisely one who is capable of laying aside preconceptions when confronted with a felicitous instant. What one really has, then, is the intersection of two disparate elements: a neutral incident and a ruse capable of transmuting it into an occasion. The disparity is between the faculty of ruse or reason, which is bent on organization and assimilation, on the one hand, and, on the other, something too minute or too insignificant to have been caught within the web of calculation. The neutral, yet propitious moment cannot be foreseen; it belongs to the province of chance. It is, in other words, so neutral, so bereft of meaning in and of itself that it could not have been assimilated beforehand into an interpretation predicting its occurrence. This is another way of suggesting that the fundamental characteristic of the moments in question is their singularity, the obscure difference contained within them which makes them impossible to measure by any ideal standards. Such standards can refer only to generalizing models that have the effect of reducing difference to sameness.

In each case with which we have dealt, however, the event is seized on by someone and transmuted into a project—not just any project, but one which effects a fundamental modification in the relations of force existing prior to the occasion in question. The theoretical implications are important here. The metamorphosis in relations of force characteristic of such moments is possible, it would seem, because below the surface of the visibly organizing structure, and outside the province of direct surveillance and control, there is a teeming mass of such events ready to rise to the surface and profoundly rearrange the existing status quo. This suggests that the apparent calm of a hegemonic structure hides, in reality, potentially disruptive forces waiting to undo it if they are seized on by someone capable of using them. Or to put it another way, one must perhaps give full weight to an argument running counter to the very existence of philosophy, namely, that the disorder of chance has precedence over ordered structures.

The relation of a power structure (which is also and perhaps foremost an interpretive structure) to what is undefined by it, to its other, is a topic directly related to the question of theory and its other and therefore of theory's relation to chance. Michel de Certeau broaches this problem in the context of his analysis of tactics, to which I alluded previously, when he critiques one of the most seductive recent attempts to deal with everyday tactical practices, namely, the one conceived by Michel Foucault in *Surveiller et punir*.[18] It would be fruitful for the present argument to follow de Certeau's reasoning on these questions in some detail. Initially, the principal indicator of the dichotomy between theories or ideologies and the everyday practices outside their sway is quite simply the fact that the latter "are no longer or not yet articulated in discourse," while the former inhabit and organize discourse.[19] How, then, can the theorist incorporate such "silent" practices into a discourse whose aim is to classify, appropriate, "talk about" them? The first sign of the difficulty inherent in the procedure is the multiplicity of nouns Foucault uses to designate the practices he wishes to isolate: *dispositifs, mécanismes, instrumentations, techniques,* the list could easily be extended. Foucault traces the intersections of such practices with the dominant ideologies of the Enlightenment. Those practices undermine and "colonize" the penal theory contained in Enlightenment ideologies. The eighteenth-century reformers elaborated in great detail a new system of penal justice in reaction to what had come to be seen as the barbaric public displays of the ancien régime. Parallel to this ideological revision, however, a whole system of disciplinary procedures was in the process of being developed, most characteristically in the context of schools and military life.

The techniques, procedures, and mechanisms of the disciplinary system became more and more refined and interlocking *without recourse to ideology* but, rather, as a series of minute displacements and adjustments which succeeded in blanketing the social space without being noticed, infiltrating the blind spots of the espoused ideology of penal justice. "In such procedures, the refinement of technology and the attention to minute detail triumph over theory and result in the universalization of a single, uniform manner of punishment—prison itself—which undermines the revolutionary institutions of the Enlightenment from within and everywhere substitutes penitentiary practices for penal justice."[20] Foucault's analysis sets up two different systems of power: the doctrinal texts of Enlightenment ideology and a technology of the body elaborated outside that doctrine. That technology is without a position in language and thus lacks a strategic position of its own *(propre)*: it succeeds in imposing itself against the grain of prevailing ideologies tactically, in their interstices. Foucault's description of the whole process at stake has a double function: "to mark out a social stratum of nondiscursive practices and to institute a discourse concerning these practices."[21] One can see the interests of such an attempt for de Certeau, who in *L'Invention du quotidien* is himself in search of an approach that can give a voice to tactics functioning in the absence of any explanatory discourse or representation in language. In an ironic, even astounding, reversal, Foucault's disciplinary mechanisms, formulated in the course of an infinite series of everyday gestures outside the light of dominant theories, finish by invading the social space as a whole and founding the discourse of modern social (the French would say *human*) sciences: what was previously without language becomes the very basis of contemporary analytic discourse. The disciplinary procedures centered on the notion of the panopticon, in other words, became the model for the analytic procedures of modern social sciences.

In many ways, Foucault's story, or history, is altogether too neat for de Certeau. In particular, it never really raises the question of why panoptical mechanisms and technologies came to enjoy their privileged status. Speculation about that question must ultimately encounter the more crucial problem of why all sorts of other procedures and techniques were left behind and did not gain such preeminence. In a most suggestive manner, de Certeau calls those other practices "*an immense reserve* containing the seeds or the traces of alternate developments."[22] Why privilege one of them and how is that privileging related to the process of formulation of Foucault's own theory? De Certeau claims that the elevation of panoptical technologies to the level of a controlling theory is a prime example of the manner in which theory incorporates what is outside its domain. Since it is manifestly impossible to embrace the entire domain of the other at once, in a single totalizing gesture, the first step in invading this indistinct region is to demarcate a part of the unknown in order to treat the part thus separated as a coherent whole, as a well-defined subsystem. The next step is to raise the fragment seized upon to the level of an explanatory paradigm which illuminates the remaining obscurity characteristic of the other: "At first obscure, tacit, and distant, [the unit thus set off] is elevated into a position from which it becomes the element illuminating theory and underlying discourse. In Foucault's work, the procedures lurking in the details of school, military, and hospital discipline, micro-apparatuses without discursive legitimacy, . . . become the reasoning that illuminates both the system of our society and the sciences of man."[23] The operation at stake is metonymic: a part of the unknown domain is cut off from the rest. Standing in its place, this metonymic object becomes the guiding explanatory principle of what remains unexplored.

What if the techniques, practices, and technologies that Foucault presents as the *object* of his theory were instead the very techniques that went into building the theory, its guiding *subject*? "The question no longer concerns the procedures organizing social surveillance and discipline, but the procedures producing Foucault's text itself. In fact, the micro-techniques provide not only the content of the discourse but also the process of its construction."[24] The techniques Foucault "discovers" are, in fact, the very techniques he mobilizes as tools for his own research. The panoptical procedures he claims to unearth, moreover, figure metaphorically and quite strikingly theory's all-seeing gaze. They provide him with the means to reveal what was previously invisible: the innumerable practices that were beyond the reach of theory before Foucault's operation commenced. One begins to perceive why the optical orientation of Foucault's "discoveries" is so important and so ironic. This orientation, moreover, carries over into Foucault's writing, which it structures at a rhetorical level: "Organizing a rhetoric of clarity—or 'écriture de la clarté'—it produces an effect of self-evidence in the public. But this theater of clarity is a ruse."[25] Under the guise of the rhetoric of clarity to which the contemporary reader has become accustomed in the context of modern social sciences, Foucault introduces the murky and uncertain practices which theory excludes, and they undermine and displace theory by surreptitiously providing a place for theory's other. What Foucault constructs is not a theory at all, but a persuasive, seductive narrative. This is not a negative judgment brought against Foucault by de Certeau, at least not entirely. On the contrary, de Certeau ultimately argues that such narratives are the only way "to clarify the relationship of theory with those procedures that [both] produce it

. . . [and] are the objects of study."[26] Narrative and storytelling are necessary tools for any attempt to scrutinize or comprehend practices and tactics. One cannot simply exclude narrative on the grounds that it is merely an unsophisticated preliminary approach to be overcome. It is instead an integral part of the encounter with the aleatory—unavoidable for every theory. Seduced in the beginning by the apparent elegance and clarity of Foucault's argument, the reader is destined to discover that its real power lies not in the theory it expounds but in the story it tells, a necessary story if one is to begin the difficult task of situating aleatory everyday encounters and practices.

The above remarks have direct bearing on the narrative moments we have been studying in *La Chartreuse de Parme* and *Lucien Leuwen*. One of the major characteristics of all of them is, as we have seen, that the actions accomplished are discursively oriented and closely related to storytelling, a fact that does not in the least preclude certain powerful effects in the sphere of personal and political action—on the contrary. Let us return for a moment to Fabrice's theft on the road back to Parma. We saw how that act succeeds in the absence of bloodshed or physical violence precisely because Fabrice mesmerizes the valet by fabricating an imaginative and rather comic yarn concerning an amorous intrigue involving his brother, Ascanio. The effects of the story go further still: by impersonating and impugning his brother, Fabrice manifestly strikes a blow against a blood enemy who has always made life difficult for him. This first narrative is not the end of things, because there is soon a kind of cascading embedding and mirroring *(mise en abîme)* of storytelling set into motion by the incident. Fabrice next describes the whole scene to Mosca (tells him the story), and the count's critical remarks provoke yet another story, the one about Vespasien del Dongo. At the heart of the tale involving Vespasien is the Bellerophon story, which suggests a tactic to Vespasien and allows him to escape from dire straits. In each situation where the two protagonists, Fabrice and Vespasien, are called upon to face an event and mold it into an occasion, to draw a lesson which permits them to formulate an effective tactic, a narrative is necessary, because only a narrative can enable the character to comprehend and activate the singularity of the aleatory moment that reverses relations of force. Outside the "lessons" provided by the narratives there remain only the well-beaten paths of "theory," that is, the ordered and controlled domains of some tyrant or another. To step outside such paths is to be faced with the problem of understanding in some way a totally different potentiality—and a narrative is pressed into service for this kind of transition.

Still more fascinating in the context of Fabrice's adventure and subsequent censure at the hands of Mosca is the effort made to end the circle of narratives and to introduce a dominating and dominant order. I am referring, of course, to Mosca's commandeering of Fabrice's story about Vespasien, to his efforts at formulating an appropriate moral. The moral is clearly a weapon of closure wielded by someone who would pretend to recuperate the narrative for the purposes of a preexistent and controlling knowledge, to reinsert the singular circumstance into a circuit of wisdom encompassing it and making of it just another example of a fixed and atemporal law. We have seen, however, that the moral at stake falls short of the universal—it is applicable only most of the time, not always. It cannot, in other words, fully encompass the potential for action that the story contains, the tactical practice which the story expresses. What escapes the purview of the law formulated in Mosca's moral is precisely what has been at stake the whole time: the aleatory nature of certain events which, if properly assimilated, reveal that any law is ill-founded. The strategist cannot triumph all the time, only most of the time. Further reflection on the other incidents analyzed earlier would reveal other complex relations to storytelling that can occur during moments when occasions, as we have been defining them, arise: from the reformulation of history through the story contained in Gros's caricature to the hypothetical suspension of the workings of Parma's judiciary system attempted by Gina in the letter she dictates to the prince of Parma. The realization of the potential contained within the auspicious occasion implies the necessity to assimilate moments that fall outside the realm of ideas and laws, of the universal and the always. To seize the occasion means to mobilize narrative organizations, those shifting constellations generated in critical instances that tap the depths of experience and memory, calling on a circumstantial thickness and opaqueness the law had thought to render transparent and ineffective.

A further suggestive direction to de Certeau's argument concerning Foucault remains to be explored. If indeed the objects of Foucault's analysis seem to turn into the structuring principles of his discourse, then it is safe to assume that the chance, fortuitous nature of the practices he studies is reproduced at the level of theory. De Certeau intimates as much in *Heterologies* when he gives the following admiring and yet somewhat ironic characterization of Foucault's research "methods": "This kind of 'art' is easy to see at work. It is an art of telling: suspense, extraordinary quotations, ellipses of quantitative series, metonymical samples. . . . It also is an art of seizing the opportunity and of making a hit. . . . His reading is a poaching. Hunting through the forests of history and through our present plains, Foucault traps strange things, which he discovers in a past literature" (p.191). This is not an attempt on de Certeau's part to discredit the research and study accomplished but rather an effort to get at its extraordinary dependence on certain surprise encounters. The persuasive force of the chance convergences which concatenate to make up the Foucaldian discourse increases progressively as Foucault's argument is deployed. At some point, the surprise such juxtapositions might at first provoke is absorbed into a convincingly tight and apparently autonomous theoretical discourse that convinces the reader of the absolute determination and necessity of the relations constructed, when, in fact, those relations are built only tactically, in the extraordinary richness of circumstantial encounters.

The stalking of the prey, the constant adjustments to new and different elements met in the course of the reflective procedure, the progressive cementing of an explanatory discourse as alluded to here possess a certain affinity with the suggestive description of similar cognitive processes that Michel Serres gives in *Hermès I: La Communication,* one of his early texts discussing structuralism.[27] In that work, Serres enlists the aid of the metaphor of the chess board, a metaphor made famous (at least for contemporary critics) by Saussure. Serres is concerned, however, with particular aspects of the comparison that differ from those which struck Saussure's fancy.[28] Whereas Saussure insists on the synchronic state of the relations among the pieces on the board after (or before) each move, Serres focuses on the shifting nature of the relation of each piece to the others as a result of the progress of the game, the differences in the respective forces of the pieces, and the fact that each move has evolutionary, temporal repercussions on relations throughout the network represented by the board: "On a chessboard one sees the confrontation of two differentiated and different networks *through the fine-resolutioned copenetration of these two networks.* In the space-time of the game, there is a transformation of each network, each for itself and each according to the transformation of the other. The situation as a whole is thus of a very complex mobility, so fluid that it is practically impossible to predict what will happen after two moves" (p.17). Emphasis is first placed on the confrontation between two networks or organizations and on the complexity of the interrelations they establish on the board.[29] Not only is the position of the pieces of great importance, but, in addition, not all are of equal force: each has its own special bearing on the evolution of the game. The result of the complexity underlined by this description is an intricate and changing dynamic which renders the determination and prediction of subsequent moves in the game a task of evolving and varying difficulty. As the game begins, one is presented with a situation in which one cannot predict with any acceptable degree of certainty exactly what the next move will be. A judgment concerning the coming decision is at best approachable as a probability at the limit of the purely fortuitous. As the game progresses, however, the situation gradually changes. The determination of the following moves can be predicted with increasing probability until at some point the observer approaches a moment of certainty—the decisive moment in which the outcome of the game will be determined by the checkmate. It must be recalled that beyond a certain threshold of probability, masters will resign, considering the outcome of the game to be irrevocably decided. Serres describes the process thus: "Indeed, *globally preparatory, underdetermined* situations (in extreme cases even *undetermined*) and *globally decisive overdetermined ones* (in extreme cases even '*pandetermined*') exist" (p.17).

There is, then, a tension between the aleatory at one end of the process and the absolutely determined at the other. The passage from one to the other takes place in a gradual manner over a period of time. "To hold onto both ends of the rope would consist in understanding how a *given transformation goes from probabilistic to overdetermined*: instead of arbitrarily choosing a series of fixed and equipowerful determinations, one must, on the one hand, explore the question of fixed determination in the direction of a plurality of underdetermined possibles and, on the other, explore its univocality in the direction of overdetermination. From that moment on, an actual process could only unfold . . . between two limits" (p.19). The model suggested by Serres throws a suggestive light on de Certeau's discussion of Foucault's "method." In particular, it offers an explanation for the sentiment one retains in Foucault's writing of the necessity of a theory constructed nonetheless out of the aleatory nature of the practices that theory confronts and attempts to encircle. As the network of theoretical mechanisms encounters the obscure practices it wishes to address and ultimately recuperate, one would be hard-pressed to predict which element of those practices will be the first to stand out and upon which the theoretical effort will originally focus. As the undertaking progresses, however, the steps it accomplishes take on an increasing air of persuasively determined direction, leading ultimately to a construction that possesses all the trappings of compelling necessity. Serres's argument proposes a very interesting paradigm, which points out the important place held by the fortuitous, approachable only via a probabilistic perspective in the process of theoretical formulations.

What catches the would-be theorist's attention is a matter of certain propitious circumstances that become deterministically necessary only after the fact, when the gradual process of approach toward the unknown has reached a decisive threshold.

The model in turn has repercussions on the opposition between strategy and tactic at the heart of the present analysis. What distinguishes the two could well be characterized by differing perspectives on the theoretical process outlined by de Certeau and Serres. The tactician evolves in the domain of underdetermined, if not totally aleatory, circumstances representative of the first moves in the confrontation between theoretical ruse and uncategorized practice. The strategist, on the other hand, would represent the one who occupies the domain of finished theory in which determination is at a maximum. What the strategist forgets or neglects is quite simply the fortuitous nature present at the founding of the law, the unpredictable propensities that gave the law its particular shape and signal its temporary (because nonoriginary) status.

[As things unfold, chance makes up for chance.]

Tout marche et le hasard corrige le hasard—Hugo

CHAPTER TWO

The Encounter, the Fall, and Superstition in Stendhal

A special type of protagonist is required to meet the challenge posed by the complex, fortuitous events that occur in the arena of tactics and everyday practices and to transform them into effective acts, to project their potential. Such events are at the heart of my concerns precisely because of their intimate connection with chance. My argument has cast Fabrice, Vespasien, Gros, Gina, and Lucien in the role of the tactician as defined earlier. One must be careful, however, not to convey an impression of panoptic calculation about them and thereby bring them too close to the strategists they oppose at various moments. Gina's failure is neither the only nor the fundamental element to point out in this context. Rather, one must insist on what is always beyond the control of our respective protagonists, namely, the occurrence of the decisive moment. If there is one characteristic they share, it is that they are in a definite sense at the mercy of time. They are unable to provoke the event permitting them to reverse an unfavorable situation and must await the occasion which presents itself against all odds when it is least expected. "The encounter: what comes without coming, what confronts one face to face, but always by surprise, what requires a wait, which the wait awaits but does not achieve," as Maurice Blanchot so aptly puts it.[1] They can be compared to each other, then, in their openness and malleability. Fundamentally available and receptive, they share the capacity to recognize the promise of the fortuitous and to seize it in order to transform it into a project directed toward an effective reformulation of the circumstances in which they are enmeshed. In *La Chartreuse de Parme* the type of calculation typical of the duke, the Austrians, the prince, and the minister of the interior is denied them by the narrator and even made into an object of disdain. Through Gina, the narrator will describe the strategist as a "courtisanesque" being (2:286), one more interested in ceremony and hierarchy (the better to organize his panoptical control) than in the potentiality the decisive moment can bring. The instant during which the determining act must be accomplished is not one for which simple intelligence suffices. Gina clearly realizes this fact as she reflects on what prevented her from succeeding in her moment of strength: "On that decisive evening, I did not need his [Mosca's] wits; he simply had to write what I dictated. All he had to do was to write the expression ["unjust procedure"] *that I had obtained* through my strength of character. His basely obsequious habits got the best of him" (2:286). Mosca trusted his calculating intelligence, his wits, when he should have relied on Gina's character. The character at stake here is a more fundamental faculty which reigns during moments of crisis when the encounter with the event requires an uncommon flair in order to provoke results far outreaching what any careful strategy might permit. In the midst of a completely new and unprecedented set of circumstances, multitudinous cultural memories, the sedimentation of time, and a savoir faire beyond the mere clarity of strategic intelligence allow the tactician to discern the occasion.

Gina is perhaps the character who gives voice most directly and suggestively to the type of approach to propitious moments outlined up to this point. In fact, however, she is both exemplary and different. The difference is an element that cannot fail to attract the reader's attention. In the first place, the protagonists at stake here are all male with one exception—and that exception carries with it certain fundamental implications. If Gina is the only woman, she is also the only character who fails to transmute her encounter with her dominator into a successful occasion. Rather than simply attribute her failure trivially to her weakened position as a woman and let things go at that, I prefer to follow a more revealing route and to explore her fiasco at a structural level. Although I maintain that the scene in which Gina confronts the prince of Parma is basically organized like the other scenes studied here, a deviation from certain common themes is nonetheless apparent. Stendhal's other characters involved in similar situations—Fabrice, Vespasien, Gros, Lucien—exhibit a particularly firm control over the discursive constructions they intend to manipulate at the decisive instant. There is simply no one around them to contest their respective assertive acts at the moment of accomplishment. This mastery is typically indicated by the fact that they *write* (or draw) on paper. The physical and material domination signified by the direct manipulation of paper and pen is an emblematic token of the very real political or personal ascendancy their acts will procure for them. Fabrice is an exception, but while he does not actually write the story he tells the valet—or anything else—during his scene of confrontation, his social superiority over the servant lends his remarks the kind of finality figured by the physical gesture of writing present in the other incidents: the valet simply has no conceivable rejoinder.[2]

Such is not the case with Gina. Her lack of success is built into the very organization of her clash from the start. She *dictates* her letter to the prince and never actually has her hand on the pen used to write it. What is more, there is an intermediary present who intercepts and deforms her discourse, removing and modifying the two most crucial elements. Significantly, it is the males in the scene who manipulate the writing instruments, specifically Mosca (but always with his eyes on the prince). It would be possible to maintain that as long as the conflict remains at the oral level, at the level of speech, Gina has the upper hand. When it comes to the moment of finalization, to actually writing down what amounts to a promise and a pledge abridging the prince's power, someone else pulls the strings (holds the pen). Further, the very grammatical structures employed by Gina in her dictation point to the tenuous nature of her fleeting mastery: through misplaced politeness she speaks in the conditional, almost hypothetically: "His Highness would write me a gracious letter, . . . He would tell me that . . ." (2:254). It should come as no surprise to the alert reader of *La Chartreuse de Parme* to see Gina's mastery placed at the level of speech (and not writing) in her conflict with the prince. Her domination of the social arena in the salons of Parma has always been based on this very strength; the capacity to find the right rejoinder at the precise moment necessary, the ability to take a remark made by someone else and turn it against an enemy, the irony of the double entendre—these are her weapons. The passage from speech to writing is lacking in the scene we have read; the ultimate step toward finalizing her triumph turns out to be impossible.

Gina's force in the arena of speech is represented figuratively throughout the Parma interlude in *La Chartreuse* in an unmistakable, even striking, thematic manner by the fact that she is the organizer and major actor of periodic commedia dell'arte plays arranged in the context of the social salons of Parma. The definition of this theatrical genre is provided by the narrator and is not without repercussions for the present argument: "A comedy *dell'arte* was being staged in the palace, in other words, one in which each character invents the dialogue as he delivers it—only the outline of the comedy is posted in the wings" (2:418). With only the barest outlines of the action provided before the presentation begins, the commedia dell'arte actor must be prepared to meet the unexpected and make of it a plausible stage performance. What better exercise to prepare one to recognize the potential of the event and to transform it into a viable occasion? No performance of the same play will resemble the last and therefore no preconceived notion of what to do at given conjunctures during the performance will suffice. There is a space of play in the commedia dell'arte, an interstice between what is given beforehand and what actually occurs on stage. This is the place of the occasion, the unexpected, the unpredictably fortuitous. One could well formalize the situation in terms of Michel Serres's epistemological model discussed at the end of the previous chapter. Given the bare outlines of a plot, the actor is left to focus on and seize what occurs during the performance in a way that defies any deterministic prediction. And yet, as the play progresses (if the performance has been persuasive), the denouement takes on an air of necessity after the fact, belying the fortuitous path adopted to lead to it.

Gina is at her best in just such situations.[3] Because she confronts the prince, as we saw earlier, with the same openness and receptiveness demonstrated in the theatrical context she knows so well, she almost obtains the upper hand. When the prince asks what she wants him to do to induce her to stay in Parma, she answers, "In truth, I have no idea, . . . in truth, I have no idea" (2:254). But the absence of a formulated project will not prevent her from sizing up the circumstances, judging her strength in the flash of an instant, and dictating the letter we have already analyzed. Reflecting on Gina's character at a later moment, Mosca tries to imagine what her plan will be following the arrest of Fabrice only to conclude: "She does not know herself" (2:300). Unpredictable precisely because she is forced to meet the unpredictable in the arena of political action (her only strength lies in these fortuitous occasions), Gina is a master at maneuvering within the space of play wherever she encounters it. Only when her opponent succeeds in closing that space, in removing all play, is she defeated.

This is what occurs in the scene with the prince when the passage to writing closes the gap definitively and precludes further tactical movement. A characteristic and corroborating illustration of what can happen in such instances is to be found elsewhere in the novel in the context of one of the theatrical performances Gina so enjoys. The reader will recall that after Fabrice's escape from the Tour Farnese, Gina gives Ferrante Palla the signal to poison the prince. Following the prince's death, Gina and Fabrice return to

Parma. The object of the new prince's desires, Gina now finds herself walking the same tightrope with the sovereign who has replaced her former tormentor. He soon begs her to allow him to play a role opposite her in one of the courtly comedies, and she agrees, promising to help him if his inspiration fails him in front of the audience. At ease in the uncertainty of the aleatory, Gina once again expresses her domination of the other by manipulating the theatrical context at will. To her surprise, however, "soon she was obliged to ask him to shorten the scenes; he spoke of love with an enthusiasm that often embarrassed the actress" (2:412). Having agreed to allow the prince to play the role of the suitor in the theater, the better to prevent him from obtaining an advantage over her and threatening her independence, Gina finds the space of play, the interstice on which the commedia dell'arte is founded, suddenly filled with the very discourse she had hoped to silence. Instead of mumbling or finding himself confined to an embarrassing silence, the prince speaks too much, too freely. Not only does he silence Gina, but he also threatens to suspend the very theatricality of the moment and turn it into a frank declaration of his love for her. Without the gap, the rift, the space of play in the other's discourse, Gina finds herself helpless before the monarch. Might we not say that it is more than a little dangerous for her to allow access to her privileged domain, the stage of the commedia dell'arte, to the very one who can then commandeer the space afforded him and thereby extend the panoptical span of his own strategy?

But perhaps we should not judge too hastily. Later, in precisely the context of another performance of the very same comedy, a second opportunity is afforded Gina to intercede effectively as tactician in the political domain. After playing his role to the hilt and with obvious pleasure on three different occasions, the prince is inexplicably unable to give a creditable performance on another evening: "The prince's acting was indeed terrible; he could barely be heard, and he no longer knew how to end his sentences" (2:421). Alerted to a potential danger signaled by the prince's mysteriously changed demeanor, Gina refuses to come to his aid and permits him to suffer through the first act: "The duchess remained near him, but coldly immobile" (2:412). The effect of Gina's decision is to provoke the very indiscretion on the prince's part which is indispensable if she is to protect herself in the upcoming crisis his behavior portends. The secret which troubles the prince and is of crucial interest to Gina is divulged in a characteristic context, in another of the marginal places which have been so important to the confrontations explored in the course of the present argument: in the stage wings, *les coulisses,* in a space that is neither wholly theatrical nor wholly a part of what is "outside" the fictional domain of the stage and performance: "Finding himself alone with her at a certain moment in the actors' room, the prince went and closed the door" (2:422). Once again the reader meets a region representing a rift, an interstice. In the wings, the prince is neither the actor he is onstage nor quite the monarch he is offstage. Small wonder that here he addresses Gina as if she were momentarily suspended between her own two roles as actress and as *grande maîtresse* of the prince's mother. This is a moment of interaction outside the two stages on which life in Parma takes place—the theater and the social world of the salons—and here the prince can disclose a secret of which she likely would not have been informed elsewhere or in other circumstances.

What is the information gleaned by Gina in the course of the prince's unusual private conversation with her? No less than that Rassi has assembled a dangerously accurate dossier concerning the machinations leading to the former prince's death. Although the present prince has not yet read the dossier, Gina can be fairly certain that it is damning for her. In a fleeting moment, in the drift of an uncertainty lasting only while the documents in question remain unread (the very same type of moment that allowed Lucien's intervention on Fari's behalf in *Lucien Leuwen*), in an opening at the frontier of "normal" courtly relations, Gina encounters by chance a vital piece of information and is thereby presented with an auspicious occasion for the second time. Just as the structure of the encounter is of interest to us, so also are the means she employs to make of it a moment of transformation. She persuades the prince to confide in his mother and reveal everything he has already told her, whereupon the three protagonists find themselves locked up alone in a protracted discussion concerning the response to be given to Rassi's troubling and potentially explosive documents. As before, Gina awaits the decisive moment, refusing to enter into the discussion and commit herself until she is called on directly. When her opinion is ultimately solicited, she responds in a manner absolutely in keeping with what we have encountered in our reading up to this point: she has the prince read aloud a La Fontaine fable, namely, "Le Jardinier et son seigneur." A narrative is pressed into service at the crucial moment, because in the absence of any clear law dictating the course of action to adopt, it suggests, through its illustration of a practical, everyday predicament, the very mode of action Gina wants the prince to sanction. More than anything Gina could have said had she adopted the analytic tone of courtly political judgment and discussion, the fable is persuasive, and, consequently, the sovereign and his mother choose to act against Rassi and for Gina.

Decidedly, when confronted with an original, unprecedented opportunity, the tactician in Stendhal's novels looks to the story for inspiration. The decision made in favor of Gina's counsel represents a victory which will spare the disclosure of her involvement in the death of the former prince and thus perhaps a trip to the scaffold. The manner in which her successful intervention is finalized is simultaneously different from and fundamentally related to other scenes studied earlier. We have seen how the mastery of the decisive moment is customarily expressed by the act of writing, and we have also noted that Gina, who held her own at the level of speech, failed to convert her advantage into a lasting project when her oral discourse was intercepted by a male intermediary who wrested control from her at the last moment. In a twist ironically indicating that the lesson taught by the earlier infelicity has been well learned, Gina opts to bypass the moment of writing altogether in this instance by destroying outright the painstakingly assembled written materials that were the object of the discussion in the first place: "Very well! A brief comment and nothing more: burn, in the fireplace right there, all the papers assembled by the viperous Rassi and never reveal to him that they have been burned" (2:426). Thrown into the fireplace where they will be charred beyond recognition, the written documents disappear along with the threat to Gina's position within the state of Parma. Only Fabrice's desire to return to the Tour Farnese will undo what she has accomplished—never again will the forces of the political strategists defeat her, since she has now definitively checkmated them.

Armed with the experience and manner illustrated by her talents in the domain of the commedia dell'arte, Gina is well suited, in the final analysis, to spar with the strategist in the space of play where the chance incident can furnish the occasion for a reversal and reformulation of relations of force. The concept of play, which has come to the fore in the preceding discussion, merits further reflection. Its meaning is apparently double: theatrical, as we have seen, and thus linked to performance and role, but also relational and confrontational and thereby related to the problem of play in the context of the game. The metaphor of the game has often tempted Stendhal's readers.[4] In fact, if Gina does indeed conceive of the courtly life of Parma in theatrical terms (as she says to Mosca following the auto-da-fé described above, "I am exhausted. I played my role for an hour on stage and for five hours in [the prince's] chambers" [2:429]), the metaphor of the game is never far behind. Her attempt to grasp what it might be like to take up residence in Parma with Mosca at the beginning of their liaison is couched in terms of a comparison with the game of whist: " 'A court is ridiculous,' the countess would say to the marquise, 'but it is amusing. It is a game which interests one, but whose rules one must accept. Who ever thought of complaining that the rules of whist are ridiculous? Yet once accustomed to the rules, it is most agreeable to make a slam against your adversary' " (2:130).

To set the stage, as it were, for a treatment of play in the nontheatrical sense, one must first point to some additional textual material in *La Chartreuse de Parme*. The appeal to the image of the game of whist as a structural metaphor indicated above is destined to reappear: it will once again be on Gina's lips when she gives her parting advice to Fabrice as he sets off to study theology in Naples. Fabrice is to accept what he will be taught while at the seminary in precisely the same spirit he would accept the rules of whist. There are certain rules one has to learn to apply in the world, but on no account should Fabrice become enmeshed in such ethical questions as the suitability of such rules for fundamental religious belief: "Believe or do not believe what you will be taught, *but never object to it*. Imagine that you are being taught the rules of the game of whist. Would you object to the rules of whist?" (2:137). Although Fabrice's ecclesiastical career is clearly envisaged by Gina, Mosca, and to some extent Fabrice himself as a worldly substitute for the military career Fabrice would have preferred, this is nonetheless strange advice to give one who is off to study theology! In another passage, Mosca compares his own political and social activity in the court of Ranuce-Ernest IV to a game of chess and, significantly, associates this metaphor with theatrical activity in the same breath: "Now I dress like a character in a comedy to live the good life and earn a few thousand francs. Once I had entered into this kind of chess game, . . . I wanted to be among the best" (2:111–12). Perhaps the most striking confirmation of the place and importance of play and games in *La Chartreuse de Parme* comes when the game of whist subsequently reappears near the end of the novel as an emblem of Fabrice's worldly success. After a lengthy interruption in their relationship, Fabrice has occasion to renew his contacts with Clélia Conti (now Marquise Crescenzi) on the very evening when, while making an official appearance at a soiree in the prince's palace, he is invited to be the fourth player in the prince's regular whist game: "The chamberlain on duty ran after him to inform him that he had been designated to play whist with the prince. In Parma, this was an unheard-of honor, one well above the rank that the coadjutor occupied in society" (2:459). Here the game on which Gina counseled Fabrice to pattern his public behavior suddenly reappears in very real form as the somewhat ironic sanction of Fabrice's political success. His career opens with a reference to a game which is to serve as a model of political sagacity and reaches an acme never to be surpassed in a scene where the same game has become a veritable political coronation.

What are we to make of these passages? The first point that needs to be emphasized is the confrontational nature of play as conceived here. Gina speaks first of respect for the rules when mentioning whist originally, but her statement closes with explicit reference to the notion of struggle contained in the metaphor, with a mention, in other words, of the agonistic clash elicited by the presence of an adversary against whom one must maneuver in order to assure a personal triumph: "It is most agreeable to make a slam against your adversary." Mosca soon seconds this approach, as we saw above: "Once I had entered into this kind of chess game, . . . I wanted to be among the best." At stake here is anything but a relaxed, naive approach to the idea of playing the game. On the contrary, such an activity reproduces the conflictual relations one meets regularly in the world. The act of playing the game always involves at least two people in strife: the subject and the adversary. If play is confrontational, it is, by the same token, relational. One is always pitted against someone against whom one wants to pull off the slam. As J. Bonitzer puts it at one point in his discussion of John Von Neumann's and Oskar Morgenstern's theory of strategic games, "It is obvious . . . that disinterest on the part of the players with respect to the outcome of the game deprives it of any significance. As is well known, it is without interest to play against a player who is too weak or too unmotivated. . . . To refuse to win is to do away with the game."[5] Thus although Gina might at first seem to emphasize the rules (advising Fabrice to follow the rules to the limit), clearly the real interest of the game lies elsewhere. If what is at stake here is a clash between or among parties, the second essential factor must then be the *uncertainty of the outcome*. As Bonitzer maintains, when the result is assured, the struggle between or among players is of no interest. Weakness and lack of motivation must be avoided at all costs because they immediately destroy all desire to proceed. The chances of the opposing parties must be equal enough so that either's victory remains within the realm of possibility.

The field of suspense and indecision which results from the impossibility of knowing who will triumph in a given conflict set up along the lines suggested above is the domain where the fortuitous circumstance can lead to the victory of one of the parties engaged in the struggle. It is the space of what Marcel Détienne and Jean-Pierre Vernant have categorized as the faculty of ruse in Greek thought, what the Greeks termed *metis*.[6] The study of *metis* undertaken by Détienne and Vernant begins with a reference to an emblematic episode in book 23 of the *Iliad* describing the chariot race that takes place in the context of the funeral games. Antilochus, although the youngest and thus ostensibly the least favored of the charioteers who confront each other in the race, profits from a moment of inattention on the part of Menelaus at a critical juncture and wins the race by means of a more or less fraudulent maneuver, but one which reveals the importance of cunning intelligence applied with requisite attention at the proper moment (pp.18–19). This episode reveals what Détienne and Vernant call "the unpredictable nature of every agonistic situation and the profit invariably drawn from this by the faculty of *metis*" (p.219). In fact, it does not really matter whether or not the two (or more) parties involved in the agonistic struggle are exactly matched. One may appear weaker than the other and thus to have less chance to triumph. Yet the slim possibility that the weaker party may pull off a victory maintains sufficient suspense concerning the outcome. This is so precisely because the space of the agonistic confrontation is fraught with incidents and moments which can suddenly turn into occasions radically transforming the relations of force between players—even when it might appear that one of the adversaries has but little chance to prevail. The critical moments encountered on the field of agonistic struggle are compared by Détienne and Vernant to the dangers and uncertainties faced by the navigator:

If the athletic contest seems to take place in a kind of closed field where limits are fixed by referees and where movement is subject to rules, every agonistic activity—whether it be a test of speed or a chariot race—takes place, in reality, in a space homologous from a certain point of view to that of the sea. With its dangerous points, with its critical moments, the agonistic space is the site where all reversals are possible, where the path fixed by rules is doubled by all the passages that *metis* knows how to open and to clear. (pp.222–23)

The confrontational domain in which parties brave one another is thus a further incarnation of the critical junctures already encountered in our reading in the form of certain other liminal spaces. At the moment when there seems to be no viable path (because there are too many paths), circumstances can appear and suggest an exit. The figure of the navigator, Vespasien del Dongo, finds its double in that of the cunning player, Gina.

The uncertainty, so crucial in the analysis of play developed above, may be approached from a different angle. The rules of the game define with precision a certain number of the aspects involved in the encounter between the two players. According to Geneviève Even-Granboulan, "Real games themselves are the fruit of artifice or, rather, can take place only in the context of precise rules."[7] Within the domain of those rules, however, all is not definitively set forth. What remains undefined once the rules are agreed upon is the space of play, in a very precise sense of the expression. Roger Caillois explains this beautifully: "The word 'play' [*jeu*—also meaning "game" in French] ultimately evokes an idea of latitude, of freedom of movement, a useful liberty, but not an excessive one, as when one speaks of the *play* in a gear mechanism or when one says that a ship *plays* at anchor. This latitude makes an indispensable mobility possible. Play permits the functioning of the mechanism. . . . It is appropriate to leave some empty space or free play at the heart of the most exact economy."[8] Caillois, one of the most astute modern observers of the anthropological characteristics and significance of play and games, insists forcefully on an aspect of the concept of play which must never be overlooked. Play also refers to something like the play in a machine, to the part of the mechanism that lies at the borders of the strict relational and structural ties that keep the rest of the machine from flying apart. A machine, like a confrontational game, is paradoxically highly structured and yet unstructured. Or perhaps one should put it in a slightly different way: the structure provides for a space of nonstructure. Clearly, if all the parts fit together too precisely, the mechanism freezes and movement is precluded. Likewise, if every situation in a game were exhaustively defined, there would be no game at all, for the points of interest in the game's unfolding are those specific instants when decisions are required and bifurcations can occur. In the uncertainty of the space of play, the unexpected befalls the player, chance rears its head, and the tactician reveals himself or herself. This space of play stands in clear correlation to the area of maneuverability left open for the actor of the commedia dell'arte and thus clarifies the link between the metaphor of theater and that of the game so prevalent in *La Chartreuse de Parme*.

The space of play in question here corresponds structurally to the numerous points of rupture and the various interstices encountered in our readings both of crucial passages in *La Chartreuse de Parme* and of the Fari incident in *Lucien Leuwen*. If Gina has been viewed as a representative example of action at the tactical fringes of social and political situations, in other words, as the consummate player in an ongoing agonistic game, a preliminary approach to Fabrice reveals many of the same elements. He is a character adept at maneuvering in passageways, a veritable amateur of liminal areas. His decision to join the emperor following Napoleon's return from his first exile marks a point of rupture in his life which will henceforth constantly put him outside, at the fringes. It will prevent him from living any semblance of a "normal" life within a society bent on forgetting all that the emperor has wrought. Fabrice becomes an outlaw in many senses of the word, condemned to a series of exiles and to a sometimes perilous tightrope walking at frontiers and borders, in the margins of social organizations and discourse. One might cite as an example in this context the ploy he invents to record his feelings while in prison and deprived of proper writing utensils. He writes in the margins of a copy of the works of Saint Jerome lent to him by Don Cesare: "Fabrice was generous to call notes the infinite scribblings with which he had filled the margins of an in folio copy of the works of Saint Jerome" (2:392). Forced to endure the kind of overbearing surveillance that only a prison sentence can impose, Fabrice succeeds nonetheless in invading and transforming the space inevitably left blank by an oppressive power structure. This space, as always, furnishes an unexpected and chance potential. Pressed into service ostensibly to inform Don Cesare of Fabrice's plight, it soon veers toward something else: the expression of Fabrice's love for Clélia. Clélia will read as a confirmation of his passion a discourse originally destined for her uncle but which ultimately does double duty.[9] Vespasien del Dongo reasserts his presence as a model for Fabrice down to the very act of seizing upon and writing in discursive margins, of turning them away (*détourner*) from their original purposes. In a general sense, Fabrice's success in transforming the rigors of prison into a context within which he not only will function with a minimum of difficulty but will also be able to express his desire (his love for Clélia) is testimony enough to his adeptness at maneuvering within the limited range afforded him.

An analysis that attempts to set forth the specific characteristics of Fabrice as actor in the spaces of chance constructed in *La Chartreuse* would ultimately, however, have to follow a course slightly different from the one appropriate for Gina and, in so doing, would have to see him as someone I would call "a man of encounters," someone, in other words, whose existence is deeply marked by a series of chance meetings.[10] Let us take the first confrontation with Clélia as a point of departure, opening not only onto the question of Fabrice himself but also onto the enigma of the encounter in general. Fleeing Grianta toward Milan with his mother and Gina in order to seek the mercy of the Austrian officials after the Waterloo interlude, Fabrice meets Clélia Conti for the first time: "Fabrice, who was quite attentively looking in every direction seeking the means to save himself, saw a young girl fourteen or fifteen years old, crying timidly into a handkerchief, come out of a small path across the fields" (2:98). At the heart of a tense moment during which Fabrice fears for his own safety after his party has been detained by a patrol of Austrian police, a quasi-miraculous vision appears—the woman destined to become the object of Fabrice's desire. What one has in this instance is a Cournot-like occurrence evincing a structure familiar to every French schoolboy and girl who has heard Henri Bergson's story of the roof tile and the passerby recounted by his or her philosophy teacher.[11] The exemplary story at stake almost canonically illustrates Cournot's definition of chance as the intersection of two causal chains as far removed from one another as possible. A passerby happens along a street for reasons pertaining to his own existence alone at precisely the moment when a roof tile from a building along his path accidentally falls on him. The intersection brutally and mortally brings together two causal chains unrelated to one another. The passerby knows nothing of the existence of the building or its roof or those who constructed it—and vice versa—until the fatal instant when the trajectories of the two intersect. Although the passerby's death is rigorously determined by a series of mathematical laws dealing with the gravity, speed, and trajectory of his body and the tile's mass, it is also simultaneously undetermined because it was beyond human foresight before it happened. The causal chains which led up to the intersection were too far removed from one another ever to have been calculated or calculable.

The nature of the intersection at stake in the Fabrice/Clélia encounter resembles the emblematic incident described above and prompts one to reflect on the structure of such meetings. At a first level, an encounter of this type would seem to be the concrete expression of a new or at least unsuspected relation between two series which previously had appeared different but now seem significantly interconnected. In other words, one is immediately tempted to see in it a junction marking some underlying wholeness or harmony, which was invisible prior to the convergence of the two series. But that would be to posit a bit too hastily an essential unity restored or at least designated by the moment of intersection. Such an approach would place the interpreter squarely in the wake of the Hegelian view of the unfurling of world history—what Luc Ferry and Alain Renaut call the Hegelian *ruse de la raison:* "the theory of 'the ruse of reason,' the theoretical model made explicit by Hegel in his philosophy of history, consists in affirming that 'in history everything occurs rationally,' in other words, everything is explainable, intelligible. One thus asserts that the historical real is, in this sense, rational, that nothing in it is without rational justification, that there is no chance, that everything is deducible or necessary in itself—even if we are incapable of effectively perceiving this necessity."[12] If one views in this manner the coincidence represented by the type of intersection created when Fabrice first meets Clélia, one ultimately empties it of all strangeness, of all surprise. The Hegelian "principle of unity . . . makes of coincidence not an irreducible *strangeness,* but a promise of coherence or a reminder of concordance," as Maurice Blanchot claims when reflecting on the Hegelian approach to such occurrences.[13]

In fact, a second and diametrically opposed understanding of the encounter lurks potentially in the wings to refute the easy reduction tantalizingly offered by the first. Blanchot continues: "At the point of junction—the unique point—what comes into relation remains without relation, and the unity thus evidenced is only the surprising manifestation (by surprise) of the nonunifiable, the simultaneity of what under no circumstances could be together. Thus one must conclude, even if this forces us to damage logic, that where junction takes place, disjunction reigns and explodes any unitary structure" (p.609). The intersection represented by the encounter, maintains Blanchot, may also be interpreted as a mark of the essential heterogeneity of phenomena, the impossible distance between them illustrated by a point of convergence which, although it may immediately suggest unity, underlines just as powerfully the radically noncontemporaneous nature of phenomena foregrounded in the very moment of intersection. In other words, the moment of convergence also contains an implicit, if not explicit, allusion to their prior separation, to the absence of any significant link between them: "The encounter thus designates a new relation, because at the point of coincidence—which is not a point but a gap—noncoincidence intervenes (is affirmed in the inter-vention)" (p.609). Blanchot's willfully antithetical formulation of the nature of causal intersections attempts to turn the tables on any Hegelian recuperation. The proper geometric figure expressing the encounter would not be a point but, rather, an *écart,* a separation, distancing, or gap. The case of Fabrice and Clélia is an exemplary one for the perspective Blanchot defends. At the outset, the reader of *La Chartreuse de Parme* can take their meeting only as a sign of an inevitable destiny which links their existences by englobing them in a mutual passion and desire, a narrative ploy announcing a coming plot fulfillment not unlike the incident in *Le Rouge et le noir* when Julien finds the torn newspaper article on the floor of the church in Verrières. But this would be to forget that in fact Fabrice and Clélia will never be together in the sense that a superficially romantic reading might imagine. Their relationship will be one marked by obstacles and failures, destined to be impossible within the social bonds of marriage and leading ultimately to the premature death of both parties. At the center of the encounter between the two is not a structure of unity but one of radical discontinuity between Fabrice and Clélia—mortal for them both. Instead of signaling the union of disparate lives in a more encompassing wholeness, the encounter is the beginning of a relationship characterized fundamentally by solitude and finally by death. The prison bars, Clélia's untimely marriage to Crescenzi, and her vow to the Madonna never to look on Fabrice nor to allow him to look upon her are all elements bearing witness to a crucial distance between the two protagonists which cannot be expunged.

The preceding remarks raise some further important questions about the nature and implications of the famous example commonly cited to illustrate Cournot's thesis concerning chance. The intersection of the separate existences of the passerby and the roof tile results in the passerby's death.[14] The essence of the chance encounter now become accident is linked intimately to mortality. In a hasty concentration on the moment of conjunction and the causal chains leading up to it, the reader tends to overlook this rather obvious fact. One could well assert, however, that the mortal threat inherent in the structure betokens very precisely the essential and radical indeterminacy and distance at stake in chance convergences. Whatever causal chains lead up to the moment of death, whatever explanations one may concoct to explain and rationalize it, death itself always remains other, impossible to imagine. No explanation can account for it if this means making sense of it. Lingering beyond the existential purview of mortals, death figures starkly as the unexplained, that which forever remains mysterious because it is inexplicable. As such, it represents the fundamental surprise within the chance occurrence, impossible to dismiss by means of an interpretation that would sublate it and incorporate it into a more encompassing Hegelian view of the unfolding unity of historical phenomena. The shock of the chance meeting is in the essential noncoincidence symbolically marked by its mortal nature. Fabrice's first meeting with Clélia may well signal the narrative union of the two characters, always tempered, nonetheless, by a distance they cannot surmount, one that is eventually fatal. Other encounters that are a part of Fabrice's story confirm the deadly content of such moments. We have already seen how the theft of the horse takes place at gunpoint with the very real threat of bloodshed skirted only because of Fabrice's quickly invented fiction. Another notable meeting in the novel takes place on a road near the site of the archaeological dig Fabrice is conducting for Mosca, namely, the confrontation with Giletti, which effectively results in Giletti's death—with all the subsequent consequences for Fabrice's own existence.

The Clélia/Fabrice encounter is really a reenactment of a classic narrative scene, perhaps the emblematic sequence of novelistic fiction in general. This is quickly and easily verifiable by reference to one of the first analytic novels in the French tradition, Mme de Lafayette's *La Princesse de Montpensier*. The heroine of that story, Mme de Montpensier, becomes embroiled in an impossible love for the duc de Guise, which leads eventually to the death of her closest friend, the destruction of her marriage, and her own premature demise. The essential element for the present analysis is the means whereby de Guise and Mme de Montpensier come into contact. Although de Guise had been one of her admirers in his youth, a sentiment reciprocated by Mme de Montpensier at the time, the two protagonists ultimately lose touch with one another and go their separate ways. One day, however, de Guise is leading the duc d'Anjou through an unfamiliar shortcut in a forest on the way to the village where d'Anjou is headquartered during a military campaign. De Guise loses his way and leads the party off in the wrong direction. Everyone realizes a mistake has been made as the group of riders nears a river which is not supposed to flow next to the road de Guise has chosen. Significantly for the present argument, what later transpires in this scene results from this wrong turn, which sends the members of the party into the midst of the forest and leaves them unable to make their way to their original destination. We have seen how liminal areas (forests, bodies of water, even roads) and the inevitable disorientation they bring are almost a necessity for meeting with the fortuitous.

Upon the river, de Guise and d'Anjou espy none other than Mme de Montpensier engaged in an afternoon promenade. The apparition is enough to rekindle de Guise's desire to conquer Mme de Montpensier. The description given by the narrator brings together all the ingredients that have been the subject of the preceding analysis of Fabrice's first meeting with Clélia: "This adventure gave the young princes and all their followers a new joy. It appeared to them to be the stuff of fiction. Some told the duc de Guise that he had led them astray on purpose in order to show them this beautiful person. Others said that after what chance had accomplished he simply had to fall in love with her. And the duc d'Anjou maintained that, on the contrary, it was he who should be her lover."[15] Originally irritating for the members of the party because they are lost in the forest, the incident abruptly veers toward adventure with the chance encounter of a beautiful woman. The fortuitous intersection of the existences of male and female protagonists immediately transforms a banal, rather uninteresting trip into a scene which can only be "the stuff of fiction." "Love is a lottery. Grace is a lottery. This is the essence of the novel," says Michelet, when comparing novelistic narrative to historical narrative in the *Bible de l'humanité*.[16] But once again, what seems to lead toward a union of the two existences, toward their ultimate coincidence, in fact results in the devastation of Mme de Montpensier's life and verifies the axiom we have been formulating. The intersection issuing from the chance encounter always marks an essential distance represented by the unknown, by death itself: "She died shortly thereafter, in the prime of her life, one of the most beautiful princesses in the world, and the one who would doubtless have been the happiest if virtue and prudence had directed all her actions," reads the last sentence of the novella some pages later (p. 33). De Guise never succeeds in regaining a position within the inner region of Mme de Montpensier's life, a fact made clear by the disaster that occurs when he tries to visit her inside the walls of her husband's château. The reference to virtue and prudence in this final phrase is significant. To live a life of virtue and prudence would mean, very precisely, never to be exposed to the kind of chance encounter which provokes the very downfall the narrator of *La Princesse de Montpensier* deplores. It would imply, moreover, that the rules of prudence govern all events if one would simply respect them. We have seen, however, that the truly significant incidents always seem to be singular, fortuitous, and portentous—not easily assimilated by the strictly prudent or the narrowly virtuous attitude.

Let us now return to *La Chartreuse de Parme*. As important and representative as Fabrice's encounter with Clélia may be, there is notable material for a further development of this same problematic even prior to the meeting as it was described earlier. In particular, the interlude in the novel dealing with Fabrice's Waterloo fiasco is full of wildly diverse encounters: from the vivandière to Aniken (one wonders, in fact, whether meeting Aniken is not just a preparatory rehearsal for what transpires in more detail when Clélia finally appears).[17] Moreover, and I think more fundamentally, an encounter with Lieutenant Robert (who has become a general when it takes place) is to be found at the heart of the portion of *La Chartreuse de Parme* devoted to the battle at Waterloo. When the existential trajectories of Fabrice and the man who may be his father intersect in the midst of a raging military clash, certain new elements in the structure of the chance encounter not yet explored in our analysis become manifest and bring further complexity to the question. In the first place, the distance/separation we have discovered at the point of copresence, a copresence supposedly accomplished in the intersection of causal chains, is more than ever at the fore in this instance. Having set off with an escort of hussars in the company of Field-Marshal Ney, Fabrice suddenly—without warning or any means of anticipating the incident—finds himself following Count d'A***, who is none other than Robert: "He noticed upon coming out of the hollow that the escort was no longer with Field-Marshal Ney. The general they were following was tall, thin, and had sharp features and fierce eyes. This general was none other than Count d'A***, the Lieutenant Robert of 15 May 1796" (2:68). The distancing tendency foregrounded in the preceding analysis is represented first in this passage when neither Fabrice nor Robert realizes he is in the presence of the other: "What joy he [Robert] would have felt to see Fabrice del Dongo!" (2:68) But, of course, he does not have time in the heat of military action to notice anything of the sort. As for Fabrice, he is in a state of excitement rendering him incapable even of recognizing the emperor himself when he glimpses him—much less of noticing Robert (whom the reader cannot even be sure he knows): " 'So that was the emperor who passed by there?' he asked his neighbor" (2:67).

At stake in this passage, therefore, is an incident that both brings Fabrice and Robert together and cleaves them utterly apart. For an instant they are in the closest possible proximity to one another and yet in a state of crucial noncoincidence. A central factor of this most curious and essential chance encounter on the battlefield is, then, that it marks a gap or distance at the center of the link between the two characters. Moreover, the material structure of the moment under consideration—proximity and distance simultaneously signified as the two characters ride almost side by side—most certainly serves a wider symbolic purpose. The convergence of destinies that both happens and does not happen at Waterloo clearly underlines the complexity of Fabrice's relationship with Robert. Presented— albeit between the lines—as a lover of Fabrice's mother during the occupation of Milan and Italy by the French, Robert simultaneously is and is not Fabrice's father: in many ways an ideological father, perhaps a biological one, but with no certainties on either of these scores. The blank that Stendhal arranges to leave in the novel with respect to the paternal question is precisely what is figured in the nonintersecting intersection occurring at Waterloo. The reader experiences here a variation on the problematic of noncoincidence suggested by the theme of the chance meeting.

There is a good deal more to be said about the incident in *La Chartreuse de Parme* outlined above. The context in which it occurs is of primary interest and must be described in some detail. Counseled by the faithful vivandière, Fabrice buys a horse as the battle of Waterloo commences and sets out on a chaotic ride across the battlefield.[18] As he gallops over the muddy terrain in pursuit of a group of generals to whose escort he has become attached, the confusion augments incessantly and renders the possibility of perceiving exactly what is happening more and more difficult: "The smoke prevented him from distinguishing anything in the direction in which they were advancing. At times one could make out galloping men set off against the white smoke" (2:65). The celebrated question formulated by Fabrice as he rides along is the result of this impossibility to distinguish anything with sufficient clarity: "Is this a real battle?" (2:65) To make matters worse, he stops to refresh himself with a large dose of aqua vitae: "Fabrice felt completely tipsy. He had drunk too much eau-de-vie, and he was rolling a little in his saddle" (2:67). Dulled even further by this excess, he becomes more disoriented than ever: "He remembered in timely fashion a remark repeated by his mother's coachman: When one has downed a few too many, one must fix one's gaze between the horse's ears and do as those around are doing" (2:67). Amid the commotion of cannon shots, falling cannonballs, crisscrossing soldiers of all types, dead and wounded bodies lying on the ground, Fabrice's disorientation becomes such that he misses the emperor himself. Precisely at the moment of maximum confusion, as the light of the battlefield is beginning to fade and become more treacherous ("the sun was already quite low" [2:68]), as Fabrice succeeds ultimately in losing even the escort with which he has been riding, he suddenly finds himself in the presence of Robert. Their encounter itself is extremely brief. It is abruptly cut short when a cannonball falls among the members of the escort, unhorsing four of the hussars and General d'A*** himself. Whereupon Fabrice precipitously finds himself on the ground as well, unhorsed by the others to provide a mount for the general: "He felt someone taking hold of his feet; they were lifted up while his body was held under his arms; he was swung over the hindquarters of his horse and then allowed to slip to the ground where he fell in a sitting position" (2:69). The encounter with Robert is also—almost simultaneously—marked by a fall, itself in a clear sense the acme of the chaos and confusion which has reigned since the moment when Fabrice's horse decided to gallop toward the battlefield some hours earlier.

What are we to make of this material? The emphasis in the passage detailed above is much more on chaos and multiplicity than it was during the encounter with Clélia. The singularity of the Fabrice/Clélia meeting is emphasized, somewhat falsely, by its isolation. The contrary is true when Fabrice meets Robert on the battlefield at Waterloo. There is almost too much happening, certainly too much from Fabrice's perspective. As a result of the tumult, he never seems to get his bearings. The difference in emphasis may well allow one to begin to formulate a definition of the chance encounter which avoids to some extent the limitations of Cournot's explanation. Michel Serres puts the problem in the following terms in an article devoted to Jacques Monod's *Le Hasard et la nécessité*: "Chance would be unthinkable—merely pathetic—without a set, a variety to serve as a basis. What is important here is indeed the plurality, the number of 'factors,' the pure multiplicity."[19] Cournot's attempt to sketch out the notion of chance appeals to a rather elementary, abstract, and isolated geometrical intuition. It is a simplified conception of what happens on a chess board, maintains Serres: "And what imposes the definition is the geometrical *staging* in which intuition is completely at ease: the event is produced, the intersection of lines renders the product geometrical or set-like. A given trajectory of the knight brings the downfall of the queen" (pp.64–65).[20] Geometric clarity is impossible on the shifting ground of the many incidents unfolding as the battle rages at Waterloo. Instead of visualizing the chance encounter as the intersection of causal chains, one might well employ the more suggestive notion of the signal, an element which sets itself off from a background of indistinguishable noise and aleatory constellations. Serres remarks: "The fortuitous event, whatever it might be, is a figure set against a background. And this background in not a cosmos, it is a cloud. If it is immense, it is no longer mastered: chaos. . . . The name of chance is cloud" (p.66).[21]

With disparate troops swarming over an uncertainly delimited expanse of terrain and cannonballs raining down at random, the multifarious happenings on the battlefield emblematically figure a chaotic structure not unrelated to a cloud. Simultaneously, however, there is something more—a flux, a flow of bodies across the space in question. Fabrice rides endlessly over hill and dale in pursuit of some unknown goal in the company of a group of horsemen themselves uncertain of what is actually transpiring: into valleys, up inclines, across rivers, forever on the move in a stable flux marked only by small and trivial interruptions. Suddenly, the encounter occurs and, simultaneously, the fall; everything comes abruptly to a halt as Fabrice finds himself seated on the ground, motionless, left behind by the unfolding Napoleonic defeat. The reader is plunged into the midst of a Lucretian universe as it has been imaginatively described by Michel Serres: the laminar flow of atoms, the physics of fluids and fluidity, turbulence, the clinamen. The escort of hussars, its trajectory cut periodically by projectiles generating pockets of turbulence soon left behind, flows over a surreal landscape. Ultimately, however, one pocket of agitation takes on proportions sufficient to interrupt the process. The clinamen appears, the fall occurs at the point of encounter, and nothing will ever be the same for Fabrice. As Serres maintains: "The atomic cascade is a laminar flow in an infinite canal without edges. The vacuum is a generalized body. Thus the clinamen comes about of its own, it announces a turbulence. As experiments show, it is produced in aleatory fashion, in uncertain times and places."[22] At the heart of the inaugural chance encounter of *La Chartreuse de Parme* is a discourse of the clinamen, spontaneously adopted as a figure for the aleatory in the meeting between Fabrice and Robert. Even Fabrice's drunkenness can only seem narratologically premeditated here: tipsy, his head in a whirl spinning like a tourbillion, he tips over, inclines to the side, loses his equilibrium, and (with some perfidious prodding) falls. This is the founding clinamen in an undetermined place at an undetermined time—*incerto loco, incerto tempore*. Chance is, after all, the fall (*cadere*), a case (*casus*) among a multitude of other potential cases. The noncoincidence marking the encounter is thus doubled by another approach toward its description that associates it with the clinamen, the originary, nondetermined swerve initiating a new state of affairs. The fall is hence Fabrice's birth into a new set of circumstances forever marked by this nonencounter.

Fabrice's bewilderment, his ignorance of the significance and structure of the events occurring around him are not without further symbolic import. The uncertainty at the heart of the movement on the battlefield results from the large number of elements and events composing the structure of the military confrontation. There is no possibility of controlled experimentation here—only the encounter with the elements which make up the real. The participants in the battle are at the fringes and limits of possible knowledge in this instance. They are in a locus where artificial and rigidly controlled structures encounter the teeming, swarming mass of the real. "The old notion of adequation oscillates at its fringes, and this aleatory trembling affects everything. . . . Uncertainty is what is given. . . . I do not master large numbers, the uncertain is at the origin, the exact is infinitely beyond the conditions of any possible experiment. Thus the residual aleatory nature of the given remains at the limits of possible experimentation, it founds those very limits"[23] Thrown into the midst of a swirl of events, Fabrice experiences dizzying effects beyond his comprehension and confronts the fortuitous, which is depicted here by the convergence of his existence with that of Robert. It would be wrong to think that Fabrice is the only one left in the dark as the battle rages. The attempt to surmount the uncertainty and chance which lie at the heart of the military confrontation is symbolically represented by the actions of the first generals with whom Fabrice rides. They stop at one point to survey the terrain from the top of a knoll with their field glasses: " 'Do you mind stopping, you greenhorn!' shouted the sergeant. Fabrice noticed he was twenty paces to the right and in front of the generals, precisely where they were looking with their field glasses" (2:63). The field glasses in question represent the scientific instrument focusing on the real in an attempt to render it with a clarity impossible in the absence of such a tool. But the resolution of the instrument is limited, and perhaps even more striking, its aim reduces the field of vision to an extremely small part of the totality of what is occurring. As soon as one endeavors to gauge what is transpiring away from the focal point encompassed by the glasses, things rapidly fade back into obscurity. The generals' attention, in addition, is trained on objects in the distance, far removed from what is closest at hand: the chaos of raining cannon-balls and the noise and movement of clashes threatening the very persons of the generals. The artificial découpage accomplished by the instrument cannot silence the seething chaos of the aleatory outside the narrow field of application for which the instrument is appropriate.

If this encounter with the limits of knowledge has a familiar ring, it should come as no surprise in the context of the present argument, for we have already explored such a boundary in de Certeau's discussion of the limits of theory as illustrated by Foucault's *Surveiller et punir*. We saw how theory had to accomplish an artificial move to restrict the tumultuous unknown of the territory it was attempting to circumscribe by cutting off a portion of that unknown and elevating it through a metonymic operation to a position as representative of what necessarily remained in the shadow of theorization. Precisely in this kind of locus, at the frontier where rational analysis meets the teeming mass of untheorized practice, tactic takes over as the only way to deal with the innumerable events whose potentiality will otherwise be reduced and thereby ignored through a stubborn and finally ineffective appeal to strategy. Tactic addresses the unexpected, the rich potential of what is different, singular, and aleatory, allowing the one whom we termed the navigator to confront the chance event and transform it. Setting out from the perspective of the scientific approach to the real, Michel Serres suggests a comparable situation. The instrument's exactness is limited, its field of application but a narrow portion of the total events. At the borders of the field toward which it is aimed, an irreparable fuzziness exists, an aleatory mass of events from which, periodically, a signal sets itself off, an event catches someone's attention, a clinamen is formed. Serres concludes in *Hermès III*: "To revive archaic distinctions, it is as if chance, since we must call it something, were the very matter that a given form multiplies, repeats, and distributes. Yes, in any case, chance is the very matter of science" (p.67). Fabrice lives that experience in the form of an encounter with Robert in the midst of the chaotic mass of happenings composing the battle, and this incident signifies the acme (although at first glance seemingly a nadir!) of his Waterloo experience. After the encounter and the fall will follow the retreat and the return to Italy, but Fabrice is forever marked by what has occurred, both individually and in his relation to the society within which he must spend the remainder of his life.

With this material now in mind, it would be useful to reflect further on several elements prominent in my earlier discussion of Fabrice and his relationship to Vespasien. The figure of the navigator held a special importance in the parallel between the two characters. Just as Vespasien accomplishes his greatest coup while sailing on Lake Como, so Fabrice is presented from the earliest period of his life as one who is at home in the midst of the tempests that periodically beset the lake on which his family château is built. The fluid, unsteady, incessantly changing environment so fundamental to the description of Waterloo outlined above reproduces a childhood experience and represents a structure within which Fabrice has always thrived. Serres's treatment of the chance event as a kind of signal setting itself off from a chaotic, cloudlike background brings the reader abruptly back, moreover, to the whole problematic of signs and superstitions in Fabrice's life and inserts it into the context of the clinamen and the chance event. It will be recalled here that the first sign mentioned specifically as such in the story of Fabrice's life appears within the framework of the periodic escapades at night on Lake Como. In other words, the confusion brought about by the darkness and stormy weather of the aquatic environment Fabrice so appreciates is an ideal setting within which singular elements are set off against a turbulent background: "At the moment they embarked, if they caught sight of a priest on the hillside, or if they saw a crow fly off to the left, they hastened to replace the lock on the chain of the boat and everyone went back to bed" (2:40). The somewhat halfhearted attempt by the novelist to make of these signs (later the eagle or the state of Fabrice's tree at Grianta) a problematic of superstition—the character of Blanès is fundamental here—cannot ultimately obscure the fact that they are also and perhaps especially indications of an affinity for chance incidents fundamental to the novel as a whole. This approach to the idea of superstition in *La Chartreuse de Parme* leaves some unanswered questions, however, and will require further reflection.

For the moment, I would like to take up once again the idea of the fall from the horse, which plays such a central role in the scene set on the battlefield at Waterloo. As any Stendhal reader knows, the falling rider is a leitmotif for practically the entire cycle of Stendhalian novelistic fiction. From M. de Moirod's ungracious fall into the mud puddle in *Le Rouge et le noir* (1:312) to Sansfin's vitriolic tumble into the creek in *Lamiel* (2:898), Stendhal seems obsessed by such moments. If Fabrice's disequilibrium at Waterloo marks a crucial instant in *La Chartreuse de Parme,* the same may certainly be said of Lucien's clumsiness in *Lucien Leuwen.* Lucien's fall is undoubtedly the most famous one in all of Stendhal's fiction. What might not be immediately apparent is its structural similarity to the Waterloo incident. A close reading of the passage where it occurs reveals some important parallels. The setting reminds one of some of the characteristics used to describe the battlefield in *La Chartreuse de Parme.* Earlier I insisted on the idea of the chaotic, confusing din marking Fabrice's experience at Waterloo. As Lucien enters Nancy in *Lucien Leuwen,* he certainly is not immersed in the hectic movements of a military confrontation. The narrator insists heavily, nevertheless, on the drab nature of the panorama surrounding Lucien as he rides with his regiment into Nancy for the first time: "The 27th regiment of lancers was approaching [Nancy], crossing the most desolate plain in the world. The dry, rocky terrain seemed incapable of producing anything. . . . The foreshortened distance was marked by a series of barren hills. Some sickly vineyards were visible in the gorges formed by the valleys" (1:792). This is a veritable lunar landscape in which everything seems to dissolve into a distressing sameness; nothing notable stands out against the overbearing background of gray which seems to defeat any attempt to categorize it by identifying salient features. The theme of disordered uniformity will be taken up again in a different manner once the horsemen penetrate the town itself: "The narrow, poorly paved streets, full of nooks and corners, were remarkable only for their abominable filthiness. In the middle flowed a gutter full of muddy water which seemed to him to be a concoction of slate" (1:793). The flat, utterly unremarkable plain in the episode's beginning, the shadowy, labyrinthine nature of the streets once the lancers arrive within the walls: all the descriptive brush strokes emphasize a certain dark disorder. Even the citizens of the town participate fully in the bleak spectacle the soldiers encounter: "Filthiness, poverty seemed to permeate all aspects and the physiognomies of the inhabitants perfectly matched the desolation of the buildings" (1:792).

In a much less dramatic but nonetheless unmistakable manner, the confusing lack of order manifest on the Waterloo battlefield reappears in this scene. Into the now-familiar setting ride columns of meticulously aligned riders, the fluid note corresponding to the shifting flux of Fabrice's escort in *La Chartreuse de Parme*. This element is all the more intriguing because the movement of the regiment's horses is parallel to the muddy sewer which becomes the very emblem of the filthy disorder the town exudes from Lucien's vantage point. "The horse belonging to the lancer who was marching to Lucien's right deviated from his line and splashed black, putrid water on the nag that the lieutenant colonel . . . had assigned [to Lucien]" (1:793). The laminar flow of the well-aligned lancers is abruptly disturbed by a slight deviation from the equilibrium point, which not only disgracefully sullies Lucien but initiates a chain of events interrupting the unhindered progress of the regiment's columns. At first Lucien is distracted by thoughts of how to avenge himself for the affront to his dignity. Then he looks up and perceives the first note of color in the Nancy landscape, the first element standing out in his perception against the drab background: "In the middle of a large, white wall was a shutter painted a parrotlike green. 'What gaudy colors these ill-bred provincials choose!' " (1:794). One thing quickly leads to another: the window to a glimpse of Mme de Chasteller, the glimpse of Mme de Chasteller to a traffic jam which impedes the advance of the column: "An encumbrance under an arch at the end of the street had forced the regiment to stop" (1:794). The first disturbance, the horse's jump to the side, thus inaugurates a series of incidents which ultimately induces a turbulent disturbance which leads to Lucien's unhorsing: "The second squadron, to which Lucien belonged, suddenly began to move. Lucien, his eyes fixed on the parrot-green window, spurred on his horse, which slipped, fell, and threw him to the ground" (1:794). The detailed description of the scene at hand reveals an almost canonical Lucretian situation. Within a disordered landscape marked by its nondescript grayness combined subsequently with darkly chaotic, labyrinthine elements, a flux of horsemen moving across the terrain leads to a slight turbulence, the deviation of one of its members from a careful equilibrium. In turn, this sets off a series of occurrences resulting in a fall, a clinamen just as inaugural in *Lucien Leuwen* as was the one described in *La Chartreuse de Parme*.

It is instructive in this context to recall the circumstances of Julien Sorel's near fall in the first part of *Le Rouge et le noir*. Mme de Rênal has procured for him the right to ride in the cavalry escort during festivities marking the visit of the king. For the first time in his life, Julien can indulge his military fantasies. As he rides down the street, he barely avoids tumbling from the saddle at one point: "His joy knew no bounds when, on passing near the old ramparts, the noise of a small cannon caused his horse to jump out of line. By the most incredible chance, he did not fall, and from that moment on he felt like a hero" (1:312). One finds in this incident the same well-aligned military formation with columns of riders going down a street. The laminar flux is once again disturbed by a slight deviation of one of the horsemen, here the hero Julien himself, which immediately threatens a major disturbance, a fall. The potential remains unfulfilled in this instance, or perhaps one could say more correctly that it is actualized indirectly with respect to the main protagonist. Someone else will fall eventually, namely, M. de Moirod—and right in front of the king's carriage to boot (1:312).[24] Proof if there ever were any that something like an inconspicuous fall cannot exist in Stendhal's fictional world. Equally as important as this parallel with *Le Rouge et le noir,* however, is that the fall in *Lucien Leuwen* is also simultaneously the moment of the encounter. Because he is distracted by a glimpse of the blond figure in the window, a surprising encounter with a vision corresponding to nothing else around him, Lucien pays the price with his tumble. Or is it the contrary? Could it be that Lucien himself stands out, provokes the intersection of his existence with that of Mme de Chasteller *because he and he alone falls*? In any case, what is manifest in this narrative moment is once again the intimate link between the chance encounter and the fall. The crossing of paths that takes place between Lucien and Mme de Chasteller resulting in (or from) the ungracious tumble shares with the intersection of Robert and Fabrice the same problematic of distance at the heart of an apparent convergence. Bringing the two protagonists together for a time, it will ultimately fail to accomplish the union it at first seems destined to precipitate. The distance between Lucien and Mme de Chasteller will never be bridged—at least in the completed portion of the novel—just as Fabrice and Robert or Fabrice and Clélia remain fundamentally apart.

The link established between the fortuitous encounter and the fall in the scenes described above calls nevertheless for a measure of caution and some theoretical clarification. The word "chance" itself, from the Latin *casus,* past participle of the verb *cadere* (to fall), has always been etymologically coupled with the idea of falling (in German, *Zufall* is, in fact, the word for "chance"). It is less certain, however, that the definition of "chance" implied by this semantic network is exactly what I have been trying to sketch out in the preceding pages. "Chance," or *casus,* contains within it the notion of the encounter in Cournot's sense, the intersection of two or more causal series. "One then speaks of a fortuitous occurrence: not because the series encountering one another in this way possess in themselves a chance character, nor even, moreover, because the place and time of their encounter is exactly fortuitous, but because the references of this encounter are unforeseen. No human intelligence is able to anticipate to the last detail all the possible encounters among existing series"[25] This conception of chance, maintains Rosset, remains subjective. It defines chance by means of a reference to the possibilities of human intellect, an approach that does not, in the final analysis, face the question of whether chance is an objective phenomenon (in fact, it assumes that it is not).

It remains for us to ask why the notions of the encounter and the fall became linked originally. Rosset speculates that the origin of such a connection may well be in the gesture of throwing bones or dice, one of the most primitive possible images of the intersection between disparate causal series—represented by at least two objects thrown which fall together (p.75). In any case, evident in this approach to the question of chance is the necessary affirmation of the previous existence of causal series in the definition itself. The explanation it proposes thus assumes the preexistence of an order, of immutable laws of nature or society in the form of causal series against which chance stands out in relief. Our earlier discussion of Blanchot's remarks on the question at stake here was meant to challenge the straightforward nature of that seemingly harmless and obvious assumption. In the examples put forth in the preceding pages, the persistent undercurrent has been the suggestion that at the heart of each encounter a certain distance remains between series converging at the propitious moment. And we have seen that to call attention to this distance means to raise doubts about the reassuring notion of a founding order preceding the chance encounter. Such is also the motivation underpinning the use of the Lucretian idea of the clinamen. For the clinamen is nothing if not the claim that what is most important in the development of the world cannot be encompassed by any causal approach to order or, for that matter, by any other explanation based on the originary existence of an ordered organization. The deviation it suggests surges into the world in an absolutely unpredictable manner, not because any imagined observer lacks the detailed knowledge necessary to foresee its occurrence, but, more essentially, because what is at the origin is, in the most essential sense, chaos and disorder. Chance is, concomitantly, an *objective* phenomenon characteristic of that chaotic state. It is therefore of great significance that the encounters between Fabrice and Robert and between Lucien and Mme de

Chasteller are couched in terms of a description so attuned to the Lucretian elements we have been able to expose and develop. They challenge the reader to abandon the comfortable notion of chance as a mere momentary aberration within an underlying order it does not really threaten, and they redefine the notion of the fall, forcing it to exceed the boundaries of traditional etymologies.

In an extended reflection on the link between chance and falling, Jacques Derrida approaches the constellation of ideas explored above from a slightly different angle, as it were (one might well imagine that the whole question is one of angles, the clinamen being the smallest imaginable deviation from a straight line). In an attempt to get at the significance of the vertical direction implied by the fall, Derrida cites Epicurus on the problem of direction in the movement of the primitive chaotic atomic rain. For the atomist, there is no conceivable direction to the atomic flux; no up or down of the innumerable atoms can be plotted when the tumultuous cloud of elementary particles is viewed as infinite in scope, because no fixed reference point from which to gauge direction is identifiable. Thus the clinamen, the instant of chance, is not related to vertical falling if one takes it from the absolute viewpoint of the infinite flux. Only when there is a defined reference point, only when systems have formed as a result of vortices created by the clinamen, can verticality come into play. The point of origin for direction and thus for the verticality of the fall becomes, in fact, human finitude, the finite time and perception of a system destined ultimately to be reabsorbed into the endless flux after a given (and necessarily limited) time. As Derrida puts it: "The fall in general is conceivable solely in the situation and places or space of finitude."[26] The vertical orientation of chance is the result of the horizontal orientation of human consciousness. What is before us can be seen and anticipated, but what falls from above strikes unexpectedly like a thunderbolt. He continues:

Is not what befalls us or descends upon us, as it comes from above, like destiny or thunder, taking our faces and hands by surprise—is this not exactly what thwarts our expectation and disappoints our *anticipation*? Grasping everything in advance, anticipation (*antipare, ante-capere*) does not let itself be taken by surprise; there is no chance for it. Anticipation sees the *objectum* coming ahead, faces the object or *Gegenstand* which, in philosophical German, was preceded by the *Gegenwurf* in which the movement of the throw (*jet, wurfen*) can once again be perceived. The *ob-jectum* (*ob-jet*) is kept under view or hand, within sight or *intuitus*. (p. 5)

Thus the coupling of the notion of chance with falling has the effect of evacuating chance out of the structure of conscious perception. The fortuitous comes from above, outside the visual, anticipated field of human experience. It becomes, therefore, an inexplicable phenomenon, an aberration not subject to being encompassed by rational thought, secondary with respect to the primary place given to the activity of reason and the order it produces.

The preceding reflections have permitted us to situate the complexities of the problematic of the fall more precisely. But there is more in the Stendhalian text. One would be remiss to abandon the problem of Lucien's fall at this stage, for, as every reader of *Lucien Leuwen* knows, Lucien will take a second tumble at almost precisely the same spot. After buying a very expensive horse to parade in front of Mme de Chasteller's house, the better to wipe out the memory of his humiliation, he is thoroughly disappointed in his attempt to play the role of the skilled cavalier, because she does not look out the window when he returns, or so it seems. Thereafter, Lucien makes a habit of riding in front of the house as often as possible but to no avail. There is never any response from the fascinating window. One day, when he least expects it, however, the window shade is open for the second time. Unfortunately, as was the case originally, he is not riding his best horse, and his attempts to prance end in disaster: "One afternoon the shutters were open. Lucien saw a pretty, checkered curtain of embroidered muslin. Almost without thinking, he began immediately to put his horse through its paces. This was not the prefect's English horse, but a small Hungarian pony that responded very badly to its rider's solicitations. . . . Finally, Lucien had the extreme mortification of being thrown to the ground by the little Hungarian horse perhaps ten paces from the place where he had fallen the day of the regiment's arrival" (1:895). One of the interesting elements in this scene of repetition is Lucien's reaction to the events: he takes the incident as a sign that he is predestined (*prédestiné*) to appear ridiculous to Mme de Chasteller. What is the reader to make of the concept of predestination appearing here and, perhaps more important, of the very repetition of the first fall, which seems to turn it into something more than a chance occurrence, which seems, in short, to transform it into the sign of a certain destiny, a certain order of things? The definition of a chance event must always insist on its singularity, a characteristic captured by everyday wisdom in the form of the remark that lightning never strikes twice in the same place. The episode at stake here would appear to contradict the commonsense dictum.

In the preceding chapter we had occasion to address the question of repetition and discovered that the domain of chance does not exclude repetition: on the contrary, it implies it in the form of what was termed "differential repetition." Repetition in the context of the fortuitous always harbors at its center the singular. This singularity appears in the incident cited above in two ways: Lucien falls not at precisely the same spot but ten paces or so from the original point, and he is riding a horse different not only from his habitual mount, the English pure-bred Laura, but also from the horse he was using during the first falling episode. Paradoxically, the very element the narrator cites to underscore what is the same in the two instances ("perhaps ten paces from the place") simultaneously identifies a singularity making the second incident at once the same and different. In addition, the fact that Lucien is riding a small Hungarian pony both establishes a relation with the first incident (at which time Lucien was also riding a horse of questionable quality, "the nag that the lieutenant colonel . . . had assigned [to him]") and distinguishes between the two, since in the second instance, we are dealing with a different animal. Whatever divergences there may be between the two incidents, Lucien focuses immediately on their similarities and makes of the repetition a sign mapping out his destiny—to be interpreted much like the signs encountered periodically by Fabrice in *La Chartreuse de Parme*: "It must be fate! . . . I am predestined to be ridiculous in the eyes of this young woman" (1:895).

The juxtaposition of repetition with interpretation is crucial in this passage, because repetition would seem to be the very thing that permits interpretation: the return of an event signals similarities which are then formulated as propositions or laws. But the aleatory works against interpretation; one of its essential characteristics is its resistance to interpretation, as Clément Rosset maintains in his reflections on this problem. Lucien faces the dilemma of the choice of approaches here and opts for overdetermination, for interpretation to the maximum. It is as if paranoia, on the one hand, and the aleatory, on the other, collapse together in this passage. What is the relation of one to the other? Paranoia is habitually presented as a mental disorder characterized by an excess of interpretation; it would be something like logical thinking gone wild. Not only is every detail down to the most inconspicuous and minor one incorporated into the paranoid's world view, but, in addition, each of those details is enlisted in the service of an explanation meant to prove that malice of some sort is intended toward the paranoid himself or herself. The specialist of mental disorders would claim that there is a difference between "healthy" thinking on the one hand and the "deranged" thinking of the paranoid personality on the other. But such a distinction might well be a procedure hastily devised to protect the assumed innocence of logical thinking itself. In point of fact, no criteria authorizing the differentiation of a permitted and normal logical thought process from an excessive and abnormal one have ever been convincingly defended. The absence of an indisputable distinction means that logical thinking slips indiscernibly from the normal to the pathological. This state of affairs carries a potentially devastating lesson (devastating for the proponents of logic, at least): "It is possible," suggests Rosset, "that paranoid logic is the *only* logic there is."[27] Perhaps there is not a proper logical thinking process to be distinguished from an improper one. It might well be that any logical process risks running wild and eventually incorporating the whole of existence into its circle. If this is the case, then all logical thinking and, consequently, all interpretation obscure the presence of chance from the outset. But that very chance, originary in nature, if it is to be taken seriously, renders all analytic attempts at ordering the world in any ultimate sense null and void. Rosset concludes: "In the eyes of the tragic thinker [i.e., the thinker of chance], all logic—as soon as it does not limit itself to nonaffirmation—is always and already of a paranoid order. There is no 'delirium of interpretation' possible, since all interpretation is a delirium" (p.21). Anyone who would grant a fundamental importance to chance phenomena is thus confronted with a dilemma: how can one reason and yet avoid total denial of chance's presence? The "normal" attitude toward existence is thus of necessity an admixture of the affirmation of chance, on the one hand, and the attempt to interpret and repudiate it, on the other: "Every so-called 'normal' man differs, moreover, from those who are characterized as paranoid, because he is a *mixture* of paranoia and tragic intuition: at times an interpreter, at other times someone who affirms the existence of chance" (p.23).

Confronted with the repetition of an event which is both extraordinary and humiliating, then, Lucien plunges almost inevitably into the exaggeration characteristic of such moments—he reduces and obscures the aleatory by means of an interpretation insisting on repetition as same and therefore as sign of his destiny. His destiny, moreover, takes a typically paranoid tack—Lucien is apparently to be ceaselessly tormented by Mme de Chasteller. The so-called delusion of the paranoid (so-called because it can now be seen as simply a degree within the tendency of any logic of interpretation), that is, of Lucien in this moment, is closely linked to the problem of superstition, because the superstitious person also forges interpretations of reality which attempt to incorporate everything and to deny the aleatory, albeit without the persecution delusion characteristic of the paranoid personality. This analogy between paranoia and superstition leads back both to Fabrice and *La Chartreuse de Parme* as well as to Jacques Derrida's article "Mes chances," alluded to earlier, and permits us to take up the question of superstition, held in abeyance when it occurred previously. My point of departure will be Derrida's "Mes chances," because this short essay formulates the problems at stake so clearly. Toward the end of his article, Derrida turns his attention to Sigmund Freud's *The Psychopathology of Everyday Life* and squarely encounters the question of superstition at the heart of Freud's work. I will set the stage for a discussion of superstition in Freud by providing a broad outline of the argument put forth in the Freudian essay on parapraxias. This will lead inevitably to an analysis of the bind elicited by the approach Freud adopts toward such phenomena. The thesis of *The Pyschopathology of Everyday Life* is quite simply that every forgetful or accidental deed accomplished by the subject is not accidental at all, not the product of chance, but the result of unconscious psychological processes which profit from moments of inattention by expressing themselves in surprising and unsuspected ways: "My hypothesis is that [these] displacement[s] [are] not left to arbitrary psychical choice but follow . . . paths which can be predicted and which conform to laws."[28] The principle put forth on the second page of *Psychopathology* will then be supported by an extraordinary series of examples gleaned from a wide, extremely eclectic group of sources. Perhaps more than with any of his other works, Freud returned to *Psychopathology* in the course of the years following its first publication to add to it countless examples meant to support the thesis proposed in the first chapter—this accumulation of examples is one of the essential structural elements of the essay. It is quite ironic that the text grew in such a haphazard way, since the whole project aspires to discredit the notion of chance. The diversity of examples and sources used is highlighted by the clearly artificial categorization Freud had to invent in order to organize them and cannot but attest to the chance nature of his encounters with those illustrations in the years subsequent to the original publication of the book.

Be that as it may, the line of argumentation Freud adopts puts him on a collision course with the obsessive personalities his method originally set out to treat and cure. If psychoanalysts maintain that nothing is arbitrary or aleatory in psychic life, what distinction will they then invoke to separate themselves from the superstitious or paranoid personalities who are the very subjects of their method? The conflict comes to a head in the twelfth and last chapter of *Psychopathology,* entitled "Determinism, Belief in Chance and Superstition." The chapter begins with a restatement of the hypothesis present from the inception of the book: "If we give way to the view that a part of our psychical functioning cannot be explained by purposive ideas, we are failing to appreciate the extent of determination in mental life. . . . Nothing in the mind is arbitrary or undetermined" (pp.240–42). Freud soon realizes that there are similarities between this outlook and the one illustrated by the paranoid personality: "A striking and generally observed feature of the behaviour of paranoics is that they attach the greatest significance to the minor details of other people's behavior which we ordinarily neglect, interpret them and make them the basis of far-reaching conclusions. . . . The category of what is accidental and requires no motivation . . . is thus rejected by the paranoic" (p.255). Another way of stating this idea would be to say that there are, in fact, no minor details in human behavior for one who believes every act or gesture to be related in a more or less direct way to an underlying psychological process. Unlike one who would reject out of hand the suppositions of the paranoid person, Freud, having spent the greater part of *Psychopathology* providing explanations that remove the element of chance from the parapraxias he puts forth as illustrations of his thesis, must admit, if only partially, their validity: *"There is in fact some truth in them"* (p.256; Freud's italics).

Related to the experience of the paranoic is that of the superstitious person to whom Freud makes reference immediately after his remark concerning the grain of truth contained in paranoid reasoning. The problem of superstition is broached by means of an exemplary story resembling the endless other exempla of which nearly the whole of *Psychopathology* is constructed—with one absolutely essential difference. This time and this time alone no explanation by reference to unconscious motivation will be invoked to diffuse the element of chance at the center of the incident recounted. The theoretical reduction of the aleatory suddenly becomes highly dangerous and problematic, as we shall see. At stake is a visit by Freud to examine a patient whom he has not seen since he left for vacation. Having provided the cab driver with the address, Freud realizes as the cab pulls up to the apparent destination that the driver has taken him wrongly to a house on a parallel street, a house possessing the same street number as the proper address.[29] Perceiving that there has been a mistake, Freud informs the cab driver, who then takes him to the correct address. A question instantly arises in Freud's mind: "Now is it of any significance that I was driven to a house where the old lady was not to be found?" (p.257). To answer yes would mean that Freud's approach to the experience differs little from a superstitious person's perspective on the matter. To answer no, which he indeed does, signifies that he refuses to partake of the delusions of superstition and will pursue the attempt to set his own activity off from them: "Certainly not to me, but if I were *superstitious* I should see an omen in the incident, the finger of fate announcing that this year would be the old lady's last" (p.257). This seemingly transparent denial is not quite as straightforward as it appears, as Derrida has shown, for the old woman (the patient he set out to visit in the first place) most assuredly represents Freud's mother, and his psychological investment in the incident is therefore far greater than his narrative admits.[30] There is, in other words, a certain level of unconscious motivation which he sets aside in this instance without revealing it.

He sets that unconscious material aside precisely because this is a theoretical moment in his argument during which a certain distance from superstition must be taken if there is to be any psychoanalytic theory. Freud makes an attempt in *Psychopathology* to draw a line between psychoanalysis and superstition, to establish a borderline to be crossed only at the risk of endangering the scientific ambitions of psychoanalysis. The passage goes as follows:

> I am therefore different from a superstitious person in the following way:

> I do not believe that an event in whose occurrence my mental life plays no part can teach me any hidden thing about the future shape of reality; but I believe that an unintentional manifestation of my own mental activity *does* on the other hand disclose something hidden, though again it is something that belongs only to my mental life [not to external reality]. I believe in external (real) chance, it is true, but not in internal (psychical) accidental events. With the superstitious person it is the other way around. (P.257)

The fundamental discriminatory gesture on Freud's part is to establish a border between the internal and the external. There is a certain territory covered by psychoanalysis and a remaining complementary region outside its purview. Acting as a strategy to limit what might otherwise be a relentlessly expansive invasion of totality by psychoanalysis, this move serves to stake out a domain for psychoanalysis, both to establish (define, delimit) and to protect its substance. If every mental attitude and belief were psychoanalytic in nature, then there would be no psychoanalysis, because nothing would differentiate it from mental activity in general, nothing would mark it as a distinct and therefore independent field. In "Mes chances" Derrida captures the ontological thrust of Freud's strategy eloquently: "In other passages, in other problematic contexts, Freud carefully avoids ontologizing or substantializing the limit between outside and inside, between the biophysical and the psychic. But in the *Psychopathology* and elsewhere he requires this limit not only to protect this fragile, enigmatic, threatened defensive state that one calls 'normality' but also to circumscribe a solid context, . . . the unity of a field of coherent and determinist interpretation, that which we so calmly call psychoanalysis *itself*" (p.25). This distinction, so laboriously sought, is still far from remaining unproblematic, for the projection by the superstitious person of unconscious factors and relations onto the outside world is a sign of the same "hermeneutic compulsion" (Derrida's term) that is to be found in psychoanalysis itself: "If the superstitious person projects [*projette, projiziert*], if he throws [*jette*] toward the outside and ahead of himself the 'motivations' that Freud claims to be looking for on the inside, if he interprets chance from the standpoint of an external 'event' at the point where Freud reduces it or leads it back to a 'thought,' it is because essentially the superstitious person does not believe, any more than Freud, in the solidity of spaces circumscribed by our Occidental stereotomy" (p.25).[31]

There is, consequently, a much closer relationship between the psychoanalytic attempt to interpret and the types of interpretation found in a superstitious world view than Freud can comfortably admit at this point in his argument. When the superstitious person projects causal relations and hidden motivations onto external reality, his gesture *mirrors* the activity of the psychoanalyst, is *analogous* to that activity, in short, remains in a troublesome, awkward proximity. Freud's own remarks in *Psychopathology* underline the space of a certain hesitation: "The obscure recognition . . . of psychical factors and relations in the unconscious is mirrored—it is difficult to express it in other terms, and here the analogy with paranoia must come to our aid—in the construction of a *supernatural reality,* which is destined to be changed back once more by science into the *psychology of the unconscious*" (pp.258–59). We must ask how such a "scientific" transformation can take place, on what notions it can possibly be based. Given the experimental and theoretical nature of Freud's own constructs, namely, the topology of the unconscious developed through his speculative efforts, one cannot help but begin to wonder which "reality" is the most supernatural: Freud's or the one championed by the superstitious person. The basic problem occurs when Freud attempts to transform a metaphysical outlook into a scientific one and immediately becomes bogged down in the same concepts that originally served the metaphysical construct so well. Derrida comments in "Mes Chances": "It [Freud's discourse] projects the reconversion into science or into metapsychology of the metaphysical discourse *from which it nonetheless obtains the concepts themselves for this project* and operation—notably, the oppositional limits between the psychic and the physical, the inside and the outside, not to mention all those that depend on them" (p.27).

The relationship between the discussion of these issues and de Certeau's distinction between strategy and tactic is evident here. In an attempt to "save" psychoanalysis as a well-defined domain of practice, the psychoanalyst does his or her best to mark territorial limits. Within that space certain laws are considered to hold as a valid description of the territory in question. As soon as the borders become contested and the sharp distinctions more vague, however, the whole system threatens to collapse. The extension of the theoretician's territory always jeopardizes the distinctions necessary to define such a territory and mark it as one's own. In the present context, it has become evident that psychoanalysis, as it develops and attempts to define its domain, constantly encounters the supernatural, the tendency on the part of the subject to project onto the world a structure reflecting his or her own psychic structure, to *interpret* to such an excessive degree that what is *other* becomes ultimately always the *same,* always an image of the self. The questionable distinction between outside and inside is undone almost as it is constituted, in the same breath, as it were.

The case of mental telepathy immediately comes to mind as a further illustration of the dangers referred to here. François Roustang has written suggestively on this topic, and his subtle argument merits attention.[32] Roustang traces Freud's attempt to deal with the subject of mental telepathy beginning as early as 1899 and spanning nearly the entirety of Freud's career. Why the fascination with this topic? The question of telepathy is intimately tied to the relation between the psychoanalyst and his or her patient, because the bond existing between the two people involved in the psychoanalytic cure is in part reproduced in the relationship between the two people who supposedly exchange thoughts in cases of telepathy. The notion of thought transmission, therefore, immediately and inevitably raises the problem of the transfer. "[Freud] clearly feels that psychoanalysis has an interest in thought transmission, not only in the passage of thoughts from the client to the fortune-teller, astrologer, graphologist, and thus to the analyst, but also in the inverse passage from the analyst to the patient," claims Roustang (p.80). As soon as one crosses into this territory, doubts inevitably arise concerning the influence of the analyst on the patient and vice versa, what might be termed their independence from one another. How can one be sure the analyst is not projecting his or her own interpretation onto the discourse of the patient to such an extent that the interpretation takes precedence, invades the space of the analysis thoroughly, and obstructs the discourse of the unconscious? The opposite danger is just as menacing: the patient could also conceivably take control and begin manipulating the analyst. In either case, what occurs if some separation and balance cannot be maintained is a frightening and dangerous encounter with the very essence of the uncanny, namely, the experience of the double, what Freud describes in his essay entitled "The 'Uncanny'" as "the transferring [of] mental processes from the one person to the other—what we should call telepathy—so that the one possesses knowledge, feeling and experience in common with the other, identifies himself with another person, so that his self becomes confounded, or the foreign self is substituted for his own—in other words, by doubling, dividing and interchanging the self."[33] Roustang comments: "It would be sufficient to multiply the passage of thoughts or of psychic processes from one person to another for one to become progressively the double of the other, as in a drawing, when the sketched outlines become sufficiently filled in, and thus one would no longer know who is who" (p.82).

Under these conditions, it behooves the psychoanalyst to find a solution to the dilemma. The resolution of the difficulty will come in the form of the "scientific" concept of the transfer designed to keep the person of the analyst at a distance during the work of analysis. "What is demanded of the analyst," says Roustang, "is to transform himself into a pure recording apparatus. . . . Thus he can pretend to succeed in receiving the message of the other with no 'selection or deformation.' The passage of thoughts from one person to another is indeed at stake here, but the transmission of thoughts in the sense of telepathy is out of the question, not so much because the message has language as its medium, but especially because at no time does the thought of one become the thought of the other" (pp. 83–84). To reinforce the absence of the person of the analyst in the cure, the analyst has at his or her disposal a series of devices represented perhaps most explicitly by the silence kept as the analysand develops a discourse originating in the unconscious. The act of maintaining a distance from the analysand by refusing to respond and remaining silent (even out of sight) has a further historical significance. One can be fairly certain, as Roustang claims, that the aim of this evolution in psychoanalytic technique was to avoid falling into the trap of *suggestion*. The technique of suggestion is essential to the success of the *hypnotic cure*. The rejection of suggestion as a valid direction for the cure was, as historians of psychoanalysis have demonstrated, one of the extremely charged gestures marking the founding of psychoanalysis by Freud.[34] Having spurned the practice of suggestion, Freud made repeated efforts to avoid the accusation that anything like hypnotic suggestion could make its way back into psychoanalysis. But it is perhaps not quite so easy to sweep aside the monster, even with the help of draconian preventive rules outlining the manner in which the psychoanalyst should behave during the analytic session, as Roustang so aptly points out: "This would be to forget that silence is a language the analysand quickly learns. . . . If punctuation is decisive for giving meaning to a sentence, one can rest assured that silence by itself is capable . . . of sending all sorts of messages to the analysand" (p. 94). Try as he might, Freud never quite succeeded in laying the problem of telepathy to rest. It is a notion that continued to fascinate him and a danger never quite surmounted. Telepathy is ultimately a seductive concept, because it is the figure of an allusive ideal in human relationships, namely, identity in difference, a kind of perfect communication simultaneously uniting two parties and yet respecting their independence. Roustang again: "If telepathy was so seductive for Freud, this is because it bears within itself a myth, the myth of the most total communion at the greatest distance, that is, the myth of identity in difference" (p.96).

Paranoia, superstition, telepathy: are these maladies of interpretation or simply different facets of an always-invasive interpretative activity? Without answering the question (is an answer possible?), we can at least begin to see the significance of the juxtaposition of chance and superstition in *La Chartreuse de Parme*. It might at first have seemed paradoxical to claim that a novel well known for the place it devotes to superstition and astrology, *La Chartreuse de Parme*, could at the same time be the locus for a meditation on chance and its processes. The preceding discussion, however, should begin to dissipate the apparent paradox. Superstition (and the related idea of mental telepathy),[35] if followed to its logical conclusion, calls into question any attempt to confine chance to an exterior of some sort, to a domain outside the series of mental events making up the individual psyche. To put it another way, the superstitious person ultimately threatens a whole tradition of logical organization characteristic of Western thought, as Derrida indicates in "Mes Chances":

The superstitious person does not believe, any more than Freud, in the solidity of the spaces circumscribed by our Occidental stereotomy. He does not believe in the contextualizing and framing, but invented limits between the psychic and the physical, the inside and the outside, not to mention all of the other connected oppositions. More so than Freud, . . . the superstitious person is sensitive to the precariousness of the contextual circumscriptions of the epistemological frames, the *constructs* and the *artifacts* that enable us, for life's convenience and for the mastery of limited networks of knowledge and technics, to separate the psychic from the physical or the inside from the outside. (pp.25–26, translation slightly modified)

Like de Certeau's strategist, the proponent of logic and analysis proceeds by circumscribing, defining a territory, and marking the inside off from the outside. What obtains within is lawlike, causally explainable ad infinitum; what transpires without is chaos which must be either assimilated or ignored. Like the tactician, although in a different manner, the superstitious person chips away at the organization relying on such a distinction. The tactician, who cannot even conceive of a well-defined domain, must always, then, maneuver on a shifting terrain whose fluctuations will never cease. The superstitious person, on the other hand, expands the boundaries of what was originally a clearly delimited domain (the human psyche) so excessively that the distinctions such a delimitation implied are destined to be obliterated. It might seem as if one were dealing with an irreducible opposition here: for the tactician, all is chance; for the superstitious person, all is seamless causality. Like most such diametrically opposed alternatives, however, the two ends of the spectrum ultimately tend to merge. For, in the case of the superstitious person, the concept of causality, having been forced to an excessive limit, is emptied of effective content and threatens at any moment to cross over into its opposite, namely, chance. If everything is linked so impeccably by a certain type of causal explanation, then there is nothing to distinguish causality from anything else, and it simply collapses into its opposite. Without the benefit of boundaries marking oppositions, categories such as chance and determinism no longer quite obtain. *La Chartreuse de Parme* seems to thrive at this uncertain, almost dangerous limit—at once the story of an unbounded, primitive superstition *and* the locus of a stunning meditation on chance and the tactics it elicits.

[He told himself vaguely that Paris was the capital of chance, and he believed in chance for a moment.]

*Il se dit vaguement que Paris était la capitale du
hasard, et il crut au hasard pour un moment.*—Balzac

CHAPTER THREE

The Demon, the Police, and
Cacophony in Balzac

In the preceding discussions, an extended reading of Stendhal's
La Chartreuse de Parme—which branched out into other works as
well—has allowed me to bring up and explore a number of theoretical repercussions implied by an approach that takes chance seriously. The questions raised have by no means been treated exhaustively and will be addressed again in subsequent analyses. It
would be worthwhile at this point, however, to interject a series of
remarks calculated to situate historically the presence of the element of chance in Stendhal's and, in the coming pages, Balzac's
texts. Specifically, it would be of great interest to know what position the question of chance occupies within the cultural field in
which these two writers participated during the first half of the
nineteenth century. What is the relationship between the structures
and views one encounters in their texts and evolutions occurring
elsewhere with respect to the treatment of chance?

The question takes on an interesting hue when one begins to
consider developments in science during the early part of the nineteenth century in France. This moment in the growth of the scientific establishment in France is marked by the triumph of Newto-

nian doctrine as reformulated and codified by Pierre Simon de Laplace. An anecdote, doubtless apocryphal, has the emperor Napoleon asking Laplace why there is no god contained in his cosmology and Laplace responding: "I have no need for such a hypothesis." "The Newtonian agenda . . . had become the official agenda of the most powerful and most prestigious scientific group, the Laplacean school, which dominated the scientific world at a time when the [Napoleonic] Empire dominated Europe."[1] Such preeminence was aided not only by political developments (the military and diplomatic triumphs of Napoleon) but also by very specific cultural factors. During the period of the Revolution and the First Empire, the French university system was reorganized and a scheme of higher education for an elite conceived, a reform contributing powerfully to the specialization of scientific personnel. The prominent men of science of the day were converted into teachers and professional researchers who, for the first time in a systematic way, were in charge of the education of their own successors. Institutional conditions clearly favored the formulation of an official scientific doctrine to be imposed on the coming generation in a very generalized fashion.[2] At the moment when Laplace was working toward his codification, his allies and students were obtaining key positions in the newly emerging higher education system for the French intellectual elite.[3]

The victory of the Laplaceans, however, was in no sense due simply to the play of external forces—it was also a direct result of the perceived success of the Newtonian paradigm itself. The scientific theory that had evolved out of Newton's laws was both convincing and powerful. The world had taken on the appearance of a unified and stable system fully comprehensible by means of the principles Newton had discovered: "The world is a system, unique, deducible, coherent. But it is a system for a second reason: the apparent exceptions, inequalities, residues are in fact periodic, sometimes secular variations. . . . The world system is closed, finite, comprehensible for the god of the differential equations table, indefinitely predictable because it oscillates, and readable for that very reason all the way back to its origins."[4] Michel Serres's description of the Laplacean paradigm underscores some important themes. Evident first is the drive toward totalization implied by the Laplacean approach. Even if there were still discoveries to be made and verifications to be accomplished, even if man's knowledge needed to become more precise, the theoretical framework for understanding the universe already existed and simply needed to be perfected. No further, more-englobing theory was required. The universe was closed in the sense that no new, surprising, or unexplained occurrence could be expected. Not only should one theoretically be able to trace the development of the universe back to its origins, but Newtonian theory possessed predictive powers beyond what had been the case prior to its constitution. Although it is true that even very early, specific portions of the theory were strongly contested, (Newtonian optics is a case in point), the Newtonian paradigm, especially as embodied in classical mechanics, provided the only framework for scientific discussion. It implied the possibility of an exhaustive knowledge of natural processes through its application, a claim no other theory developed since the beginning of the scientific revolution in Europe could make, and in many ways it redefined the very notion of what scientific theory and practice meant.[5]

Perhaps the most characteristic statement of Laplace's own confidence in the progress brought about by classical mechanics can be found in the introduction to his essay on probability. It is highly significant that Laplace addressed the issue of the degree of certainty to be found in Newtonian theory at the very moment he was writing the introduction to an essay on probability. Laplace's attitude toward probability is deeply colored by his buoyant belief in the efficacy of the Newtonian doctrine. Far from treating the problem of uncertainty and chance as an objective phenomenon, Laplace writes about probability solely to affirm in the strongest manner the nonexistence of chance as a potentially objective class of events. If there is such a thing as chance, it is a subjective phenomenon destined to vanish as scientific knowledge progresses:

All events, even those which, due to their minuteness, seem to escape the grand laws of nature, are no less the result of those laws than the revolutions of the Sun. Ignoring the forces that link them to the total system of the universe, we have attributed them to final causes or to chance, depending upon whether they occurred with regularity or without apparent order. But the explanatory strength of these imaginary causes has been successively weakened as the limits of our knowledge have receded. They disappear entirely in the face of true philosophy, which sees in such causes merely the expression of our ignorance as to the real causes of events.[6]

We might as well say that there is absolutely no place for chance in Laplacean theory. Choosing to deal with the question of chance under the guise of probability, Laplace indicates his attitude from the outset. The mathematization of chance, its transformation into a series of calculations applied to large numbers, is a denial of the singular, of events potentially breaking the chain of predictable continuity. Although the universe may be too large and therefore complex for mere human intelligence to encompass in its entirely, *in theory* it would be possible to know everything—the evolution of the universe is entirely determined and determinable.[7] The position of the ideal observer who would be omniscient is provided for *within the theory itself* and is expressed in terms of a superior intelligence, the famous demon: "A mind that could, in a given instant, know all the forces which act in nature and the respective positions of the bodies which make it up—if, in addition, it were vast enough to be able to submit these givens to differential analysis—would incorporate in the same formula the movements of the largest bodies in the universe and those of the lightest atom: nothing would be uncertain for it, and the future, as well as the past, would be present before its eyes."[8]

Much ink has flowed in the course of various discussions concerning the validity of the image of the demon, and I could not pretend to give any full account of the arguments it has provoked.[9] Suffice it to say that Laplace assumes a continuity between the simplest systems, which we can fully describe, and the more complex ones, which are beyond the scope of exact measurement and comprehension. The claim of continuity is what contemporary science criticizes in its attempt to explore the differences between macroscopic and submicroscopic (atomic and subatomic) phenomena, revealing in the process that the postulation of an unproblematic continuity between various levels of the universe is more a metaphysical gesture than a scientific one.[10] Irrespective of the modern response to Laplace's demon, his image of an ideal observer is a clear expression of the finality and predictive powers claimed for classical mechanics, a discipline in which chance and indeterminism have no place.

Subsequent attempts to deal with the question of chance in France in the first half of the nineteenth century were strongly colored by Laplace's theoretical presence, as the example of Auguste Cournot amply demonstrates. Cournot's *Exposition de la théorie des chances et des probabilités*, published in 1843, wrestles with the Laplacean straitjacket in ways that are closely related to what occurs in Balzac's work.[11] Unable to envisage a world in which strict causality does not reign supreme (even chance must have laws) and yet loath to accept the rigidly mechanistic consequences of the Laplacean world view, Cournot tries to steer a middle course. It consists in accepting the Laplacean deterministic view while maintaining simultaneously that there are causal sequences sufficiently far removed from one another to be treated operationally as if they were wholly unrelated. As Cournot puts it, "Events brought about by the combination or conjuncture of phenomena belonging to independent causal series are what we call fortuitous events or the results of chance" (p. 73). The farther removed one series is from another, the more their intersection can be considered to belong to the realm of chance. It would be instructive to quote an example provided by Cournot in a later work: "Suppose a citizen of Paris decides he wants to make a trip into the country and boards a train to take him to his destination. If the train is wrecked, and the traveler is a victim, it will be accidentally so, for the causes leading up to the wreck are independent of the presence of this particular person. These causes would have developed in the same way even though, because of unanticipated changes in his affairs or for other reasons, he had decided to go by another route or to take a different train."[12] The causal sequence representing the plans and intentions of the traveler has no apparent bearing on the one provoking the train wreck, as was the case in Bergson's related example studied in our previous chapter in which the falling roof tile and the passing pedestrian belonged to this same type of disparate series.[13]

Cournot's reasoning clearly does not escape the dilemma posed by Laplace's demon. The problem for his argument is that Laplacean causality simply does not provide any space for causal series unrelated to one another. The distance between series may be great, even infinitely great, yet the deductive and calculating powers of the demon will always be able to trace them to a common source. In other words, Cournot's argument is not yet structured to contain a theoretical stance which directly confronts and refutes the possibility of the Laplacean viewpoint (the demon) from which the separate series mentioned in the above example could be linked. Until one destroys the demon, one cannot avoid succumbing to its power. This does not disqualify Cournot's reflections entirely, however. His quest for the slightest play in Laplacean theory to allow the possible existence of chance leads him to outline a type of situation in which the very idea of a search for the common causal origin of two given sequences becomes, at least from a practical point of view, extremely problematic, almost absurd. This very absurdity is destined to become more and more threatening to the calm mastery of the Laplacean doctrine.

Just as Cournot questioned a scientific theory that would exclude chance entirely, so also we have seen how Stendhal's text searches for means to represent the space of play in which the aleatory reigns. It becomes evident that such explorations are a wider cultural phenomenon than is at first apparent when one begins to consider certain other literary developments characteristic of the early nineteenth century. In particular, recent essays by both Peter Brooks and Christopher Prendergast have insisted, although for quite different reasons, on the importance of the melodramatic imagination as the century opens.[14] For all else it might be, melodrama is surely a literary mode depending heavily on chance, predicated as it is on surprise encounters and revelations of all sorts. Thus at a time when scientists and philosophers of science dreamed of a world fully determined by mechanical laws (an "immense tautology"),[15] novelists and playwrights in France were creating a genre marked specifically by its attempts to produce effects intimately tied to the fortuitous. Because Balzac is often considered to be not only the inventor of the nineteenth-century French novel but one of the premier practitioners of melodrama in the novel, it is irresistible in the context of the present argument to turn to his writing and explore the workings of the aleatory in his novelistic praxis. The unexpected encounters, confusions of identity, plot twists, and surprise confrontations so common in Balzacian narrative are impossible to account for and analyze without addressing the question of the importance and meaning of the fortuitous in Balzac's writing. To cite in passing one of many possible examples, when Raphaël de Valentin is drawn inexorably into the gambling house in the first scene of *La Peau de chagrin* and there wagers his whole existence on one spin of the roulette wheel, the reader simply cannot ignore the fact that chance has been transformed into a decisive narrative element.

I shall have occasion to return to the opening pages of *La Peau de chagrin* to reflect on Raphaël's gesture, but I would like to begin my remarks on Balzac by turning initially to *Ferragus*. I have chosen this novella, published first in 1833, in part because it begins with what could be called an archetypal structure in Balzac's fictional world: a chance meeting between two characters which creates a situation containing various implications explored and developed in the course of the narration. Any number of other Balzac stories employ a variation on this structure, which, given its repeatedly prominent position, commands attention. In order to construct a first approach to an understanding of the status of chance in *Ferragus,* one must therefore reflect carefully on the organization of the novella's incipit. The narrator begins his story with a series of remarks in which he attempts to create a typology of Parisian streets: "In Paris there are certain streets just as disgraced as a man guilty of some infamous deed, and then there are noble streets, and simply honest streets" (5:793). This typological exercise recalls the beginnings of two of the other novellas in the *Histoire des treize* series, namely, *La Duchesse de Langeais* and *La Fille aux yeux d'or*. Both of those other stories show a certain hesitancy and difficulty at the moment of transition into the actual narrative material. After a mysteriously unexplained preliminary incident, *La Duchesse de Langeais* lingers for a while on a discussion of the weaknesses in the position of the French aristocracy within Restoration society and politics before getting on with the narration meant to explain that incident. *La Fille aux yeux d'or*, on the other hand, begins with a veritable treatise on the class structure of Parisian (and French) society. All three stories, then, dawdle at the threshold, at times seemingly unable to begin. We shall subsequently consider this element in their composition.

The typology of streets constructed by the narrator as *Ferragus* opens is directed toward a specific type of reader: "These observations, incomprehensible beyond the confines of Paris, will doubtless be understood by those thoughtful, poetic men of pleasure who, while idly walking [*en flânant*] around the city, know how to harvest the mass of delights floating within its walls at every moment" (5:794). Balzac often attempts to seduce the reader by appearing to endow him or her with membership in the select group of sophisticated Parisian readers. But there is something more here. The *flâneur*, that category of idle observer invented by Balzac, Baudelaire, and their contemporaries, is not only a Parisian, he is the very embodiment of the potential for chance encounters. Wandering aimlessly about the city, but always alert to what he sees, the *flâneur* is simultaneously waiting for nothing in particular and yet awaiting anything and everything. He expects nothing, and yet his attitude is one of perfect expectancy. There is no way to predict whether or not the *flâneur* will witness an occurrence somehow implicating him in a chain of events from which he was previously excluded. Nonetheless, he represents a state of potentiality ripe for transformation through some surprise provocation. In certain characteristic ways, then, the *flâneur* resembles the tactician defined in the course of my argument. Like the tactician, he is not the master of the domain in which he finds himself, but his experience prepares him to meet the unexpected. The *flâneur* deliberately tempts chance to see what it will bring him, certain that he will make an occasion of what transpires.

The state of expectancy and wandering attention cannot be attained easily and without penalty, as the narrator is quick to point out. It is, in fact, a "costly luxury" (5:795). The *flâneur* must spend much time at his occupation (or, rather, nonoccupation) and see many a morning or evening wasted in pursuit of what may result in nothing tangible. This is the way of the poet. It is not surprising, therefore, to see the narrator place himself in the very category he has just created. Not only is he a Parisian, like the understanding reader of his text, but he himself is given to wandering aimlessly in search of an occurrence. The *flâneur*'s path is a vagabond one like the narrator's in his opening paragraphs: "Those readers [who have engaged in activities akin to those of the *flâneur*] will excuse this vagabond beginning" (5:795). Here the narrator presents himself as one who knows the streets of the city as any *flâneur* does, but also as one who, in this specific instance, repeats the same kind of activity at another level, namely, within his own textual work. He too must wander in search of the beginning of his own story, and he encounters it only after an incipit which allows him to speak of other things before he happens on his subject. Thus there is an intimate connection established between the artistic work of the narrator and what appears to be his own propensity in his idle hours of Parisian life.

The narrator now proceeds to actualize further the very category of the *flâneur* he has just defined (and of which we now know he himself is a member) by giving it a second member in the form of the first character to be introduced in a story which only now, after a wealth of preliminary reflections, begins. A young man, later to be identified as Auguste de Maulincourt, is strolling aimlessly (*il marchait fort insouciamment* [5:796]) down one of the streets about which the narrator has been talking: "At eight-thirty in the evening in the rue Pagevin, at a time when absolutely no wall in the street was bare of disgusting graffiti . . . , a young man, as a result of one of those chance happenings which occur only once in a lifetime, was turning the corner of the rue Pagevin on foot in order to enter into the rue des Vieux-Augustins" (5:796). Because he is there at that very moment—extraordinary *kairos*—Auguste happens to espy a woman who turns out to be none other than the one he has admired and loved at a distance for months: "*She,* in this filth, at this hour!" (5:797). The narrator strongly insists on the chance nature of the encounter. It is not enough simply to say that it happens fortuitously—it can, he continues, be lived only once in a lifetime. This is a pleonasm, of course, because by definition something occurring by chance can only happen once, cannot, in other words, belong to a series characterized by any regularity attained through repetition. It must be absolutely singular and exceptional. But this is a significant pleonasm, because it serves the attempt to make the unique nature of the encounter stand out even further from the background of everyday events.

The situation described here is one with which the reader should now be more familiar. Once again we are presented with a Cournot-like intersection of two sequences unrelated to one another. The *flâneur* Maulincourt's presence in the rue Pagevin bears no relation to the appearance of Mme Jules at the same place. The two causal series leading up to the point of intersection between the two characters' paths are, for any discernible purpose, totally independent. This chance encounter will resemble all the others we have considered thus far in at least one telling manner. It will lead only to an increasing distance between the two characters instead of toward their union and will once again put into question the common understanding of the meaning of an intersection. The topography of the scene as constructed by the narrator, moreover, is of interest even outside the context of his lecture on the *flâneur*'s aimless strolling. It quickly becomes evident that one is dealing with something akin to a labyrinth here. The darkness of the hour makes it difficult for Maulincourt to identify his prey, much less to follow her: "The young man hastened his step, passed the woman, and turned to look at her . . . Swish! She had disappeared into an alley. . . . [He] doubled back and saw the woman at the end of the alley climbing up . . . a twisted staircase" (5:798). The experience encountered in the labyrinth stops short of a radical confrontation with the real viewed as the manifestation of chance. In the labyrinth, knowledge may not appear in its normal guises, intersections never imagined may become manifest, but the belief that there is in the end some kind of knowledge in the form of a possible law is never fundamentally shaken. Between the incipit of *Ferragus* and its conclusion the image of the labyrinth will be abandoned in favor of a more extreme topography, one clearly more chaotic, less ordered, less playful, altogether more tragic.[16]

Swallowed up in a labyrinthine pursuit, Auguste de Maulincourt naturally assumes, then, that there is an explanation for what he has observed. Ignoring the possible difficulties and the dangers to which he might expose himself, he immediately commences an "investigation." As we have seen, he does not hesitate to follow Mme Jules (the young woman he has identified in the street) once he has observed her in such questionable surroundings. He is able to identify the destination of her foray into the rue Pagevin neighborhood, namely, an old, rundown building on the rue Soly, thoroughly unsuitable for anyone of her social standing. She disappears into the building, as we saw above, and Maulincourt takes up a station outside to glean whatever information he can concerning the actions of the woman he secretly adores. At precisely the moment when he perceives the shadow of Mme Jules through a fourth-story window, he receives a blow to the shoulder, administered accidentally by a workman carrying a piece of wood: "The young man heard a warning: 'Watch out!'. . . . It was a workman's voice. . . . It was the voice of providence telling his curious spirit: 'What business is this of yours? Take care of your own affairs'" (5:799). Maulincourt's experience on this fateful night combines both chance and providence. Although in principle providence would seem quite different from chance because it implies purpose and final cause, the two are traditionally close to one another. One must remember that the Greek goddess Tyche combines the two functions: simultaneously she is providential in her actions and haphazard in her interventions. Chance and providence share the common characteristic of residing beyond the scope of human control.[17] Baffled once by an inexplicable meeting, Maulincourt now receives a providential warning to let well enough alone. Why? The answer, at an abstract level, is that a chance occurrence is irreducible to rational experience, uninterpretable in the sense we have set forth, because it is by definition something else entirely—as is the very warning given to Auguste to cease and desist. His efforts to understand can only be in vain and ultimately even fatal.

Despite the warning, Maulincourt throws himself into an attempt to solve the mystery which surrounds the dingy apartment of apparent interest for Mme Jules.[18] The chance meeting initiates a series of events which will seem governed by an increasingly inevitable causal logic. In terms of plot, a mystery demands a solution, and the solution will draw an ever-tighter web around the four main characters in the story: Auguste de Maulincourt, Mme Jules, her husband Jules Desmarets, and Ferragus, the father of Mme Jules and the person she was visiting when Auguste glimpsed her in the rue Pagevin. The efforts by Auguste to penetrate the mystery, never to be completely successful, would be halted totally from the outset, however, were it not for another fortuitous meeting. Inexperienced in the skills necessary to conduct an investigation into Mme Jules's private life, he is unable to progress despite long efforts: "A novice in this kind of work, he hesitated to question either the doorman or the shoemaker who lived in the building where Mme Jules visited" (5:813). In fact, the description given of Auguste's investigative technique in itself already suggests that he is not and will never be quite the cold rationalist he believes himself to be: "He wandered about [*flânait*] full of hope" (5:813). Clearly, his "method" as it is first described is simply another form of the aimless activity [*flânerie*] in which he was engaged when the story began. His procedure for testing conjectures, furthermore, is also closely tied to the exploitation of chance: "Jealous lovers imagine everything, and by imagining everything, by choosing the most probable conjectures, judges, spies, lovers, and observers guess the truth they are after" (5:818). Unable to envisage in a calculating, rational manner what the significance of Mme Jules's behavior might be, Auguste simply blankets the whole field of possibilities with his fertile and wandering imagination in hopes of stumbling on the most probable explanation. Totally mystified by what he has seen, yet on the path of something momentous for his own existence, Maulincourt spontaneously adopts the only approach he knows—to increase the potentiality for another occasion, for an intersection of circumstances required to fuel and further propel his knowledge.

To move forward in the attempt to solve the mystery of the first encounter with Mme Jules, Maulincourt will ultimately need help in the form of a second occurrence, namely, an additional chance encounter. One does in fact occur, and the manner in which this encounter is structured is of great import to the present argument. While spying to no avail on the building which has become the center of his attention, Maulincourt is unexpectedly caught in a rainstorm. This first element in the scene at hand is not without significance in itself. The weather is the epitome of unpredictable, fortuitous events: nothing intervenes in a more haphazard way to undo plans carefully laid or to suggest unsuspected bifurcations. Stymied in his own calculations, Maulincourt will find an exit only in the aleatory. Driven by the storm, he takes shelter in a doorway along with several other passersby as the rain begins to fall. It so happens that Ferragus is among them, something Auguste begins to suspect as a result of what the narrator calls "one of those vagabond reveries [*rêveries vagabondes*] which begin with a vulgar question and end in the understanding of a whole world of thoughts"

(5:817). A vagabond and *flâneur* at the beginning of the story, just as the narrator himself, Auguste is now served by the same wandering attention which leads him toward the heart of the matter. Confirmation of his suspicions is offered when he finds a letter on the ground, apparently fallen from the pocket of the suspicious stranger, who disappears quickly after the storm. As we have seen, the idea of the fall is intimately linked to the aleatory. It is significant, therefore, that the confirmation Auguste receives of his suspicions originates in an incident provoked by the falling rain and ends with a letter fallen to the ground beside him. Maulincourt is once again guided by an occurrence beyond his own predictive control and becomes definitively caught in a plot unfolding in a manner rapidly beginning to escape him.

The question of mastery is, of course, a fundamental one here. Chance and mastery are the two opposite ends of a spectrum: at one extreme is a totally unexpected and unpredictable encounter; at the other is the ideal vantage point, Laplace's demon, the observer for whom every causal sequence can be linked to every other. Auguste's attempts to discover the causes of Mme Jules's attachment to a poor, undignified stranger (Ferragus) are the result of his desire to dominate (meaning to interpret in this context), but also, in a less abstract sense, to master the woman whom he has not succeeded in approaching in any other way. Failing more respectable means to get her attention in the salons they both frequent, he will blackmail her by threatening to reveal her nocturnal visits to the stranger, a weapon he has happened on by accident. But in his own attempt to assume the position of the demon, Maulincourt will confront someone who is more than his match, always in possession of a better vantage point—a veritable demon in the Laplacean sense. For every move Auguste makes, Ferragus will have a response, a superior, englobing strategy. The means used to express Ferragus's position of superiority in this now-deadly game of cause and effect, moreover, will be a series of apparent chance occurrences, accidents which turn out to be attempts on Maulincourt's life arranged by Ferragus. He who would assume mastery must master even accidental occurrences. A victim of the fascination aroused by two chance encounters, which instilled in him a false confidence in his own deductive powers, Auguste now becomes the target of a devious criminal.

Let us briefly consider the "accidents" at stake here. A most striking element catches the reader's eye immediately. All the accidents are textbook illustrations of Cournot's definition of chance— but this time travestied, mere simulacra of chance occurrences. First incident: as Maulincourt drives out of his courtyard, a piece of stone from a scaffolding falls on his carriage, narrowly missing him and killing his manservant. Second incident: in the course of another carriage ride, the axle of his vehicle inexplicably collapses and he is nearly crushed. Third incident: the marquis de Ronquerolles, provoked by an apparently harmless remark Maulincourt makes concerning his (Ronquerolles's) sister, challenges him to a duel in which he wounds Auguste, although not fatally. While these "accidents" may appear superficially haphazard, the weight of repetition ultimately leads to the perception that they are all attributable to Ferragus. Indeed, the second incident already provokes Maulincourt's suspicion, a feeling confirmed by evidence that the carriage axle was weakened in order to make it fail. What appear to be accidents at one level, therefore, ultimately turn out to be planned attempts on Auguste's life. At this point, Maulincourt realizes that he has locked horns with a master of causal series. To parry his own amateurish insufficiency, he enlists the help of experts in matters of cause and effect. First, the police: "What one can reasonably expect of them is to look for the causes of an event," says one of his confidants (5:826). In addition, he uses the services of an "old Figaro," a servant who is a skilled detective in his own right, having arranged many a confidential amorous pursuit. All is to no avail—Ferragus always succeeds in remaining one step ahead of his adversary, and he finally poisons Auguste: " 'This Ferragus, this Bourignard, or this Monsieur de Funcal is a demon,' cried Maulincourt. . . . 'Into what hideous labyrinth have I stumbled? Where am I headed?' " (5:859). The image of the labyrinth recurs here, I would note in passing, as Auguste realizes that he is rapidly becoming lost in the confrontation with Ferragus. What will become important for us shortly is the transformation of the labyrinth into something else entirely as the narrative ends.

For the moment, however, the idea of mastery suggested above deserves more detailed attention. Earlier, I situated mastery and chance at two ends of a spectrum, but this approach does not really go to the heart of the matter. *Ferragus* is marked by an open-ended series of dramatic reversals as various attempts to master events and people in the narrative fail. The narrative seems thus to be characterized as much by ruptures as by opposing approaches that could be measured on any continuous scale. For example, as indicated earlier, Auguste at first believes himself capable of competing with the criminal Ferragus only to discover that Ferragus always seems to be one step ahead of him. Ferragus, on the other hand, will himself fall victim to a reversal provoked by Jules Desmarets, who is in turn one step ahead of him—and this reversal will undermine his plans and destroy his position. The narrative is structured as a series of levels of comprehension characterized by limiting boundaries at which transformations occur. Because he is unable to gain any all-englobing observational position, a given character regularly finds himself confined to a space ultimately defined by what appear to him to be chance occurrences—events whose connection to an ordered complexity can become manifest only when they are shown to be at a threshold, a liminal frontier at which their significance can be reinterpreted. From this point of view, the three "accidents" befalling Maulincourt are symbolic of the dilemma at stake. From Auguste's original point of view, they necessarily appear as unconnected and aleatory. Only when he begins to suspect that he will have to attain another vantage point integrating and subsuming the first does he realize he must enlist help to penetrate the mystery and discern the hand of Ferragus.

The relationship between information and the aleatory suggested by this structure contains similarities to that between chance and noise evident in certain aspects of information theory. In particular, the position of an observer within a communicational structure can determine whether he interprets what passes through a circuit as noise or information. Michel Serres states succinctly the elements involved in this theoretical approach:

If one writes the equation expressing the quantity of information exchanged between two stations through a given channel and the equation which provides this quantity for the whole unit (including the two stations and the channel), a change of sign occurs for a certain function entering into the computation. In other words, this function, called ambiguity and resulting from noise, changes when the observer changes his point of observation. Its value depends on whether he is submerged in the first level or whether he examines the entire unit from the next level.[19]

At the limits of a given level, an observer confined solely to that level perceives certain phenomena as noise (chance events), whereas an observer at another level is able to perceive them instead as information. In other words, a reversal in the perceptual significance of certain events occurs at such a limit.[20] An analogy to the situation of social interaction described in *Ferragus* is clearly discernable. Each new observer/actor in the story gains a new and different perception of the events as they unfold. What appeared as aleatory for one character can thus become ordered for another. The open-ended repetition of this process, however, demonstrates that no one will attain an ultimate observational position from which all noise can be transformed into interpretable and therefore mastered information, as we shall see in a moment.

The example analyzed above of the three "accidents" befalling Maulincourt is perhaps not the best one available to illuminate the principles just introduced. The most pertinent illustration of what can happen at the limits of transformation between levels is undoubtedly the climactic scene of recognition which finally brings Ferragus, Mme Jules, and Jules Desmarets physically together in the story. The background leading up to the scene in question sets the stage for a reading of the events it contains: Auguste, defeated and poisoned by Ferragus, has been brushed aside, but not without having first passed the torch of the desire to know to Mme Jules's husband, Jules Desmarets. "Ah! I want to know everything" (5:850) is the fatal phrase that sums up Jules's obsession and his coming tragedy. It is important to note that Desmarets is a banker and stockbroker, a man of figures [*chiffres*] and logic, one skilled, therefore, in the investigative and deductive talents necessary to pursue the inquiry initiated by Maulincourt: "After having toiled over his figures, he occupied his leisure by obstinately attempting to acquire the set of skills necessary for any man who would make his mark in the contemporary world," as the narrator says of the young Desmarets (5:806). Where Auguste has failed, Desmarets will succeed, albeit to his own chagrin and detriment. Having been informed by Maulincourt of Mme Jules's trysts with Ferragus, Desmarets does what Maulincourt never thought to do as the narrative opened: he goes directly into the building where the meetings now take place, tricks the concierge, and bribes an acquaintance of Ferragus in order to obtain a vantage point from which to survey a meeting scheduled for the following day. Jules's burning interest in the meeting is kindled because he incorrectly believes Ferragus to be Mme Jules's lover.

On the morning of the meeting, Jules goes to the apartment of Ferragus's friend, the widow Gruget, whom he bribed in order to observe the events: "She showed him . . . an opening the size of a . . . coin, created during the night in a position corresponding to the highest and darkest point in the pattern of the wallpaper covering Ferragus's room. . . . It was extremely difficult for anyone to detect this peephole [*meurtrière*] in the shadow" (5:874). What Jules actually does, then, is to put himself in the raised position of the observer, above and removed from the level of the scene about to be played out before him. His post behind the backs of the principals in the unfolding spectacle assures him of a vantage point outside the circuit they themselves will occupy. The narrative emphasizes the height at which Jules is forced to stand: "He was obliged, in order to maintain his position [at the level of the peephole], to remain in a rather tiring position perched on a stool which the widow Gruget had been careful enough to provide" (5:874). These details are highly symbolic. In order to master those whom he observes, Jules must be placed at a level separated from them, behind and above them (outside the channel between them). He proceeds to witness a conversation between Ferragus and Mme Jules in which the mystery of his wife's behavior is finally fully divulged. He learns, in other words, both that Mme Jules is Ferragus's daughter and that Ferragus is planning to cover his criminal background by assuming the identity of a Spanish nobleman, M. de Funcal. The calm, almost detached knowledge Jules thus obtains is simply too neat, however. As one could invariably expect in a narrative marked by so many such moments, an occurrence Desmarets could not have anticipated, much less prevented, in short, a chance event, intervenes to destroy his cool detachment. The widow Gruget, who has allowed Jules to witness the scene by looking through the peephole, receives at precisely the same moment a letter from her daughter Ida announcing Ida's impending suicide: "A terrible scream echoed in the room where Jules Desmarets was standing" (5:877). Needless to say, a tremendous commotion ensues during which Mme Jules discovers her husband's ruse, and the carefully laid plans of all three characters collapse.

Certain elements in the description of the scene outlined above are vital. Whenever one of the characters believes himself safe and fully in control of a given situation, someone appears behind or above to undermine him: Ferragus, calmly revealing the details of his complex plot aimed at producing his future destiny, is discovered by Jules, and Jules, after carefully arranging his foray into espionage, is undone by the widow Gruget. Moreover, the precise moment when the whole house of cards comes tumbling down is marked by noise, by a commotion striking terror in the hearts of all those involved in this crucial scene. The noise at stake is the very embodiment of the aleatory, I would maintain, of that which is necessarily neglected by the various interpretations constructed in the minds of the principal characters. As soon as a level behind or beyond them in the structure of the plot appears, the order they had sought to construct at their own limited level breaks down. What had appeared as orderly structure is suddenly transformed into disorder; what was once information becomes noise. And there always appears to be a next actor who can accomplish yet another transformation capable of changing order into disorder and vice versa. Ultimately, however, as the scene suggests, behind and beyond every state of order is another, more profound disorder, a chance occurrence waiting to undo any stasis. We might put this another way by saying that there can and will be no ultimate master among the characters in *Ferragus,* or rather, that the only master will be chance (and disorder). I shall return shortly to this observation and treat it from a slightly different angle.

A further emblematic element in the narration serves to confirm the analysis attempted above. At stake is the method whereby Jules learns of the time and place of the rendezvous described in the preceding paragraphs. Having discovered that his wife has sent a message to Ferragus, Desmarets knows there will be a response. The precise manner in which the response will come (the means to be used to disguise it), however, remains a mystery. As he speculates on the many possibilities, Jules finds himself in a situation not unlike the one experienced earlier by Maulincourt: "And he was suspicious of everything, and he traveled across the immense fields, the endless sea of suppositions. Then, after having floated for some time among a thousand contradictory choices, he felt stronger in his own house than anywhere else and resolved to stay there" (5:862). Like Auguste de Maulincourt, whose wandering attention led him to discovery, Jules roams about until he hits upon the best solution. Instead of exposing himself needlessly, he decides to wait, certain of his ability to recognize and seize the time to act. Choosing the only terrain on which Ferragus is not fully master (the private, the hidden) and thus creating for himself the potential to muster a superior force should the occasion arise, Jules succeeds and indeed intercepts the response he has anticipated in the form of a letter. Things are not quite so simple, however, because the letter, incomprehensible, is of no use in its original form: "[It] was unrelenting nonsense, and one needed the key to read it. It had been written in code [*en chiffres*]" (5:862). Jules, *homme de chiffres,* the man of mathematics and figures, is now presented with a different *chiffre*. The important point is that the letter appears at first to be nothing but a jumble of words and letters. For Jules, it is *pure noise, pure chance*. Only by addressing the problem from a different level will he be capable of resolving it. Specifically, he calls on a longtime friend, a man who works in the Foreign Ministry and has experience with diplomatic codes, to decipher the message. The incident is symptomatic of the process of transformation occurring at limits, a process reproduced in a more mortal form once Jules actually goes to the meeting place and finds himself exposed to view by the unforeseen suicide of Ida Gruget (he who cannot foresee will infallibly be seen). The case of the letter demonstrates, then, what the disaster at the Gruget apartment will confirm. Phenomena perceptible only as noise and chance at one level become order at another—and so on, in an endless and reversible chain.

A further lesson concerning the structural characteristics of the aleatory in the novella can be drawn from the material describing Jules Desmarets. Although at the critical narrative moment represented by the incident of the letter he bears some resemblance to Maulincourt, I earlier insisted on a significant difference—as a man of figures, he is better suited to the task Auguste could only fail to accomplish. There is something more to this portrait of Desmarets, however. As broker and banker, he is also a man of contracts and agreements. The most striking proof of this is his own marriage to Mme Jules. Too poor to pretend to the hand of a daughter of the aristocratic or moneyed classes, Desmarets falls in love with Clémence, the future Mme Jules, for her beauty and not a little out of the desperation of the hopelessly poor man. When he discovers that Clémence has neither name nor fortune, he is able to win her hand as he would not have been able to do under any other circumstances. Soon after the marriage, a series of lucky events (*une série d'événements heureux*) ensues which make Jules a rich man: "It was impossible for him not to notice, in the manner in which business deals came to him, some occult influence attributable to his mother-in-law or a secret protection he ascribed to Providence" (5:808). Ordinarily based on a legal contract, which in this instance is never mentioned and whose existence is therefore always in doubt, the marriage will come to be defined by an implicit agreement between Jules and his wife, a contract of silence never directly alluded to by the two principals but tacitly applied: Jules will not mount any attempt to identify the source of his success or the familial origins of Clémence but will accept both without comment. In a sense, this arrangement is a necessary substitute for the normal marriage contract, because Clémence has no legal basis, no other ground on which to stand in her dealings with Desmarets: "She had no official birth certificate [*état civil*], and her name, *Clémence,* her age, were established only by a subsequently notarized statement [*un acte de notoriété publique*]" (5:807). Her lack of status would make it difficult, if not impossible, to enter into the normal contractual relationship implied by legal marriage. Thus, despite lingering suspicions, no question will be asked concerning Mme Jules's past and the events which have led to the couple's well-being. Only once prior to the chain of events provoked by Maulincourt's intervention is the pact tested. Someone suggests too hastily to Desmarets that his financial success is not his own but, rather, the product of his wife's family's influence. Desmarets promptly dispatches the calumniator to his grave in the course of a duel.

What I am suggesting is that far from being the kind of immediate and natural love relationship at which the narrator coyly hints, the agreement between the two characters is an artifice. It is based, in other words, on a convention, a temporary arrangement destined to hold only for a certain time. Confirmation of this fact is provided subsequently by a lengthy description of Mme Jules's strategy within her marriage. It is one of continual seduction aimed at prolonging Desmarets's interest in her. In the first place, she lavishly decorates the private territory of her life with Jules in an attempt to maintain the constant stimulation of all his senses. To summarize Clémence's program, the narrator remarks: "You must understand love as a principle developing all its grace only on Savonnerie rugs, under the opal shimmer of light provided by a marble lamp, between discrete walls covered in silk, before a golden fireplace, in a room insulated from the noise of neighbors, the street, everything" (5:838). Mme Jules pursues her program to such a degree that she even forbids her husband from ever seeing her in disarray, preferring instead to present herself at every moment in all her seductive charm even in the privacy of her own boudoir: "Most women returning from a ball, impatient to get to sleep, throw their dresses, their wilted flowers, their now odorless bouquets all around themselves. . . . Placed before the love of a husband who is yawning one finds thus the true woman who is also yawning and who presents herself in a disorder lacking all elegance" (5:839). Not so Clémence: "Mme Jules had forbidden her husband from entering her dressing room. . . . Jules always saw a woman coquettishly adorned in an elegant robe issuing forth from the room in question" (5:840). The distinction between the public and the private persona becomes utterly blurred. Instead of appearing at her best in public, as do the majority of women, Clémence reserves the most seductive of her artifices for her private relationship with Jules, preventing him from seeing behind her artfully constructed identity and appearance. The private persona is just as invented as the public one.

The significance of these characteristics of the relationship between Jules and his wife is revealed most fully when seen in light of my previous analysis of the essential distance at the heart of every intersection of destinies. Despite the public perception that Jules and Clémence are an ideal couple, their private lives demonstrate the tension, the fault line, at the center of their relationship. The idea that the alliance of man and woman is a "natural" phenomenon, regulated by some underlying immutable law of attraction beyond artifice, seduction, and chance, is debunked in the description of the marriage of Jules and Clémence in *Ferragus*. Their marriage rests on a contract. The concomitant axiom, moreover, is that all such contractual relationships are necessarily temporary and thus fated to be undone. The order they establish will necessarily succumb at a later point to the stochastic disorder of a disaster.[21] Furthermore, in the case of Desmarets and his wife, the disorder—the gradual destruction of their marriage—is the result of a series of chance occurrences, as has become clear in the course of our reading of *Ferragus*. To express the structure of Balzac's story in metaphoric terms, it is almost as if the relationship between Jules and Clémence were a ship battered about by the unpredictable movement of the waves, of the world outside, destined to sink sooner or later.

No object is more expressive of the inevitable results of this process as it unfolds in the novella than the funerary urn containing Mme Jules's ashes, an obsessive motif as the story closes. The conclusion of *Ferragus* describes the confrontation which takes place when Jules spies on his wife from the Gruget apartment. It results in Clémence's death, when she is unable to bear the shock she receives by the mistrust of her husband and the breaking of the covenant between them in the course of this fateful moment. Shortly thereafter, unwilling to accept the idea of his wife's remains buried in a Parisian cemetery, Jules petitions the city to be allowed to exhume the body, cremate it, and retain the ashes. Doubtless a certain romantic thematics is tied to this motif, prompting in part its appearance in the context at hand. I would argue, however, that one must go further in interpreting it if one is not to miss an important point. The ashes emblematically represent maximum atomic disorder, the stochastic state toward which, in the Lucretian theory of the universe, all conventions must converge. It must not be forgotten that Lucretius described all conglomerations resulting from the clinamen as contracts, whether they be natural or social. The notion of contract is devised by Lucretius to emphasize that all conglomerations are only temporary, destined, in other words, to be undone shortly. Modern thermodynamic theory takes up this notion once again in the form of entropy when it maintains that organizations move toward a state of maximum entropy. In such a final state, no organization remains save the random movement of the atoms themselves.[22] In *Ferragus,* the marriage between Jules and Clémence is destroyed as a result of Jules's indiscretion, and, in addition, Clémence's very body finishes as a heap of ashes. *Ferragus* thus catalogs the formation and dissolution of one of the myriad of conventional organizations of which social life—and, Lucretius would maintain, nature itself—are composed and, in the process, demonstrates a hidden concern for Lucretian questions in a manner not unrelated to what one finds in Stendhal's *La Chartreuse de Parme.*

A rather fascinating dialectic is established in this part of the story's conclusion between social convention and law, on the one hand, and the random collection of ashes, disorder, on the other. For it turns out that Jules's request is not quite as simple as it first appears. Having charged his friend Jacquet (the very same friend who deciphered the letter permitting Jules to observe his wife from the Gruget apartment) with the administrative details of the cremation request, Jules waits. Jacquet soon discovers that the complexity of Parisian law dealing with burials and dead bodies admits of no exceptions and therefore does not allow Jules's request to be honored. In other words, it is as if the law refuses to release its hold and acknowledge its own temporal limitations even when presented with death and dissolution. The body emptied of life still cannot seem to escape the clutches of the social order. The narrator describing Jacquet's sentiments comments: "Constitutional, administrative legality gives birth to nothing. It is a barren monster for peoples, for kings nd for private interests. . . . Jacquet, a man of freedom, thus returned home reflecting on the beneficent effects of the arbitrary, because a man judges laws only in light of his own passions" (5:892–93). In fact, the fulfillment of Jules's petition will require a gesture beyond the law, emanating from the realm of the arbitrary and the unpredictable: the outlaw Ferragus will cut through the question of legality in one fell swoop simply by stealing the body and delivering the ashes to Jules. The lifeless, random ashes are ultimately severed from the social order only by an act which cannot be foreseen and thus forestalled by that order.

The story does not end there, however. The complexity of the conclusion of *Ferragus* contains a series of lessons it would behoove us to explore in detail. The first observation one must make is that the novella could arguably be said to possess three different conclusions—the narrator himself acknowledges this anomaly. The first one is the scene at the cemetery where Mme Jules is buried: "Here would seem to end the telling of this story" (5:891). The narrator immediately launches into a discussion of the legal implications of death in Paris, culminating in the gesture of Ferragus, who, as we saw, restores Mme Jules's ashes to her husband. The very structure of this second ending, I would insist, mirrors the beginning of the novella. There is a descriptive musing on Parisian mores that simultaneously delays and yet leads into the events marking the second ending of the story. As if this were still insufficient, the narrator promptly proceeds to offer a third conclusion, namely, the scene of a highly charged encounter between Ferragus and Desmarets. The stage is carefully set for this extraordinary third finale. Consumed by grief at the loss of his wife, Jules Desmarets leaves Paris for a trip to the provinces after receiving the funerary urn, presented to him by Ferragus in an ultimate and ferocious display of paternal love. There is a break in the narrative, whereupon the narrator begins a discussion of the bizarre characters one often encounters in the streets of Paris. The correspondence between this passage and the opening paragraphs of the novella is patent. This closing moment, like the incipit, will also be marked by a chance encounter to which we shall turn in a moment. It is crucial to note that these two instants, both stages for the appearance of chance events in the novella, are framed by the same type of detailed discussion covering some topos of Parisian life. Characteristically, a third important chance meeting outlined earlier, namely, Auguste de Maulincourt's encounter with Ferragus in the doorway during the rainstorm, is also the locus of a similar discussion, this time an artistic passing in review of the gallery of Parisian pedestrians who can conceivably find themselves huddled together during the typical Paris storm.

The narrator proceeds thus as the third and final conclusion commences: "While walking along the boulevards of Paris, at the corner of some street or under the arcades of the Palais-Royal, someplace in the world where chance provides the occasion, who has not met a being—man or woman—whose appearance provokes a thousand confused thoughts!" (5:900). Whatever Paris means to Balzac—and much has been said on this subject—one thing is clear in *Ferragus*: Paris is the setting par excellence of chance encounters. To venture out into its streets is to enter into a realm where the unexpected is the rule. And what one meets there is material inextricably linked to the artistic act. It may be the writing of a novel ("this creature becomes embedded in your memory and remains there like the first volume of a novel whose ending escapes you" [5:901]) or perhaps the conception of a painting ("How is it that none of our painters has yet attempted to reproduce the physiognomies of a swarm of Parisians huddled together under the humid archway of some building during a storm?" [5:814]). The artist is invariably a *flâneur* and the *flâneur* an artist in Balzac's universe. Once again, as he concludes his story, the narrator links his own personal artistic activity to the wandering attention of the aimless stroller, as he did in the incipit.

The discussion of bizarre characters encountered by chance in the streets serves as an opening that permits the narrator to cite one such case—a man whom he recently noticed in the area between the Luxembourg Gardens and the Observatory and who turns out to be Ferragus. The topography of this particular part of Paris is perhaps even more intriguing than the character who inhabits it. The text paints a neutral space, one impossible to classify precisely: "In this area one is no longer in Paris and yet Paris is still there. The place resembles simultaneously a square, a street, a boulevard, a fortification, a garden, an avenue, a road; it belongs both to the provinces and to the capital. Indeed, it is all that, but it is nothing of that: it is a desert" (5:901). This "place without a name" (5:901), as it is also characterized, is in-between—not outside, but not quite inside. It is located at a limit, in a region where the order and law of the city begin to weaken, where careful planning and rationality begin to lose their hold. Within the confines of the city, even the remains of the dead fall prey to the law, but here one meets the fringes, the frontier of the law's power. Into this liminal scene rides Jules Desmarets returning from his country retreat. As he passes by he espies Ferragus. " 'It's him,' exclaimed Jules upon discovering beneath this human debris Ferragus XXIII, leader of the Dévorants" (5:903). Jules's exclamation "It's him" echoes Auguste's original "*She,* in this filth, at this hour!" Once again the paths of two characters in the narrative intersect in a totally unpredictable manner. Jules happens to pass through a particular neighborhood while on a trip that is taking him to an unrelated destination. Ferragus, in his senility, has become a wandering beggar completely cut off from his former life.[23] Their destinies, once so tied together by their mutual love for Mme Jules, now have radically diverged. And yet those paths, those destinies intersect one last time. There is a moral to be extracted here, and Jules's final remarks express it: " 'How he loved her!' he added after a pause. 'Drive on, cabbie!' he called" (5:903). The fact that Desmarets stops only momentarily and then turns quickly away toward new business is clearly meant to indicate the shallowness of his love for Mme Jules when compared with Ferragus's adoration. Unlike Jules, Ferragus has been utterly destroyed by his daughter's death. But to remain at that level alone would be to miss some important implications of this final scene.

From the dimly lit, labyrinthine, chaotic streets of a poor section of Paris, haunted by a vagabond straggler in the opening scene of *Ferragus,* the narrator leads the reader, in his conclusion, to the vague, disordered, desertlike limits of the city where urban categories weaken and disappear. These two settings are complementary and demonstrate the range of the evolution accomplished in the course of the story. As made clear at the beginning of the present discussion of *Ferragus,* the labyrinth is not yet the most radical questioning of order, not yet the embrace of a view of chance affording it a status beyond and independent of structure and organization. The chaotic topography which characterizes the ending of the story, on the other hand, defies normal classifications and is no longer the locus of even the modicum of certainty provided by the labyrinth. The category of the *flâneur,* now encompassing Ferragus himself (the narrator asks rhetorically as he muses on the bizarre figures which provoke his final reflections, "Who are you? Why are you wandering about [*Pourquoi flânez-vous?*]?" [5:901]), has finally found its domain of predilection, the no man's land of civilization's limits. One could easily say that in *Ferragus* a sort of protodetective story featuring ever more complex deductive mastery constantly undone by chance is sandwiched in between two closely related scenes characterized by a curious and troubling disorder, more drastic as the narrative progresses. And whereas the beginning of the story is marked by Auguste's transformation, albeit ultimately unsuccessful, from *flâneur* into devious schemer, the end contains the image of a Ferragus who has gone the opposite route, from master of causes to senile vagabond.

The implications of the story's trajectory are far reaching indeed. In Laplace's theory, chance was viewed as a mere manifestation of the observer's ignorance. The fundamental state of the world conforms to the laws of nature, which encompass everything, including what might at first glance seem to escape them. Even in Cournot's attempt to grant a more independent status to chance occurrences, they remain aberrations, exceptions to the underlying rule of strict causality. By opening with a scene in a labyrinth already suggestive of a coming disaster and closing with a scene marked by chaos, both of which contain an unpredictable encounter, Balzac's *Ferragus* seems to suggest something much more radical. The orderly unfolding of the story is preceded by near disorder (an aimless stroll through darkened streets) concluded only by the appearance of a fortuitous event (Auguste's encounter with Mme Jules). This event in turn gives rise to an ordered chain of effects. The order attained within the main body of the narrative disintegrates at the end, and the reader is thrust back into a domain where chaos (absence of order) reigns, where the only "law" is chance, represented by the brief encounter between Desmarets and

Ferragus. What Balzac has done is to invert a traditional hierarchy. Instead of a foundation of order in the form of the laws of nature on which certain aberrations (chance events) sometimes occur—to be explained away either as examples of our ignorance or as exceptions to the rule—one is presented with a system lacking foundation in the classical sense. This system originates and terminates in disorder, in the very terrain of chance occurrences so fortuitous that no law could predict them. Order is now the exception.

Balzac's structuring choice is fundamentally a philosophical one. As Cournot himself maintained when writing on probability, mathematical or purely scientific reasoning cannot really get to the heart of the question concerning the status of chance: "One must bring in other notions, other principles of knowledge, in short, one must engage in a philosophical critique."[24] The question truly raised by the structure of *Ferragus* is whether or not one may establish a hierarchical relationship between order and disorder and what that hierarchy would be. As Clément Rosset would have it, this is "the old problem of knowing whether disorder can only be imagined from the point of view of order (Bergson's thesis), or whether, like Lucretius, one can speak of a primordial disorder or chance."[25] If Balzac had stopped at the idea of introducing Cournot-like occurrences into his narrative, he would already have demonstrated in this manner a tendency, which was to become more and more visible in the scientific domain as the nineteenth century wore on, to attempt to escape from the rigidly deterministic world view associated with Laplace's version of classical mechanics. But he would have stopped well short of a more extreme questioning. The structure of *Ferragus,* however, takes the argument one step further. The framing of the story accomplished by using two scenes of disorder suggests that disorder is not simply an aberration occasionally added to a fundamental, underlying order but is, rather, primordial. One could safely assert that this is not a position often presented or defended in the history of philosophy—for obvious reasons. Chance and disorder, when taken as primordial elements, are not very firm bases for philosophical reasoning as it is classically understood.

The debate to which Balzac alludes in *Ferragus* increasingly finds its way into scientific theory in the course of the nineteenth century in the form of a new scientific discipline, thermodynamics. It will take more than a century, however, for developments in the modern thermodynamic study of open systems to permit a theoretically interesting attempt to include chance as a productive principle of scientific explanation. Certain modern researchers, Ilya Prigogine and Henri Atlan among them, maintain that chance perturbations, or noise, as information-theory proponents would call them, can be incorporated by open systems and used by them to evolve toward increased organization and complexity—an approach suggesting at the very least that chance and organization are equals. But even this recent hypothesis concerning the status of chance has led to more than one passionate debate.[26] The problem of chance, because it necessarily probes the limits of human knowledge, is a point of intersection between science and philosophy, at the limits of interpretation in ways I have already discussed and therefore a fertile locus of polemics.

But what of the narrator in *Ferragus*? In reading the story's incipit, I suggested that we would have to return to the hesitation it evinces and thus to the figure of the narrator after studying the ending in order to try to draw some conclusions. If none of the other characters in the story succeeds in attaining a position of mastery over chance, what must we say of the narrator? In many ways, one could maintain that Ferragus is his surrogate. Just as Ferragus seems at one point to control all of Paris, so would the third-person omniscient narrator appear at times to be a sort of super-Ferragus, maintaining firmly in his grasp all the narrative strings. In fact, it could be argued that the position of the third-person omniscient narrator corresponds in a striking manner to the position of Laplace's demon, since, ideally, he is the master of all causal sequences in his story. But this would be to forget what the narrator said of himself in the opening paragraphs of the novella. We must remember that he too wanders in search of his story, unable to begin before holding forth on a subject (Parisian streets) ostensibly unrelated to the plot that subsequently unfolds. Moreover, the third ending of *Ferragus,* which we have just discussed at length, although it is entitled "Conclusion," appears to be something of an afterthought on the narrator's part and is hence much less clear-cut and conclusive than one would expect.

The tripartite nature of the story's conclusion—as if the narrator could not release the text, could not decide how to end—puts it into direct correspondence with the incipit. The edges of what otherwise gives every impression of being a sharply ordered performance by the narrator are slightly frayed, haunted by an air of hesitation, by what would almost seem an inability to get to the point. The reluctance to begin or to end is provoked by the haphazard interests of the narrator: his fascination for the city struggles against the need to get on with his story. The traditional image of the third-person narrator thus becomes problematic in *Ferragus.* The story seems instead to be bent on exposing the fundamentally vagabond nature of beginnings and endings in general. Not only do the beginning and the ending of *Ferragus* illustrate the effects of chance encounters that resemble one another to a striking degree, but the narrator himself is ultimately infected by the very structure he attempts to describe. The classic Balzacian narrative style is threatened to an extent one does not always suspect by a disintegration leading it down the path of haphazard musings.

The stochastic aspects of the narrative practice illustrated in *Ferragus* are, in many ways, just the tip of the iceberg. When Balzac directly addresses the question of aesthetic creation elsewhere in his fiction, the place and importance of chance become even clearer. One might well use another of his novellas, *Gambara,* as a nearly doctrinal exploration of what happens at the limits of artistic creation. The story concerns a musician caught between the dreams and abstract musings of his own theorizing, on the one hand, and the limited appreciative capacities of his audiences on the other. Before addressing this opposition more directly, however, I must point out that the beginning of the narrative bears a distinct relation to the structure observed earlier in *Ferragus*. Specifically, the story opens with a chance encounter, one, as could be expected, between a young man and a woman who fascinates him. This opening reproduces fundamental aspects of the topography found in *Ferragus*. To bring out the similarities, it would be best to describe the first pages of the story in some detail.

The narrative commences with the description of an unidentified young man engaged in an evening promenade at the Palais-Royal. A common and well-known Balzacian topographical entity, the Palais-Royal represents a crossroads, a sort of interchange where afternoon or after-dinner strollers (*flâneurs*) congregate and cross paths, and where, consequently, unexpected encounters are the rule. Balzac emphasizes the sexual undertones of many of the encounters which ensue by reporting the passing comments made by two prostitutes observing the young man who is the subject of the story in this inaugural scene. More important, however, is the potential for topographical transformation apparent even in this, the heart of civilized Paris. Although what occurs at the Palais-Royal may represent well-regulated social interaction in a carefully policed society, the meeting place exists, nevertheless, in an uneasy juxtaposition with something different and almost darkly threatening. A street representing anything but a part of the ordered social exchange defining the Palais-Royal leads directly off from it. The narrator follows the young man as he crosses the square in order to reach the rue Froidmanteau, which he describes as "a dirty, dark, and uninviting street, something like a sewer the police tolerated right next to the sanitized Palais-Royal in the same way an Italian majordomo would permit a negligent valet to pile up in a corner of the staircase all the dust swept up in an apartment" (10:460). The reader once again is put at the fluctuating edge of organized society, in an obscure place where carefully conceived categories are challenged by a rising disorder. We find, in fact, the same dark, labyrinthine context which marked the beginning of *Ferragus* only to be reprised in its ending as well.

In a further indication of the breakdown of social law suggested by the rue Froidmanteau, Andrea Marcosini, the young man whom the narrator tracks in these opening pages, is in pursuit of a woman with whom he has become fascinated and who appears to be grossly beneath his own social class. The foray into the rue Froidmanteau, whose subversive characteristics are made crystal clear in the narrative, is simultaneously accompanied by a potentially explosive confusion of disparate social classes. After seeing the woman who has provoked such a profound interest on his part, Marcosini, who "put much stock in social distinctions" (10:462), finds himself so bewildered by "but's and if's, . . . [so] overwhelmed by one of those furious temptations for which there is no name in any language—even in the language of the orgy—[that he] threw himself onto the trail of this woman, ultimately chasing after a target of easy virtue like the typical Parisian rake" (10:462). Just like the street, which is an almost unspeakably disordered sewer in the midst of one of the most brilliant squares in Paris, Marcosini's desire is unspeakable, incomprehensible, a temptation going against the grain of every precept hammered home in the course of his education as a distinguished Italian nobleman. There is literally no name for what he feels, even in the most disordered of languages, the language of the orgy. Like Auguste de Maulincourt, Andrea follows his prey in the dark street ("the night had fallen" [10:463]) only to lose her in the obscure maze into which he has ventured: "Andrea, who was walking behind her, saw her disappear into one of the darkest alleys of the street whose name was unknown to him" (10:463). Once again the chance meeting at the beginning of the narrative is accompanied by all the marks of the unforeseen, of what escapes the law as it is normally understood: confusion, darkness, loss of direction, and the like.

This is but a preparatory experience for what will quickly become a much more profound questioning of Marcosini's ideas on the accepted limits of order and disorder. For the woman he is following, Marianna, is the wife of a musician, Gambara (his name doubles as the story's title), whose theories of artistic creation will throw Marcosini's own well-systematized ideas concerning music into disarray. After debating the question of whether he will embark on what he fears will be a strange and threatening adventure, Andrea decides to plunge ahead. His investigations lead him to a restaurant for Italian exiles and émigrés and to the truth concerning Marianna's relationship with Gambara. The first meeting with Gambara takes place on the occasion of a New Year's dinner prepared by the restaurant owner, Giardini, and is marked by a conversation during which Marcosini's ideas seem to harmonize with those of Gambara. Although the other regular guests of Giardini's establishment consider Gambara to be deranged (Giardini chief among them), Marcosini finds him cogent and lucid during the discussion. Indeed, he succeeds in winning Gambara's confidence and thus in receiving an invitation to go to Gambara's apartment to hear some of the master's work.

The stage is set in this manner for the central scene of the story. Gambara gives a rendition of his masterwork, the opera *Mohamet*, on his piano as he sings portions of the various vocal parts. Marcosini's shock and surprise mount as he sees more and more clearly that Gambara's work is absolutely incomprehensible. Gambara not only fails to realize that the portrait painted of Mohammed's long-suffering wife in the opera corresponds precisely to the position of his own wife, Marianna, but he is also absolutely oblivious to the fact that the music itself contains nothing of what normally passes for beautiful and harmonious:

Andrea contemplated Gambara in dumbfounded amazement. At first he was gripped by the horrible irony presented by a man expressing the sentiments of the wife of Mohammed without recognizing them in his own wife, Marianna, but soon the madness of the husband was eclipsed by that of the composer. There was not even the semblance of a poetic or musical idea in the deafening cacophony which struck the ears. The principles of harmony, the first rules of composition were totally foreign to this formless creation. Instead of the carefully crafted music which Gambara was explaining [as he played and sang], his fingers were producing . . . discordant sounds thrown together by chance, apparently combined solely for the purpose of assaulting even the least delicate ears. It is difficult to explain the bizarre execution, because one would need new words for such an impossible music. (10:493)

Although Marcosini, Marianna, and Giardini can only take the sounds Gambara is producing as signs of his folly, Gambara himself slips into an almost ecstatic trance and believes, contrary to the other characters in the scene, that he has created a new and more beautiful music: "The strange discordances crying out beneath his fingers had obviously echoed in his ear like divine harmonies" (10:494).

Who is right here, Marcosini or Gambara? An answer to the question will require some reflection on a discussion of music to be found in Michel Serres's work, a discussion which sheds an interesting theoretical light on the notions developed in this passage of *Gambara*. First, however, we should underscore the repetition of a certain element which surfaced even as the narrator described Andrea's pursuit of Marianna in both the Palais-Royal and the rue Froidmanteau. The temptations driving Marcosini to stalk Gambara's wife in the street were also described as drives for which there is "no name in any language—even in the language of the orgy." Once again Marcosini and the narrator find themselves in a situation where language breaks down. The description given of Gambara's music as formless and discordant, unable to be classified in any existing system of categories, is signified here in a manner similar to what we found in the beginning of the narrative—there are simply no words to describe it.

This is the point, or more precisely, the problem and sticking point, that opens Michel Serres's meditation devoted to an experimental composition by the Greek composer Xenakis.[27] Music has rarely spoken for and of itself in the cultural history of its existence but, rather, has regularly been a hostage of other arts and other languages, Serres claims: "Rejected by the other arts because it is a primitive language, slave and prisoner of any and all, it remained [for music] to discover itself, finally to speak about itself, to make its own naked voice heard, its autochthonous ubiquity" (p.181). Annexed by other cultural activities, music has either been an ancillary embellishment or the subject of endless interpretation about what its relationship to other forms of aesthetic activity—painting, theater, opera, and so forth—might in fact be. As such, it has been discussed in countless different ways, and it has always been seen as an aesthetic domain designating or pointing to something other than itself, never quite approached on its own terms. To put it in a different way, music has always been conceived in the form of the concept of *composition,* as an organized ensemble resulting from the creation of signs set off from an original complex foundation that can be understood as encompassing all meaning:

At stake is always a meaning fading into a sign, a sign forced into a signal, a signal emerging from noise. [Music] compresses into a preliminary stage preceding communication the set of all ulterior articulated sounds. By means of the squeezing together of meanings in the direction of the sign and that of the sign in the direction of the signal, a signal which emerges from noise, it escapes the univocity of everyday messages, it is a voice containing several voices. The result is the quasi-indefinite possibility of translating it in every way, of reformulating it, of betraying it, of discussing it with (im)pertinence and with such a degree of freedom." (p.189).

What one has in Serres's conception of the traditional approach to music is an unstructured, undefined background from which a signal, in the form of a note or series of notes, sets itself off. This signal, as it emerges, is always already within the realm of other cultural languages, and they can thus annex it outright for their own purposes. The potentiality contained within the signal—it includes a whole set of undefined articulations—leaves it open to an endless interpretive discourse. It is ripe for appropriation by any language other than one able to treat it on its own terms. As the narrator of *Gambara* puts it, "one would need new words" in order to give it a voice of its own. How then can music be freed from such bondage? We would have to conceive of a music without a listener in the traditional sense, a music before all signals, one somehow able to reproduce the background, the noise, before the emergence of any sign. Serres continues:

What is emitted when no demon is there to intercept it, what can be heard in a world without man? Raw turbulence, the fluctuation of particles, the shock of individuals distributed by chance in time, the fluctuation of the cloud. . . . To erase the signal (and thus the sign and everything following from it), to compose the aleatory paths of disjoined individuals, to model the global cloud of sound, to allow the orchestral ensemble to fluctuate, means, physically, to simulate the background noise . . . to deliver the negative and the condition of all communication, to plunge the listener into the conditions of all hearing, to make him hear the unheard of all listening, the music of music, a language which speaks of itself, which populates all silence. (pp.190–91)

The characteristic of this music is its aleatory fluctuation, its lack of organization in the normal sense, its direct link to the background noise from which composition originates. It is literally cacophonous because it contains within itself the conditions of possibility of all other forms of music, an absolute potentiality figured by the indefinably chance encounters of the primordial elements constituting it.

For someone like Andrea Marcosini, a sophisticated listener steeped in the traditions of Italian and German music, the conditioning ingredients of his own cultural formation, whatever exceeds those traditions can only be heard as bizarre at the very least, if not as pure noise, a "hubbub of notes" (10:493). Furthermore, the baffled silence with which he greets the performance is the sole possible reaction of one who can approach music only by interpreting it along broader cultural lines. This is all the more so in the case of Gambara's music if one envisages it not just as another style but as a veritable attempt to get at the underlying conditions of possibility of all music. Gambara has not fallen short of the level of skilled execution required to produce acceptably his own creation. This is not what is at stake. On the contrary, what he has accomplished is of enormous complexity and demands a skill acquired only through long practice and reflection: "the execution of this demented music required a marvelous skill in order to master such a touch. Gambara had to have worked at it for several years. His hands were not occupied alone, moreover; the complication of the pedal work imposed on him the perpetual agitation of his entire body" (10:494).[28] The crucial point is, rather, that all cultural categories of listening have been abandoned. Needless to say, the listeners (Andrea, Marianna, and Giardini) are completely mystified as Giardini provides an exemplary summary of the entire experience from their point of view: "Assuredly, chance itself would not have avoided the harmonization of two notes with as much skill as this devil of a man has done for the last hour" (10:494).

Giardini, I would maintain, says a little more than he realizes in this remark. For him, as well as for Marcosini, chance cannot be envisioned as anything but the absolute contrary of what music as composition must be. But the element of chance is precisely what Gambara has reached after years of meditation and research. Those years are marked by an extended period of wandering, an *errance,* as the text itself describes the interval: "From the time I was ten years old, I thus began the wandering life [*vie errante*] to which almost all men who contemplate artistic, scientific, or political innovations have been condemned" (10:477). One must give full force to the adjective *errante* in this context. It is at once the act of putting one's life in the hands of chance encounters in a topological meandering that leads toward no goal and also the acceptance of the possibility of error. This is a spiritual itinerary not corresponding to the traditional sense of the term, because no aim is envisaged which could give the voyage any fixed point of reference. Gambara's stochastic approach to life has thus given rise to the notion of a stochastic music, just as the *flâneur* of *Ferragus* lived for aleatory experiences. Marcosini has nothing better to do, of course, than to embark on an attempt to change Gambara's ways. Ironically, Gambara seems to be more lucid on the subject of music theory when he is tipsy than when he is completely coolheaded and sober.[29] Andrea exploits this fact by plying him with wine and finally persuading him to attend the opening of Meyerbeer's *Robert-le-Diable*. Following the performance, the two protagonists engage in a protracted discussion of the work. The subject of this conversation is perhaps less important than the very fact that Andrea has drawn Gambara into a debate about the technical merits of the piece. He has, in other words, brought Gambara into the context of the endless discursive analysis of music, which can only serve to turn one away from music itself.

It is not long before Gambara comes to his senses, however. When he does, his praise of *Robert-le-Diable* quickly turns to criticism. The main reproach directed against Meyerbeer's opera should have been expected by a perspicacious reader of *Gambara*. He accuses Meyerbeer of writing music of and by everyone: "If the opera pleases everyone so much, this is because the music is taken from everyone and thus is bound to be popular" (10:513). We must be careful here not to read this remark at the first level, simply as a criticism of low culture and cultural plagiarism by some kind of proponent of a higher culture. Instead, we can now read it more significantly as a refusal to entrust music to aesthetic and cultural interpretation at all, to activities naturally turning it away from its essence. Meyerbeer has failed precisely because he used and mimicked a cultural context with his music rather than setting out in search of the quintessence of musical creation. His music elicits a discussion which can only be a distraction, causing one to miss what is most important to grasp.

The destiny the story ultimately holds for the material signs of Gambara's musical efforts serves to put the notions developed here into clear symbolic relief. Failing to modify Gambara's behavior, Marcosini, in accordance with an agreement made with Marianna, runs off with Gambara's wife and leaves the musician-composer to his fate. Without the material support of Marianna, Gambara quickly falls into debt and must sell all his possessions. The musical scores he has created, in particular, meet with an emblematic fate. They are sold as wrapping materials to the food vendors of Paris: "The day following the sale the musical scores had served as wrapping at the butter, fish, and fruit markets. Thus, the three great operas about which the poor man talked . . . had been disseminated around Paris, devoured by the stands of the street hawkers" (10:513–14). The product of a search that has led Gambara toward the origin of music in the stochastic background noise preceding all signs, in the fluctuations of molecular elements, Gambara's scores are in turn themselves undone into their separate elements in an aleatory process of circulation.

The interpretation of the meaning and place of music in *Gambara* attempted here took as its point of departure Marcosini's encounter with a certain unexpected disorder in the first scene of the novella, a disorder directly linked to a chance encounter with an unknown woman. *Gambara,* like *Ferragus,* closes with another manifestation of disorder, the scattering of Gambara's musical scores. The novella does not quite end there, however, as if it required a postscript in a manner similar to what the reader finds in *Ferragus*. The narrator proceeds to describe the return of Marianna after her break with Andrea and, more important, the dire straits into which the couple falls. The story ultimately ends with Marianna and Gambara forced to stroll in the dark streets of Paris playing the guitar and singing in a desperate attempt to scratch out a meager and hazardous existence. The same obscurity and uncertainty which was an integral part of Marcosini's first experience returns again to haunt the end of the story. In this context, moreover, a chance encounter occurs, one with which the story closes: a noble Italian couple take pity on Gambara and pledge to be his protectors. Only in the uncertain region represented by the deserted obscurity of evening streets could such an unpredictable event occur. The reader is thus once again presented with a structural framing mechanism analogous to the one used so effectively in *Ferragus*: incipit and closure marked by disorder and chance. The element added in *Gambara* is a veritable theory of artistic creation, at least in the domain of music, in the form of an attempt to reproduce the background of stochastic fluctuation, the condition preceding the formulation of any finished work of art. What Marcosini perceives as noise is, in fact, that without which no musical score would be possible.[30] The real debate in *Gambara* is not between the wildly abstract musings of a theoretician and the limited appreciative capacities of his potential audience, but between a proponent of chance and one of laws, rules, and order. No one who is not attuned to the aleatory foundations of the world could ever listen for the sounds Gambara hears.

[Chance is the greatest novelist in the world.]

Le hasard est le plus grand romancier du monde. —Balzac

CHAPTER FOUR

Balzac's Gamblers

As we saw in the preceding chapter, while Cournot's theory of chance looms large in the structure of certain encounters portrayed in the Balzacian text, there is a more essential level in the treatment of chance in both *Ferragus* and *Gambara* that radicalizes the question and abandons the safe haven of ultimate order left over within Cournot's analysis. Cournot, it will be recalled, remains within the bounds of the kind of causal structure that characterizes Laplace's world view, even though he suggests possible situations that try the limits of the Laplacean system. As is obvious in the example I cited earlier at the beginning of my discussion of *Ferragus* (Raphaël's desperate act in the gambling house in the opening pages of *La Peau de chagrin*), there is a further context to be explored in any argument addressing the question of chance in Balzac's text. Along with many of his contemporaries, Balzac evinces a persistent fascination for gambling and games of chance. It would be difficult not to take notice of the highly charged symbolic atmosphere constructed in the initial episode of *La Peau de chagrin,* not to attempt, in other words, an interpretation that explored the suggestive lines of force set forth within it.[1] Balzac critics, however, have not fully understood and commented on the experience of the aleatory undergone by Raphaël as he stands before the gaming table. I should like to organize my discussion of gambling and games of chance in Balzac, therefore, around an extended reflection on this first scene of *La Peau de chagrin*.

The obvious interest in games of chance in the context of the general problem of chance in the French tradition has a double justification. In the first place, early attempts to deal mathematically with the uncertainty manifest in situations where chance plays a large role took questions concerning gambling as their point of departure. The part of the correspondence between Blaise Pascal and Pierre de Fermat devoted to what became known as "the problem of points" is often cited as the beginning moment of modern approaches to the uncertainty characterized particularly by the presence of chance factors.[2] Only at the end of the eighteenth century and the beginning of the nineteenth did probability theory start to break its connection with the gambling and risk taking associated with games of chance and hence start to take on a more "disinterested," scientific guise.[3]

In the second place, and perhaps even more fascinating, a suggestive etymological theory concerning the origin of the term *hasard* in French demonstrates how closely the notion of chance is linked to games in French. The etymological argument to which I am referring has been put forth in Clément Rosset's *Logique du pire* (pp.73–78). According to Rosset, there are actually four related ideas covering the semantic field devoted to chance in French: (1) *sort,* or fortune, (2) the idea of the *rencontre* (encounter) contained in the Latin *casus* and maintained in European languages by such terms as "chance," *caso,* and *casualidad,* (3) the philosophical notion of contingency, and, finally, (4) the uniquely French term *hasard.* The existence of the fourth category, *hasard,* then, is a twist characteristic only of French (among the group of European languages derived from Latin, that is). It refers to an idea entirely unlike the other three. Fortune, encounter, and contingency are all concepts depending on a preexisting order for their definition.

They require a background of various ordered elements from which they can set themselves off in relief—they somehow differ from the order they presuppose. This method of analyzing chance clearly assumes that the supposedly chance phenomena are, in fact, *derived phenomena,* secondary with respect to the order their various definitions are led to postulate. Order, not chance, is primordial in the case of the first three notions that share the semantic field describing the experience of chance in French.

Hasard, on the other hand, does not depend on order for its definition. It suggests, on the contrary, that chance is primordial, that it precedes order. The term *hasard,* Rosset maintains, "designates . . . the name of a castle in Syria in the twelfth century" (p.75). This would make the etymology of the very term itself doubly fortuitous, first, because the source of the word is the arbitrary name of a geographical place (all such names contain a large dose of chance and circumstance) and, second, because within the French linguistic experience the newly discovered term replaces—by pure chance (the discovery of and contact with the castle in question)—the series of words derived from *casus.* An excerpt from William of Tyre's chronicle of the Crusades, *Historia rerum in partibus transmarinis gestarum,* written in Syria in the twelfth century, reinforces the argument: "Rodoans, the lord of Alep, disputed and fought with his baron, who was the lord of a castle called Hasart" (p.76).[4] The thirteenth-century translator of William's text immediately adds that in the said castle the crusaders had their first exposure to a dice game bearing the same name. Rosset concludes: "Before designating a certain dice game (another contested etymology would attempt to derive *hasard* from the Arab word *al sar,* meaning "the die"), *hasard* thus designates the name of a castle, then the name of a certain dice game played first in that castle, later to become familiar to all the crusaders, and finally imported into Europe by them" (p.76).

What was so different about this game? Why did it make such an indelible impression on the crusaders who encountered it? Rosset conjectures: "Perhaps the men who discovered at 'Hasard' the game which for some time bore that name were impressed precisely because such a game signified—for the first time?—an absolute exclusion of every idea but that of the *hasard* of the game itself, thus implying the impossibility of any recourse to something outside, be it chance, destiny, providence, or fatality" (p.77). The experience of absolute perdition brings one to the ultimate and radical level of the meaning of the term *hasard,* namely, the absence of any referent. Deprived of the possibility of relating the experience to anything, even of representing it outside the immediate immersion in it, the subject who lives the moment of *hasard* is unable to use language to describe it—unable to reduce it to any preexisting logical categories, to speak of it by reference to any other experience within the world. Crucial to this moment of truth is the idea that the experience of *hasard* itself precedes any ordered structure. Necessarily shunted aside in such an experience is the notion of nature, to which thought could refer in order to screen itself from the confrontation with *hasard,* in order to reduce the experience to a mere exception within an otherwise ordered "nature" governed by what we have called regularly since the eighteenth century the "laws of nature."

This analysis is manifestly driving at an Ur-experience of chance that, if is it to be comprehended, requires a definition of thought and reality more complex than one centered on straightforward causal logic and categorization. The experience at stake here is envisaged as an existential one characterized by morosity, dread, and helplessness—but also by fascination, a certain mesmerizing force drawing one inevitably toward what escapes one's control. At last the subject actually encounters the real in a manifestation unburdened by ordinary attempts to insert it into a pattern and thus to hide its fundamentally aleatory character.

The preceding discussion is remarkably applicable to the scene set by the narrator in the first pages of *La Peau de chagrin*. One is almost forced to begin a reading of the passage, for example, by mentioning the obstinate silence of the young man who is the subject of the narrator's attention. That silence is extremely polysemic and hence interpretable in a number of different ways.[5] I would like to insist here, however, on its importance in the context of an approach to the experience of *hasard*. The inability to speak is the most crucial characteristic of an encounter with chance. To speak would be to undertake a reduction of the experience to some representable form. Thus, from the moment the young man enters the scene until the moment he departs the gambling house, he will not utter a word.

The encounter with *hasard* in the episode is developed in great detail, well beyond the overriding silence which marks it. The young man in question is obviously in some sort of trance as he passes through the door of the gambling house, unable to grasp what is happening to him. The first descriptive note concerning him in the text refers to his "conspicuous surprise" as the doorman requests his hat (10:58). As he steps up to the gaming table, the narrator describes him more precisely: "The gloomy impenetrability of suicide lent his forehead a dull, sickly pallor; a bitter smile outlined almost imperceptible folds in the corners of his mouth, and his physiognomy expressed a resignation painful to behold" (10:61). Manifestly emptied of all feeling and of all desire to retain command over his own destiny, stripped of everything he has wanted to do in his life (as the reader discovers progressively), the young man, Raphaël de Valentin, is prepared to confront the real in the form of an *event*. He will come face to face with the limits of order and human mastery in the world, since he has attained the requisite state of resignation and no longer seeks to avoid the confrontation. The quintessential experience of chance awaits him at the table. A curious error in Balzac's text betrays even more clearly the experience of *hasard* at stake in the episode under consideration. If one attempts to understand exactly what game is being described as the scene reaches its climax, one discovers that in the final, corrected version of the novel, two different games have been confused. The first reference is to trente et quarante, a card game related both to blackjack and to baccarat (10:59). When the actual round is played following the bets, however, the dealer announces, "Rouge, pair, passe." This would actually be "Rouge perd," if the original card game were still being played. The Pléiade editor of *La Peau de chagrin,* Pierre Citron, astutely identifies the confusion in the passage and indicates that *rouge, pair, passe* is a phrase more likely to be heard at the roulette table. He draws only the obvious conclusion, however: "The error comes from a hasty correction in the Furne edition" (10:1238). This explanation, almost certainly correct at the factual level, has the unfortunate effect of obscuring a more significant meaning which the error strongly foregrounds. In a scene intent on describing the experience of helplessness and impotence characteristic of the encounter with *hasard,* the slippage from the card game to roulette is not without importance. Indeed, it represents an increase in the factor of chance within the game. Whereas a certain skill can conceivably change the odds and therefore invites calculation and strategy in the card game first suggested in the passage, the same is not true of roulette. Nothing can affect the aleatory trajectory of the ball, and the player can only watch, enthralled, completely given over to what is beyond his dominion.

The young man's demeanor as he arrives at the table only serves to confirm what has been set forth above. Although he walks purposefully up to the table, his wager could hardly be described as careful and deliberate, quite the contrary. His resolution serves rather to prepare him to face the effects of *hasard* head on, without any mediating circumstance, to abandon any attempt to determine what the outcome might be: "[He] walked straight to the table, stood there, and without calculation, threw a gold coin he had in his hand onto the table. It rolled onto the black" (10:62). Clearly essential in this description are two elements. First, the description of the young man's act as one accomplished without forethought is quite consistent with what is shown at other points in the episode: in this supreme moment, normal reflection and logic have been abandoned by the young man in favor of a more essential experience. Second, the manner of placing the bet is obviously a rehearsal for the very spin of the wheel itself. Like the roulette ball soon destined to fall unpredictably on the red or the black, the gold coin is dropped on the table and rolls lazily across its surface, abandoned to unforeseeable circumstances created by gravity and friction which will bring it to rest fortuitously on a black square. An attempt is immediately made by the narrator to differentiate between the young man and the fanatic gamblers who have been described as fixtures in the gaming house, a distinction ultimately based on the idea of calculation, its presence and its absence. The Italian who is observing the scene makes an apparently at least partially reasoned choice to bet against the young man: "The Italian seized with the fanaticism of a passion on an idea that occurred to him and bet his pile of gold against the unknown figure" (10:62). Unlike the young man, the Italian has an idea, and it is immediately transformed into a "system," as it might be called in gambling circles. The so-called system, however, is from the outset infected by the unstable passion of the young man. It is seized on with a fanatic singlemindedness as soon as it inexplicably "occurs" (how? by chance?) to the Italian. He later explains: " 'I heard . . . a voice whispering in my ear: the game will get the better of this young man's despair' " (10:63–64). The Italian's decision to bet against Raphaël is nothing more than a mirror reflection of the choice made by the young man; it participates fully in the desperate gesture from which it boldly attempts to distinguish itself. It cannot sustain any semblance of calculation at a first level of analysis and appears to be little more than a hunch. The narrator goes further, however. The dealer (now become banker of a roulette wheel because the game has changed) launches into an explanation of how the young man could have played more rationally: " 'This was not a gambler,' responded the banker, 'otherwise he would have divided his money into three piles to give himself better odds' " (10:64). The banker can only envisage the gambler as one who endlessly plays the odds. But this is a derivative view of the game, it neglects the game's origins in the experience of total perdition. The object of the young man—to confront the aleatory in all its fascination, to get to the bottom of the experience offered by the game—makes of him, on the contrary, the only true gambler in the room.[6] Those who, like the banker, think that there is a means of restricting the complexity and peril contained within games of chance are, in fact, off the mark in their assumptions. The young man is the only one to have opened himself up to the full effects of *hasard*.

Although, based on the first scene of the novel, Raphaël might appear to be a naive initiate to the sensations provoked by gambling, further reading reveals a somewhat different pattern.[7] A closely related episode of strikingly similar form is described in the second part of Balzac's story after Raphaël begins to recount certain episodes of his youth to Emile. It turns out that a moment of experimentation at the gaming table was a key incident in Raphaël's early career. The passage I have in mind here is the outing at the duke of Navarreins's ball, recounted in detail and with some bitterness by Raphaël, since it illustrates many of the elements of his paradoxical relationship with his father. Raphaël, under the close tutelage of M. de Valentin, has always been prevented from exercising his own will and has been kept more or less in familial bondage. The ball held by the duke of Navarreins represents the first time Raphaël's father has allowed him to experience the social world at first hand. Naturally, Raphaël has absolutely no hint of the social grace required to manage a very new and different set of circumstances. The lack of such expertise is indicated in the episode by, once again, Raphaël's complete silence, his inability to utter the simplest compliment or remark to join in the conversations he witnesses: "I withdrew to a corner so that I could easily eat ice cream and contemplate the beautiful women" (10:122–23). In the midst of the evening's activities, Raphaël's father inexplicably entrusts him with his keys and his wallet. Raphaël's first thought is to use the money at the gaming table in order to win sufficient funds to pay for a night on the town for himself: "I turned toward a gaming table holding the two gold pieces in the humid palm of my hand. . . . Prey to inexpressible anguish, I suddenly glanced around me with a translucent look. Certain of being discovered by no one who knew me, I bet on a short, stout, lively man" (10:123). The feeling of anguish is the result not only of Raphaël's secret defiance of his father. More important for the present argument, he has exposed himself to the unpredictable caprice of *hasard*. The exhilaration coupled with fear and dread is precisely the same sensation he encountered in the gaming house at the beginning of the novel, however different may be the motivations leading up to the two incidents. Raphaël's choice to bet on the appealing little man, moreover, exposes once again the impossibility of any other more rational choice in the game. The crucial nature of the moment at Navarreins's ball matches the atmosphere of the scene in the gaming house in the novel's incipit. The experience at the table at the beginning of the novel puts Raphaël face to face with his own dissolution and death, while the one at the duke's ball signals the destruction of Raphaël's youthful innocence and his ascent to manhood (albeit stunted once again by his father's heavy hand).[8]

A feeling of fascination in combination with powerlessness is thus characteristic of the two scenes directly recounting Raphaël's experiences at the gaming table. Those sentiments seem to generalize traits of Raphaël's character. Critical moments in his existence often find him helplessly watching his own fate being decided for him in much the same way he entrusts his destiny to chance when he gambles. The most emblematic of those moments is the one lived by Raphaël as he observes the conversation which takes place in Foedora's boudoir. Rebuffed by Foedora as he attempts to court her, he decides to spend the night observing her in her own bedroom thereby to obtain the ultimate truth concerning her character. Withdrawn and hidden behind a curtain, he witnesses a conversation among Foedora's favorites before Foedora goes to bed. Raphaël's friend Rastignac is the center of attention and profits from the occasion to expound on his philosophy of ministerial eloquence (10:180–81). Inevitably, the conversation turns toward Raphaël at a critical moment, and Raphaël is forced to observe his own social execution. Armed with a ridiculously ineffective weapon ("Lacking a dagger, while dressing I put a small English penknife in the pocket of my vest" [10:179]), he can only watch in horror as he is attacked and disposed of by the sharp tongues (Rastignac: "my sword is the equal of my tongue" [10:181]) of the most witty of Foedora's Parisian admirers. At once fascinated and without effective means of intervention, Raphaël is forced to let happen what may, exactly as he behaves each time he approaches the gaming table, completely given over to forces beyond his control.

The strategic position of these scenes in the narrative, especially the ones at the gaming table, makes of them veritable scenes of initiation. At the duke of Navarreins's ball, Raphaël tries his hand at a game of chance for the very first time. At the other end of the spectrum, the incipit of the novel places him before the ultimate decision of life or death and opens the way toward his projected suicide. The initiatory content at stake here is confirmed by a comparable episode recounted in *Le Père Goriot*, during which Eugène de Rastignac experiences his first taste of the aleatory in circumstances closely related to those we have observed in Raphaël's case. I am referring to the moment in the novel when the hidden misery of Delphine de Nucingen is revealed to Eugène for the first time. Delphine extends an invitation to Rastignac to dine with her and Nucingen at her house and then to accompany her to the opera. Upon his arrival, Rastignac finds her alone and distracted. When he attempts to discover the source of her distress, she responds by whisking him off in Nucingen's carriage and requesting that he enter into a gambling house to risk one hundred francs at the roulette table: "Go into a gambling house, I don't know where they are, but I know there are some at the Palais-Royal. Wager the one hundred francs at the game called roulette, and lose it all or bring me back six thousand francs. I'll tell you all about my problems when you return" (3:170–71). Just prior to this request, Delphine ascertains that Rastignac has never gambled in the past and is reassured by this fact—he will thereby be a candidate for beginner's luck.

Thus commences a scene reproducing almost step for step the one that occurs in the opening of *La Peau de chagrin*. The gaming house is designated by its street number, as was the case in *La Peau de chagrin*; Rastignac checks his hat, an element commented on extensively by the narrator of *La Peau de chagrin*; and he strides up to the roulette table. Need we insist on the importance of the choice of this and only this game? The textual slippage toward roulette in *La Peau de chagrin,* I maintained earlier, indicates the same unmitigated encounter with chance that is now detailed in *Le Père Goriot.* Uneducated in the rules of betting at roulette, Eugène asks for an explanation: "To the surprise of the regulars, one of the employees led him up to a long table. Eugène, followed by all the spectators, asked shamelessly where he was supposed to place his bet" (3:171). The appearance of a noninitiate within the confines of the house immediately crystallizes the attention of all who are present, just as was true in *La Peau de chagrin,* where, however, the exact nature of the new arrival was not quite so clear. Raphaël de Valentin's appearance was ambiguous, a sign of either naïveté or profound corruption, but whatever hypothesis the onlookers chose, his desperation nevertheless made of him a fascinating figure. In the present case, Rastignac's naïveté functions like a talisman of sorts. We might ask at this point exactly why the rank beginner so intrigues gamblers. Why are they always persuaded that his intervention will be felicitous or, at the very least, interesting? In the context of the present discussion, it is tempting to reply that the beginner represents the unobstructed encounter with the aleatory. Incapable of calculating yet because he knows nothing of the mechanics of the game, only he can experience its aboriginal significance, the unmediated confrontation with the workings of chance. Once the rules of the game have been elucidated, things will never be quite the same. What is explained to Rastignac is the bare minimum of the formalities for betting, insufficient information for him to appreciate the finer points of strategy (if indeed there is such a thing in roulette), and he immediately bets his whole sum without forethought: "Eugène threw the hundred francs on the number representing his age, twenty-one" (3:171). Just as Raphaël's gold coin rolls lazily across the table to land fortuitously on the black, Rastignac's stake falls on a number he pulls out of thin air in a completely arbitrary manner (arbitrary since it has no bearing on the mechanics of roulette), his own age. Unlike Raphaël, however, he wins. By now his actions interest those around him immensely, and, as was the case with Raphaël de Valentin, the connoisseurs are there to give immediate advice: " 'Take your money back,' said the old man, 'one never wins twice with that system' " (3:171). Having won only 3,600 francs, Eugène cannot stop now and bets the whole sum on the red, still completely mystified by what is happening. He wins a second time.

It would be instructive once again to reflect on the remarks made by the inveterate gamblers during the episode in question. We have already seen that Eugène's mentor counsels him not to wager on the same number another time. Moreover, he immediately interprets Rastignac's act not as a whim but as the consequence of a *system*: "One never wins twice with that system." The mentor cannot conceive of placing a bet in a manner as aleatory as the trajectory of the marble on the roulette wheel itself. There is more, however. Once Rastignac wins with the red, the old gentleman who has seemingly adopted Eugène now advises him to quit altogether—and for a very specific reason: "If you want my advice, you will leave, it has stopped on red eight times now" (3:171). This is an oddly comic remark for one who knows anything about the relationship between probability studies and games of chance, because the theory shows that the outcome of any given spin of the roulette wheel is unrelated to the preceding spin. The fact that red has come up eight times does not change in the least the probability of its coming up yet again on the following spin. The rules of probability only hold, in any case, on very large samplings. Eight or nine spins could hardly be called a large sampling. It is important to grasp that the old gentleman displays an ignorance of the experience of chance characteristically exhibited by one whose real interest is in turning away from *hasard,* if not in denying its very existence.

Eugène does indeed withdraw, "still understanding nothing about the game, but stupefied by his luck" (3:171). Not to have understood the slightest thing about the game (strategically speaking) is, on the contrary, to have experienced it and understood its ultimate link to chance. Mesmerized by the whole episode, Rastignac has been nearly as mute as Raphaël. Eugène's near silence in the gaming house mirrors his relationship with Delphine de Nucingen, the very thing which provoked the gambling scene in the first place. Everything was silence and mystery between the two of them before the scene began. Having experienced a confrontation with the aleatory, Rastignac now will have a claim on Delphine, certain rights that she will no longer be able to deny. The episode in the gaming house opens onto another state of social existence for Eugène, in a manner quite similar to the change of state implied by Raphaël's bets at two critical conjunctures in *La Peau de chagrin*.

There are some further lessons to be drawn from the opening scene in *La Peau de chagrin*. In a note at the beginning of the present chapter, I evoked a treatment of the scene to be found in Samuel Weber's *Unwrapping Balzac*. Weber's interpretation holds a great deal of interest in the context of the present argument, because its suggestive approach to the question of economic structures in this episode will allow us to return to a consideration of chance in the act of gambling from yet another angle. As will become clear in the course of an extended reflection on these economic elements, an important and perhaps decisive structure neglected by Weber serves to connect economics and chance in a very unexpected way as the young man wagers his last gold coin. First, some indications concerning the direction in which Weber's argument leads the reader. He begins his discussion of the evocative economy of the gaming house by focusing on the concept of need, both as it is present in the writings of Karl Marx and as it is manifested in Balzac's description of the gamblers at the table. Can one detect a relation between the worker and the gambler with respect to need? At first glance, such a relation is less than obvious because of the restricted manner in which need has been defined in economic theory. Too often it has been narrowly interpreted in a natural or biological fashion. Traditional wisdom would have it that the worker is forced to work in order to ensure his self-preservation. He is not yet in a position of sufficient freedom to have developed desires beyond the purely biological. But this is to neglect the cultural context inevitably present in the expression of any need: "Thus, even in the apparently straightforward case of the worker, . . . the external constraints of self-preservation which compel him to sell his labour power are doubtless less 'external'—in the sense of 'natural' or 'biological'—than has often been supposed. Even at its most rudimentary level, that of 'need,' self-preservation implies a distinct project of subjective self-fulfilment, which in turn is mediated not simply by natural, but also by cultural, social, and historical as well as individual factors."[9] To claim that there are parallels to be drawn between the gambler and the worker in the context of a capitalist economy is not quite as farfetched as it might at first appear. When Balzac describes the situation of the morning gambler as one of "palpitating passion and need in all its frank horror" (10:59), a purposefully vague notion of need seems to bring the gambler closer to the worker. The gambler would simply be a more distilled representation of a project he shares with the worker, namely, a self-reappropriation, a speculative recovery of his essence and identity through an attempt to fulfill needs which are always, at least in part, symbolic.[10]

What ultimately distinguishes the gambler from the worker is an increased level of abstraction in his activities. The gambler is engaged in a structure of circulation and exchange in the absence of concrete objects. He is, to put it differently, a speculator, altogether unconcerned with use value in his pure concentration on exchange value. The novelistic description of the gambling house is a direct reflection of the gambler's concerns. It emphasizes the quasi-empty and bare nature of the room—the undecorated walls, the sparse furniture, the conspicuous absence of objects per se. Only a worn green tablecloth covering the gaming table marks and particularizes the space inhabited as a locus of specialized activity. The sole object that remains highly visible here is a symbolically charged and characteristic one, gold itself. The medium of exchange is the mediating instrument of the gamblers' desires, the emblematic mark signifying that needs are never directly satisfied but instead are always forced to adopt circuitous paths if they are to be ultimately fulfilled.

The representative status of gold results from the sublimation of its origin in the sphere of production, a fetishistic forgetting which alone permits it to play its ambivalent role in the structure of the capitalist economy. Without entering into great detail here, suffice it to say that gold is simultaneously a produced object (a metal mined through human labor) and the measure of all exchange value. In addition to being a produced object, in other words, it is also an abstract unit embodying the labor that constitutes value. "By virtue of this dual function, in the developed commodity world it becomes counter-productive simply to possess money. . . . To keep it is to lose it. . . . This is why neither labour as such nor the effort to retain wealth can directly manifest the law of value: the latter only fulfils itself in a movement of disappearance and reappearance, involving the expense of energy and its transformation into objects, which in turn change into energy. The overall result might be described as a movement of *consumptive production.*"[11] The speculative movement of capitalist circulation with its attendant elements of risk, loss, and slow decline is reproduced in the organization of the gambling house, where the structures of mediation in that economy are to a certain extent abstractly laid out.

One could say, however, that Weber's analysis falters in the domain of the problem of mediation, for mediation implies certain social relations more present and obvious in the gambling scene than Weber has indicated. In particular, I would refer once again to the reaction of the Italian upon seeing Raphaël about to wager his last gold coin. Having sized up the young man, he promptly bets against him, pretexting a system we have already had occasion to discuss. Despite the Italian's act against Raphaël, he is clearly governed by de Valentin's gesture, since his own can be analyzed only as a mirror opposite. What occurs here is comprehensible only if it is seen as a mimetic act, one accomplished as the result of an imitation of the other. The claim here is that this mimetic aspect of what transpires in the gaming room is not an anomaly but rather an essential element in any viable description of speculation. The Italian's attempt to model his own behavior on Raphaël's, moreover, is integrally linked to the problematic of chance.

To demonstrate the link between the mimetic action of the Italian and the notion of chance in the domain of economic decision requires a quick reminder of some additional fundamental aspects structuring the exchange economy rapidly developing even as Balzac himself was writing. In the first place, reflections treating the notion of a market economy too often ignore the fact that the idea of a self-regulating market is a fiction. The market is always a mixture of "pure" market forces, on the one hand, and of an understanding and acceptance of certain rules in some sense external to the market, on the other. André Orléan calls this view the "heterodox" approach to the idea of the market.[12] One of the crucial capitalist acts which illustrates this mixture of the two types of elements is the contract. The contract indeed details the responsibilities of the individuals who enter into an exchange agreement and is, in that sense, a market mechanism. On the other hand, however, it introduces into exchange certain obligations imposed by structures and mechanisms outside the market itself, be they cultural or legal. As Emile Durkheim affirms: "A contract is not sufficient unto itself, but is possible only thanks to a regulation of the contract which is originally social."[13] This regulation, moreover, is necessary because the individuals involved in an exchange cannot predict everything that will occur over the life of the contract, cannot, then, act as purely calculating players in the so-called self-regulating market. One could maintain that the contract is necessary because any agreement to exchange goods in the marketplace contains a large dose of unpredictability, of uncertain elements defying prior calculation by the individuals entering into the contract, in short, of chance. Durkheim's discussion of the contract demonstrates an acute awareness of these difficulties when he states: "We can neither foresee the variety of possible circumstances in which our contract will involve itself, nor fix in advance with the aid of simple mental calculus what will be in each case the rights and duties of each, save in matters in which we have a very definite experience" (p.213).

André Orléan comments on Durkheim's approach to the contract: "If uncertainty puts into question the capacity of the contract to produce a stable social relation, this is because it designates an order of phenomena for which individual calculation is not pertinent. Individual rational calculation finds its limits in uncertainty. . . . Thus uncertainty causes the emergence of the social or the collective as the effective form of the reduction of the unpredictable."[14] The constitutive uncertainty of market conjunctures makes of the private individual an incomplete being who must seek the collective social whole as a means of protection against uncertainty. The term used by Durkheim to mark the uncertainties present when one enters into a contract is "circumstances," those attendant elements depending to a large extent on conjunctures, encounters, and occurrences, which, from the point of view of calculation, are in large part aleatory. The term will return below in the context of remarks I shall make concerning Vautrin in *Le Père Goriot*.

What do we mean by chance occurrences in this context? Are we talking about events differing in any essential way from those treated by the probabilistic and statistical mathematics characteristic of liberal theory? The response would be that the events calculated by such theorems are not really uncertain in a radical sense. Probability theory deals with only two types of situations: the one in which, as Orléan puts it, "one can determine a priori equiprobable elementary events" (p.259), managed by means of combinatory calculus, and the other in which a series of empirical observations of frequencies allows one to establish tables of great exactness, like the mortality tables which gave rise to statistical theory in the eighteenth century. There is, however, a third type of event, the unique and singular event, which does not belong to any previously constituted classificatory series and for which, therefore, one cannot establish a frequency reducible to a table. Quite simply put, there can be no basis of comparison on which one could establish the probability of such an event. Orthodox liberal theory excludes such events from the purview of economic calculation—unjustly, because a large portion of the circumstances with which the speculator must deal are of this nature.[15]

Liberal economic theory clearly has not been capable of dealing theoretically with events that are fortuitous and unpredictable. This state of affairs can be explained by the way in which singular events have been defined by the theory. Of more interest to my discussion of *La Peau de chagrin*, however, is the approach André Orléan takes to the aleatory in his "heterodox" analysis. His attempt to bring chance in the economic domain back into an ordered explanation provides an elegant theoretical description of the behavior of the Italian in the gambling scene of *La Peau de chagrin*. Orléan proposes a convincing thesis to describe the point at which chance and rule converge in the economic domain, namely, *mimetic polarization*. Confronted with aleatory conjunctures that provide no possible means to calculate the outcome of an action, *the only rational behavior is to imitate another person*. The reasoning leading to this choice is eminently logical and reminiscent of what one finds in arguments devoted to game theory perspectives on economic decision making. Orléan writes: "To copy the other in an uncertain environment improves your performance, because either the other shares your ignorance and thus your position remains unchanged, or the other knows something and by imitating him, you will improve your position."[16] This approach to the question of uncertainty in the economic domain differs quite significantly from the traditional orthodox one, which pictures the subject as an ever-separate and autonomous individual capable of calculating in his or her own solitude the outcome of decisions made in the economic sphere of exchange. On the contrary, a mimetic approach claims that each economic subject is incomplete if left to his or her own devices and demonstrates that he or she is fundamentally caught in the field of the other's gaze, driven by a desire for socialization, which represents the only escape from the aleatory encounter with events in an arena where completely accurate prediction is impossible and where chance thus plays such a large role. One could summarize in the following way: chance, the domain of those events or circumstances the farthest from lawlike behavior, paradoxically provokes a socially cohesive reaction when encountered by human beings, namely, the desire to find some kind of solidarity in imitation.[17]

The fundamental characteristic of mimetic behavior in the economic domain is the potential for rapid polarization. In a group of people given over to mimetic behavior, any news or new piece of information can become the potentially dangerous object of a cumulative contagious process. If one person or a small group of people act on the basis of the given piece of information, others may quickly do so, and as more people adopt the position in question, more of those who are originally outside its sway will become affected by it and succumb to it in turn. Once a certain critical mass is reached, the whole group of people affected by the behavior of the originator of the movement will adopt that behavior as the only rational one. Mimetic phenomena clearly are extremely volatile and violent in their effects. They introduce a fundamental instability and unpredictability into situations where they occur, a swift propagation that appears to be a radical overcorrection of the excessive individualism encouraged by the liberal market. In the presence of such rapidly unfolding mimetic processes, one might ask, what is to prevent the periodic, inevitable, and violent mimetic crystallizations which could only be destructive in the marketplace, which could only produce, in other words, repetitive crashes? Orléan's answer is what he dubs the *monetary rule*. Suffice it to say for our present purposes that the existence and the possession of money allows economic agents to allay their suspicions, thereby preventing the excesses otherwise inevitably provoked by aleatory conjunctures. The possession of money allows one to wait out the uncertainties of the moment and to make decisions later, based on increased information or a better notion of the direction in which present trends are unfolding.[18]

The preceding remarks should enable us better to grasp the details of the gambling scene at the beginning of *La Peau de chagrin*. What has just been said concerning the means of preventing mimetic behavior from becoming excessively disruptive, namely, the necessity to remain liquid, suggests that Marx's notion that to keep money is to lose it is in need of some nuances. Indisputably, Marx's observation identifies a major characteristic of capitalist economy which sets it apart from what preceded it. No longer can one expect to succeed economically by constantly hoarding what is earned; gains must be thrown back into circulation to produce further profit. At the same time, however, one cannot afford to have all of one's fortune tied up in long-term investments, for if this is the case, a waiting game cannot be played when unfavorable and dangerous conjunctures occur. In other words, the roulette banker's reaction during the opening scene of *La Peau de chagrin*—the belief that Raphaël should have divided his money into three different piles—is the eminently social response to a confrontation with the aleatory. It is best to wait and see in order to be able to try again later. As we have seen, however, Raphaël's act is designed primarily to set himself off from society, to establish a break, allowing his projected suicide. His encounter with chance must, therefore, be total and unmitigated—he can only risk all in one shot and thus refuse any act that would have as its goal a certain safety or a desire for social cohesiveness.

The mimetic hypothesis, moreover, tends to suggest an even closer parallel between the behavior of the gamblers, especially the Italian who has been the subject of preceding reflections, and the speculator's thought processes in a capitalist economy. The Italian's decision to bet against Raphaël, a decision based on observation of and imitation of de Valentin, is perhaps not quite as impulsive as I first suggested. It mimics, in fact, the only rational decision-making process available to the speculator, given a situation of maximum uncertainty. Unable to predict the outcome of the coming spin of the roulette wheel, the Italian looks for a sign in Raphaël's own behavior indicating a source of possible knowledge. As I said earlier, it makes little difference whether the experienced gambler wagers with Raphaël or against him, for in either case, his behavior is modeled on Raphaël's act.[19] The other gamblers, moreover, are well aware that by not following Raphaël's and thus the Italian's cue, they have made a mistake: " 'If we had imitated the gentleman?' said one of the old men to his colleagues while pointing to the Italian. Everyone looked at the lucky player whose hands were trembling while he counted his bank notes" (10:63). De Valentin's conduct at Navarreins's ball is a further example of the same type of situation. Unschooled in the rules of the game, Raphaël spontaneously adopts the only strategy available in any case (whether, in fact, he understands the game or not): he imitates the bet of another, and the act of imitation is an eminently social one—the only way Raphaël can demonstrate solidarity with those around him at the ball.

The discussion of rules and circumstances lends a particularly fascinating light to the analysis of modern society offered by Vautrin, Balzac's master criminal, in a crucial passage of *Le Père Goriot* to which I would like to direct attention for a moment. Having gauged the profound ambition of Eugène de Rastignac to succeed in the highest circles of Parisian society, Vautrin decides to use Eugène for his (Vautrin's) own ambitious plans. In order to do so, he must persuade Rastignac to follow his advice, and he attempts his seduction by laying bare the hidden and none too pretty workings of modern social organizations, thereby undoing Rastignac's respect for certain guiding principles instilled in him by the archaic social schooling provided by his provincial family. The culminating moment of Vautrin's argument is a justly famous and often-quoted remark: "There are no principles, only events; there are no laws, only circumstances. The superior man shapes himself to the events and circumstances in order to direct them" (3:144). We are in a better position to reflect on this remark following our discussion concerning rules and the liberal market. Vautrin's apparent mastery of the workings of modern society lies in his understanding that despite the ideology of contractual exchange on which capitalist society is constructed, with all its implications of the potential to calculate risks successfully, there is a largely unexplored and unexploited region of circumstance which can always undo the best-laid plans and the firmest contracts. Like the tactician in Stendhal's *La Char-treuse de Parme,* Vautrin knows that to succeed is to be alert to the potential for maneuver provided by unanticipated circumstances, by *occasions,* as I termed them previously. The trick is to be capable of meeting such circumstances and incorporating them into one's tactics. But Vautrin goes perhaps too far here when he suggests that circumstances can be directed (*conduire*), because he appears thus to bring them back into the realm of possible calculation. This be-comes even more evident when one steps back to take an analytic distance from the striking remark quoted above and views the whole of Vautrin's reasoning a bit more carefully.

What precisely is Vautrin planning? To put it succinctly, he wants Rastignac to seduce Victorine Taillefer. Disinherited by her father, Victorine stands to obtain the family fortune only if her brother is somehow removed from the picture. Vautrin plots to have him killed in a duel provoked by a military expert whom he has recruited for this purpose. Thus Eugène will be able to marry her, get his hands on the money, and pay back Vautrin by giving him a percentage of her dowry. The revelation concerning the duel comes at the end of the conversation with Rastignac, who is appalled when the project is clearly outlined and abruptly breaks off contact with Vautrin. It is immediately curious and highly significant, I be-lieve, that the whole dialogue during which Vautrin's project is laid out is framed from beginning to end by the notion of the duel.[20] Vautrin and Rastignac begin their conversation at a moment when Eugène is exceedingly angry at Vautrin and ready to provoke him in a duel (Vautrin has just ridiculed Rastignac at Mme Vauquer's din-ner table and Eugène wants revenge). The goal of the dialogue Vautrin initiates with Eugène is thus first to forestall the moment when the two will be forced by their honor to confront one another in a manner a good deal more risky and violent than a polite talk. In fact, the question of risk is at the very heart of observations Vautrin makes concerning the possible duel, observations with which the conversation actually commences. Vautrin has full confidence in his ability to kill Rastignac easily at thirty-five paces: "Even if I proved to you that at thirty-five paces I can put five straight bullets through an ace of spades, . . . this wouldn't take away your courage" (3:135). Just as Eugène would refuse to back down from the challenge, so Vautrin himself would not hesitate to face him in a duel, ostensibly secure in the knowledge of his mastery of the skills necessary to triumph. And yet he does hesitate—for a very particular reason. Vautrin recounts a similar event in his past: "I can put five straight bullets in an ace of spades—and at thirty-five paces! When one possesses that nice little talent, one can be sure of killing an adversary. Well, I shot at a man at twenty paces, and I missed him" (3:136). Not only did Vautrin miss him, but the uninitiated antagonist put a bullet right through Vautrin's chest and nearly killed him. Circumstances—a gust of wind, a moment of inattention, a reflection—something on which Vautrin had not counted, intervened to undo all the skill that should have permitted him to prevail. How to calculate such events? The implication is that such calculation is well-nigh impossible. To expose oneself needlessly to uncontrollable circumstances is less than intelligent.

And yet Vautrin's whole plan concerning Victorine is constructed squarely on still another duel: " 'I have a friend whom I helped out, a colonel in the Loire army. . . . He would put Jesus Christ back on the cross if I told him to do it. One word from Papa Vautrin and he'll provoke a quarrel with this fine fellow [Taillefer's son] who hasn't even sent a hundred *sous* to his poor sister, and . . .' Here Vautrin stood up, put himself into fencing position, and imitated the movement of a master swordsman who attacks. 'And into the grave!' he added" (3:145). Vautrin has forgotten the essential point he himself made at the beginning of the conversation while telling the story of his brush with death, namely, no one fully masters the very circumstances to which he alluded as he summed up his notions of the workings of society: "there are no laws, only circumstances." Now fascinated by his own calculated project, he does not hesitate to picture himself removed from the warp and woof of the aleatory, to portray himself, as he puts it, under the guise of providence: "I myself will take the role of Providence, I'll make it the will of God" (3:144). The incident recounted at the very beginning of the conversation (Vautrin's own near-fatal duel) implies that Vautrin's scheme is tenuous at best. What can assure him that some type of chance circumstance will not again occur to undo the skill of even the most expert swordsman? Indeed, just such a circumstance does intervene to undo Vautrin's plan—someone stumbles by chance on his identity and sells him out to the police.

It is evident, on reading the dialogue between Rastignac and Vautrin, that there is an appreciable distance between theory and practice in Vautrin's performance. The very one who seemed to realize best of all that chance occasions had to be expected and used proceeds to exclude them when it comes to conceiving a plan allowing him to escape and retire. This is all the more clear in the way Vautrin manipulates the metaphorical network he chooses to employ in order to describe his confidence in the success of his projects—the metaphor of games of chance: "To court a young person whom you meet in conditions of solitude, despair, and poverty when she has no inkling of the fortune that is to come! Well, it's like having a straight flush and four of a kind in your hand,[21] like knowing the winning numbers in the lottery, like playing the stock market while being privy to the news before anyone else" (3:142). The confrontation with the aleatory is conjured up only to be dismissed immediately in favor of an artificial certainty designed to elude the *hasard* which is the founding element of games of chance. Vautrin imagines playing solely with the triumphant hand. The fact remains that situations of uncertainty correspond much more realistically to experiences in the world. Vautrin himself is destined to rediscover this as he is ultimately undone by a totally unexpected denunciation toward the end of *Le Père Goriot*.

The position of Vautrin with respect to the question of chance is ambiguous, then, despite his apparent embrace of a philosophy of society which concedes a large place to aleatory phenomena. One should take advantage of the occasion with an act of mastery, maintains Vautrin ("To get rich, one has to accomplish great deeds"

[3:140]). The point of such acts, however, is then to remove one-self from exposure to the unexpected dangers brought by circumstances.[22] The ambiguity is evident again in the projected outcome of the plan Vautrin yearns to have Rastignac share with him. He wants the money Eugène would give him from Victorine's dowry in order to invest in a plantation in America to escape the uncertainties of the unruly society in which he is now forced to live: "My idea is to go live the patriarchal life on a large property, a hundred thousand acres, for example, in the United States, in the South. . . . I'll be fifty years old, not yet senile, I'll have fun in my own way" (3:141–42). The oscillation one detects in the complex motivations of Balzac's master criminal makes his later conversion at the end of *Splendeurs et misères des courtisanes,* at which point he joins the very police force that has been pursuing him all along, comprehensible and striking. We saw in the context of *Ferragus* that the reputation of the police lay in their capacity to calculate cause and effect: "What one can reasonably expect of them is to look for the causes of an event," one of Auguste de Maulincourt's confidants had said (4:25). A part of Vautrin yearns for the false sense of clarity and mastery such an approach provides, for a kind of straightforward social existence perfectly regulated by the structure of Laplacean causality, for the end of his own uncertain position as the outsider within society.

I should like to return now to the opening of *La Peau de chagrin,* the significance of which has been anything but exhausted in the remarks made up to this point. The encounter with chance described in the gaming room scene is only the first in a series of experiences with the aleatory that Raphaël de Valentin is destined to undergo in the beginning pages of the novel. The narratological structure of the scene in the gambling house is curiously (and certainly not intentionally) annunciatory of the series. Three times the young man's entrance into the room is described, just as he will experience the aleatory in three different manners in the initial portion of the novel: (1) "He walked resolutely into the room" (10:58); (2) "At the moment when the young man entered the room, several players were already there" (10:60); (3) "The *dealer* and the *banker* had just given the bettors that pale look which kills and were saying in thin, high-pitched voices: 'Place your bets!' when the young man opened the door" (10:61). The triple entrance mimics the triple encounter with chance Raphaël is about to undergo: the moment of perdition in the gambling house will be followed by a random walk, in recognizable ways a reflection on the fortuitous, and both experiences will in turn be followed by the jumbled disorder of the antique dealer's store, where Raphaël signs the pact that sets the story in motion. I shall turn first to the exit from the gaming room and the walk that takes place subsequently.

Raphaël ventures out of the setting where he has just lost his last dime in what can only be called a daze. Removed from mundane concerns in his focus on what will now be his suicide attempt, he has severed all connection between himself and the exterior world he encounters in the streets. He simply does not know where he is going: "He soon found himself [*se trouva*] under the galeries of the Palais-Royal, went on to Saint-Honoré Street, turned in the direction of the Tuileries, and crossed the garden indecisively [*d'un pas indécis*]" (10:64). The suggestive literal force of the expression *se trouver* is ironic in this instance; lost in confused thought, Raphaël abruptly wakes up to find himself somewhere without knowing how he arrived there.[23] But he does not really find himself, because the jolt of awakening brings no enlightenment, and he remains lost in what should be for him a familiar setting. The subsequent progress of his walk is hesitant, irresolute, dependent on the traffic. Instead of being the anticipated Paris topologically laid out on a customary map with which Raphaël is deeply acquainted (Parisian that he is), the landscape has become unfamiliar, lacking the orientation points required to plot a course: "He walked as if he were in the middle of a desert, jostled about by men he didn't see, hearing in the midst of street noises only a single voice, death's voice, lost in a torpid meditation" (10:64). The Cartesian strategy for the disoriented traveler, namely, to decide to walk straight in one direction in order to create a path that goes somewhere, is no more applicable here in the desert than it is on the undulating and polymorphous surface of water. The desert, the sea, the forest: all symbols for the impossibility of choosing a direction when presented with an infinite number of them. No longer are there any fixed points to guide de Valentin; he is condemned to err in the fullest sense of the word. The well-laid-out city with its grid of streets, each attached to the other in a recognizable and analyzable manner, has become a jumbled collection of points bearing no identifiable relation with one another, a random conglomeration matching the wandering of Raphaël's own psychic processes. "The unknown young man was assailed by a thousand thoughts of the sort, passing in tatters through his soul, like the torn banners flying above the melee of a battle" (10:65). I had occasion previously to call attention to the elements of chance inevitably present on the battlefield.[24] The movements of soldiers, however well planned beforehand, unavoidably confront the unstable region of chance once the troops throw themselves into the fray. The image employed by the narrator to describe Raphaël's mental landscape thus bears a close relation to the description of the strange, alien topology of Paris emerging in the course of his walk.

De Valentin is headed in his own roundabout way toward a catastrophe, that is, a bridge: "He proceeded toward the Pont Royal" (10:65). The river divides the city in two, makes of it two different spatial varieties separated by a fault, an abyss, a chasm that represents the menace of a disastrous split and that must perforce be spanned. The bridge paradoxically connects the disconnected in a place of maximal danger and difficulty, where order threatens to disappear and where, consequently, disorder can and must be confronted.[25] Raphaël faces his own dissolution in one of those very crucial vicinities where the aleatory imperils the regulated structure that defines the capital city and the society it represents. Not only does the heart of the city contain other such pockets that regularly captivate (if not to say, capture) certain Balzacian characters, but its exterior limits are also in troubling proximity to disorder. The nearly bewitching fascination displayed in the text for the method of suicide Raphaël contemplates, namely, throwing himself into the river, is not without historical justification—the period is marked by numerous such suicides. As always, however, the appeal to a historical explanation is insufficient; there is within the factuality of these circumstances a symbolic significance. Where better to express a revolt against an attempt to deny disorder and the fortuitous (a denial accurately characterizing the new generation of bureaucratic statisticians who are formulating a different type of political power) than at the pivotal location of a topological fault, or fold, in this case the river and the bridge, that vicinity where the seamless, joining bent of strategic discourse is most threatened? In fact, Raphaël grapples with the problem of bureaucratic statistics and classifications as he contemplates the deed he wishes to accomplish. The narrator may well see in each suicide, or especially in those of great men, "a sublime poem of melancholy" (10:64), and suicide can thus become another one of Balzac's attempts to expose an underside of contemporary history fraught with singularity and interest. Raphaël, on the contrary, believes that for the vast majority of people, his projected death will become just another paragraph in a newspaper, another anonymous case, another tidbit of local news [*fait divers*].[26] The narrator imagines the style of that *fait divers*: "*Yesterday, at four o'clock, a young woman threw herself into the Seine from the Pont des Arts*" (10:65; Balzac's emphasis).

There are, moreover, public health services that deal with the problem of suicide in the river in an attempt to recuperate it morally and sociologically: "He suddenly shivered as he saw in the distance, on the Tuileries port, the cabin above which rose a sign where these words were traced in foot-high letters: 'AID FOR DROWNING VICTIMS' " (10:65). Ultimately, if Raphaël is successful, his body will become nothing more than an object of study with a specified price on it. We are once again confronted with the problem of singularity and statistics raised in the preceding discussion of liberal economy in the context of the gaming room. Raphaël's projected act could not be more singular, unpredictable, uncertain, and therefore fortuitous—thus a most appropriate place (the bridge, the river) has been chosen—and yet he will not escape "the nets of Saint-Cloud," mentioned by Vautrin in *Le Père Goriot* (3:136), that is, the nets stretched across the river at Saint-Cloud to catch the bodies of drowning victims downstream.[27] The grid composing those nets is a very striking figure for the structure imposed on society by the statistical methods of an impeccably ordered bureaucracy, which sees everything as just a number and loses track of nothing, not even the most insignificant event. The authorities are incapable of dealing with events not couched in terms of statistics, and worse, they simply annex those events into an interpretive methodology which cannot do them justice. Small wonder that in order to recuperate a certain identity and singularity, Raphaël must remain anonymous for such a society: "He resolved to die during the night, the better to turn an undecipherable corpse over to this Society which ignored the grandeur of his life" (10:66). The paradox is patent and stunning: to be singular and to protect whatever identity one has, one must remain anonymous with respect to the controlling forces of the society.

Raphaël's melancholy walk will ultimately lead him to a state of utter moral chaos. The narrative description of his culminating mood bears quoting in its entirety: "Thus nature herself conspired to plunge the dying man into a painful ecstasy. Under the influence of the maleficent power whose dissolving action finds a vehicle in the fluid circulating in our nerves, he felt his organism imperceptibly slide toward the phenomena of fluidity. The torments of this agony imparted on him a movement resembling waves, prompting him to see buildings and men through a fog in which everything undulated" (10:68). I have called attention first to the disorder implied by the new topology within which de Valentin experiences the city after he leaves the gambling house and then to the fascination necessarily exercised by the river and its bridge for someone in his state. They symbolize a certain chaotic disorder in Raphaël's experience, they drive him toward a paroxysm of suffering during his wandering after his losses at the gambling table. The reader is ultimately confronted with the figure of the cloud, that fetish of our own contemporary meditations on aleatory phenomena. At this moment de Valentin sees the antique shop, a chance encounter brought about by his aimless walk through the streets of Paris.

Before plunging into the subject of the antique store I would be remiss not to reflect for a moment on the problem of the encounter during Raphaël's promenade. There are, in fact, a series of encounters while Raphaël meanders about the city streets rendered unfamiliar by his desperation—encounters with both people and things. The two most striking and obvious ones are when he stumbles upon the beggars and when he crosses the path of an elegant woman in an engraving shop. The latter incident is both significant and representative, and it confirms my analysis of the notion of the encounter in chapter 2. Once again we have a potential union of disparate causal sequences: on the one hand, Raphaël, whom I have been following since the beginning of the novel, and on the other, a beautiful woman of mysterious origins about whom we know nothing. This is the ideal novelistic moment, one might say, because it is almost as if a second potential story were waiting in the wings, ready to be exploited as yet another exemplum in the long novelistic tradition of such chance meetings. Balzac himself, as I have remarked on several occasions, was particularly infatuated with this configuration. The encounter, the moment of intersection, however, in this case as in others, is not a moment of actual convergence; rather, it is but a further confirmation of a distance, the mark of an unbridgeable rift precluding any real union between Raphaël and the coldly beautiful woman he beholds. Maurice Blanchot's antithetical analysis of the intersection of causal sequences portrays the crossroads as a point at which, far from realizing the relation between events in the world, we are presented instead with the distance that always remains between them, the gap, the *écart*. The exchange of glances that occurs in the engraving shop demonstrates quite clearly the separation at stake here: "The young man, on the doorstep [of the shop], ostensibly absorbed by the contemplation of the engravings displayed in the stand, vividly exchanged with the unknown woman the most piercing glance a man can muster, only to receive in return one of those uncaring, haphazard glances directed toward passersby. It was, on his part, a good-bye to love, to women, but this last and powerful questioning was not understood, did not move the heart of this frivolous woman, did not make her blush or lower her eyes" (10:67). The moment of the encounter, as we saw earlier, is particularly affected by the presence of death. Indeed, at the very point where things should come together and coalesce, on the contrary, *La Peau de chagrin* is leading us toward Raphaël's impending doom (his suicide), the profoundly unanalyzable fatal event that suggests the hidden and unreachable essence of the aleatory, as I argued earlier. Once again the mystery of death underscores the irreducible chance content of an instant when one might instead have expected an opening onto a new and different kind of life (or narrative), an encounter staging a true convergence of causal series.

The idea of the "other" novel, stumbled upon and quickly forgotten in the unsuccessful meeting between de Valentin and the young woman, is one we shall have to keep in mind as I turn now to the famous scene in the antique shop. The relation between the experience Raphaël undergoes in the shop and his wanderings preceding his entry into it is manifest, especially with respect to the notion of disorder developed above. De Valentin's plunge into the universe of the shop is tantamount to his insertion into a context of chaos far exceeding even what he has endured up to this point in the narrative. A series of quotations from the first page of the description of the antique store will suffice to reproduce the flavor of the passage in question:

The beginning of the world and yesterday's events were joined together in a grotesque simplicity. . . . Instruments of death . . . were thrown pell-mell together with instruments of life. . . . Several portraits of French magistrates, of Dutch burgomasters, as unfeeling now as they were during their lives, rose above this chaos of antiques. . . . It was a kind of philosophical dung heap where nothing was missing. . . . Further, these monstrous tableaux were prey to a thousand accidents of light due to the bizarre nature of a multitude of reflections caused by the confusion of nuances. (10:69–70)

One could continue, but I think the point is clearly made. Lost in the disorder of a chaotic mental fog translated into a Parisian landscape he can no longer recognize, Raphaël enters a shop which reproduces, even magnifies, that very disorder. Not to be overlooked is the replication, once again, of an exterior landscape by an interior one. A single passage will serve to underscore the interior/exterior parallel reestablished here as it was in the two preceding scenes: "He fastened on to all the joys, seized on all the sorrows, took hold of all the formulas for existence by scattering his life and his sentiments generously on all the simulacra of this plastic and empty nature. The noise of his footsteps reverberated in his soul like the distant sound of another world" (10:73).

Despite the jumbled juxtaposition of the innumerable objects within the store, the narrator does not despair of making sense of it all. We are, he maintains, citizens of a new scientific modernity represented by the great biologist and naturalist Georges Cuvier. Cuvier is a master at reconstructing the past given only the slightest evidence with which to work. "Our immortal naturalist has reconstructed whole worlds from whitened bones, rebuilt, like Cadmus, cities with teeth, repeopled a thousand forests with all the mysteries of zoology using only fragments of coal, found populations of giants enclosed within the foot of a mammoth" (10:75). The disorder is only apparent; one can get beneath it and restructure a whole system of classifications which will allow one to recreate the world behind the tangled mass of objects and artifacts. Cuvier is something like the Laplace of the biological realm. Give him a biological relic, and he can predict the previous states of the system. Thus the antique shop is an exemplary context for illustrating the activity of revealing the underside of history mentioned above as Raphaël reflected on the danger of having his suicide transformed into a *fait divers*. In other words, each object, event, and person contains, hidden beyond the surface, on its underside or reverse side, a story waiting to be told, one that exposes the previous states which form a continuous chain subtending the present, one that matches in fascination the wildest novel. This is all well and good, but to force the descriptive passage concerning the antique shop back toward an exercise in classification waiting to be accomplished is at the same time to neglect the lesson of disorder and the aleatory to be found within the portion of the novel that precedes the text treating the antique shop. Such a gesture is tantamount to a refusal to take seriously the lavish elaboration of the semantics of disorder contained in the language used to describe the shop itself. Confusion, chaos, accidents, monstrosity, madness, fog, oceans—figures for primordial disorder in the midst of which chance rears its head, notions prominent in my own analysis now return in profusion in a culminating moment that occurs just before the narration of Raphaël's life begins in earnest in *La Peau de chagrin*.

Instead of being tempted by the demon of order and classification in reading this passage, I should instead prefer to see in the antique-shop scene a kind of chaotic reservoir or source of potentiality. It is as if the narrator were exposing the underside *(envers)* of his own narrative practice, but this *envers* is no ordered sequence of causes and effects. It is, rather, a primordial disorder which forms the backdrop subtending the narrative structure emerging in this particular story. In a manner directly related to what we found in the story of Balzac's musician, Gambara, the narrator conjures up the fluctuating mass of objects and events at the origin of the miraculous, unexpected coalescence that produces this and only this story. Gambara's opera is the antique dealer's inexplicable collection, and Raphaël can make no more sense of the collection than Marcosini did of the bizarre opera. Shimmering in the distant background, at the origin of narrative, at its limits, are hundreds of other potential stories that could have emerged from any one of the objects Raphaël encounters as he browses in a daze. All those objects and stories are present just beneath the surface of the decision he makes to choose the wild ass's skin and nothing else. In my analysis of Balzac's *Ferragus,* I spoke of the fundamentally vagabond nature of beginnings and endings in narrative. Aleatory wandering is evident once again in the present text, as the main character of the novel stumbles through its first pages, finally to become conscious only at the moment when he makes a risky decision to accept the talisman—at which point a more "normal" or familiar narrative structure begins to unfold as he is accosted by friends who invite him to dinner. The narrative style of the text itself reproduces the wandering and disorder of the hero it creates, represents it, one should perhaps say, not only in the delay occasioned by the triple experience Raphaël undergoes, but in the obvious, almost sensual pleasure derived from the meticulous description of the objects in the antique shop, a stylistic tour de force that constantly tempts the narrator to turn permanently astray. At some point the readers must ask themselves whether or not the narrator is going to get on with the story, as was the case in *Ferragus,* where, at the beginning of the story, the narrator lingered with conspicuous delight on his typology of Parisian streets.

The confused array of objects presented in the opening part of the antique-shop passage exemplifies a fundamental definition of primordial chaos, namely, the complete absence of *difference.* No classification has been imposed on the objects (despite the narrator's claim that this could be done), no ranking suggested, no means provided to differentiate in any significant way one article from the other. De Valentin's incremental progress within the shop will be toward increased difference until ultimately one object stands out from all the rest, captivates him, and motivates an act of will. Many Balzac commentators have analyzed the structure of initiation present in the passage by showing how Raphaël advances toward a culminating moment when a secret is revealed to him. I would define Raphaël's progress instead as a process that carries him away from the chaos produced by lack of difference and toward the moment when a single item will be definitively set off and thus differentiated from the rest. The progress at stake takes the form of a slow ascent up the different floors within the antique shop, marked by the increased worth and preciousness of the things encountered, until de Valentin reaches the place in the shop where quite literally priceless articles are stored. What identifies those objects as inestimably valuable is the increased expertise, skill, and artifice required to produce them. So extreme is the proficiency they illustrate that it strangles all desire to attempt to match it: "These were works capable of inspiring distaste for artwork, masterpieces accumulated such as to make one hate the arts and lose all enthusiasm" (10:74).

In the midst of these priceless artifacts, the wild ass's skin appears. It quickly becomes the hyperbolic symbol of the distance between a consummate artistic work and the disorganized, everyday matter to be found in nature, a distance some profound artistic skill has created. The description provided by the narrator is clear: "The black grain of the skin was so carefully polished and so skillfully tanned, the capricious lines so clean and flawless, like the facets of a garnet, the irregularities of this oriental leather formed a number of small foyers vividly reflecting light" (10:82). And later, " 'I must confess,' exclaimed the young man [Raphaël], 'that I can hardly guess what process was used to engrave those letters so deeply into the skin of a wild ass. . . . Levantine ingenuity has secrets all its own' " (10:83). All the narrator's descriptive verve is mustered here to establish the singularity of the ass's skin, the manufactured perfection of which removes it from the dissolution and disorder habitually affecting objects and artifacts. The concept of entropy in thermodynamics predicts that organized systems tend toward dissolution and disorganization precisely because disorganization is the point of stable equilibrium, where energy is evenly distributed throughout the system and no pockets of difference in the form of energy differentials exist. Balzac's insistent description of the finely worked nature of the ass's skin establishes its status as an artifact, as far from the entropic equilibrium point as possible. Later on in *La Peau de chagrin,* when Raphaël realizes that his life is governed by the rhythm of dissolution imposed by the skin, he attempts first to alter its organization (to make it bigger), and then to destroy it. His failure once again emphasizes the hyperbolic nature of the difference produced in the wild ass's skin by an artifice which has given it an almost supernatural systemic compactness.

The material feel and behavior of the wild ass's skin itself are not the only elements that point to its emblematic significance. Traced on its surface is an Arabic inscription (mistakenly indentified as Sanskrit by the antique dealer).[28] If one ignores for the time being the actual meaning of the inscription at a linguistic level, one notices immediately that it is typographically marked in a highly visible fashion—it is presented in the form of an inverted pyramid.[29] This suggestive shape could conceivably lead the reader in a multitude of different interpretative directions. In the first place, the pyramid is in a real sense the prototypical geometric object, since the founding of geometry is inextricably linked to it. Thales is said to have discovered the principle of measurement at a distance, geometry, in the course of a trip to Egypt during which he undertook to measure the height of the pyramids.[30] The pyramid is associated, furthermore, with one of the most highly developed cults of the dead in ancient history, the one found in Egyptian culture. Small wonder that La Peau de chagrin would feature such a highly charged object in its own extended meditation on death. There is something more, however, something essential to my present argument. One cannot forget that the pyramid is inverted, upside down. I described the wild ass's skin above as an emblematic object for a very specific reason, namely, its extraordinary artifice and organization, its *difference,* which is defined by its enormous distance from entropic equilibrium. I maintain that the inverted pyramid created by the inscription is a highly visible replication of the same problematic, because a pyramid perched on its head is a profoundly evocative figure for a systemic state radically removed from an equilibrium point. To be at the farthest extreme from equilibrium is simultaneously to be at a point of greatest instability. The slightest force, the most negligible puff of wind, even an unpredictable molecular collision, would suffice to set the pyramid irreversibly in motion toward its state of maximum stability, the state from which it could move again only by means of the application of a further energy to create a new potential, a new energy differential.

The point of maximum difference, I would stress, is also the apex of instability where, perhaps unexpectedly, one confronts the aleatory in yet another of its guises. The force required to precipitate the fall of the pyramid on one of its sides (and it is impossible to know which one) is extremely small, as small as possible, so small as to be aleatory, impossible to predict. De Valentin's fascination with the wild ass's skin is thus subtly related to the experience of chance, the keystone of the opening portion of *La Peau de chagrin*. Navigating with difficulty through a chaotic collection of artifacts, Raphaël stumbles on an object as differentiated from the preceding chaos as possible. That very difference, however, is the seat of a fundamental instability that promises a catastrophic fall back toward an ultimate equilibrium point, described in the text as a process of slow dissemination leading inexorably toward the final total dissolution of the skin into its molecular components, in short, its utter disappearance as a constituted object. Raphaël's own dissolution can only parallel the skin's, inevitably. But the skin is more than a mere symbol of de Valentin's descent toward dissemination, it is also a figurative representation of the story itself. The story's tight structure, prepared and now ready to unwind like a well-tooled machine as it suddenly appears in all its rich potentiality, is destined, in its descent toward a denouement, to jettison bit by bit parts of its own potentiality until nothing is left for it at the end but to disappear with Raphaël himself.

The inevitability that apparently permeates the narrative once Raphaël has made the pact may seem troubling for an argument that has insisted on the appearance and representation of chance in the opening sequences of the narrative. How is it possible to speak of chance in the context of a narrative that positively revels in the determined unfolding of a tragedy even the best science of the day cannot deflect?[31] But to speak of chance is not to deny all possibility of order, of regularities detectable on the backdrop of chaotic beginnings. Far be it from me to deny the relentless nature of the middle and final thirds of *La Peau de chagrin*. On the other hand, however, the unswerving progress of Raphaël's dissolution cannot lead us away from the lessons of the novel's beginning. The notion we must be capable of grasping and of maintaining is the coexistence of chance and regularities. Improbable events can indeed give rise to regularities, but those regularities in turn will disappear when other chance events intervene. However determined and inevitable Raphaël's destiny appears in *La Peau de chagrin,* it remains nonetheless true that the narrative is once again, in what I hope to have shown to be something of a Balzacian trademark, framed by chance moments. For if indeed the beginning of the novel focuses for significant reasons on the scene in the gambling house and its immediate sequel, the ending of the novel is no less attached to the questions the incipit raises.

Not surprisingly, then, the narrative does not conclude neatly and cleanly—it reenacts yet again the problem of troubled endings we discovered in *Ferragus.* Troubled beginnings breed troubled conclusions. The final scene in Raphaël's drama, in all its theatricality, might appear sufficiently succinct and striking to provide immediate closure, but the narrator is once again unable to let go, to release his hold on the narrative. An epilogue follows Raphaël's death. The untidiness of the epilogue, its supplementary character, is reason enough to point to it as a rather chaotic moment, on the order of the troubled beginning of the story. The epilogue is constructed, moreover, around an image bearing a direct relation to the problematic we have been exploring. An imagined reader sits in an armchair and gazes into the oscillating, wavering, fluctuating flames given off by a fire—a suggestive constellation recalling the topos on disorder with which the narrative began, in particular, the mental fog that characterizes Raphaël's walk in the streets following his loss in the gambling house. A kind of simulacrum of the Pauline character appears indistinctly in the flames and coalesces instantaneously, only to fade back just as quickly into molecular oblivion. The aleatory production and disappearance of the simulacrum repeats that of the narrative itself, which, at its limits, sputters and finally dies. The narrative closes in the vicinity of aleatory chaos, just as it began in an encounter with *hasard* before a roulette wheel in a gambling house at the Palais-Royal. The epilogue, an afterthought, is thus directly related to the problem of chance raised in my analysis and reproduces once again the inextricable intermingling of chance and order always present in Balzac's universe, functioning, in fact, as a major characterizing element of that universe.

Tempest in a Teapot?

When René Thom published an article in *Le Débat* in 1980 in which he portrayed himself as an avowed Laplacean who affirmed that there was no science without a belief in determinism, he touched off a lively debate possessing all the characteristics of the typical Parisian intellectual joust, in which the wit of the various players matched the passion of the positions they assumed.[1] Because certain researchers in the French tradition have recently been particularly interested in the notion of the aleatory, both in scientific and in epistemological terms, Thom's article elicited a series of impassioned written responses.[2] The exchange of ideas that took place proved beyond a shadow of a doubt that the question of the relation between chance and determinism remained in 1980 as difficult and intractable as it has always been. The confrontation produced in the pages of *Le Débat* is of interest even for the nonscientist and nonmathematician, because it demonstrates what Cournot (among many others) clearly realized in his work on chance, namely, that the problem of chance and determinism cannot be solved by science or mathematics alone—it is a deeper, philosophical question. As a fitting closure to my own thoughts set forth here,

I should like to look briefly at some of the important points brought out by three of the main participants of the discussion in question.

Thom, a mathematician, decries the appearance of the notions of noise and chance in science, because from his perspective such notions are simply indefinable. The best approximation one can give of randomness is, of necessity, negative. If that which is random is by definition that which cannot be reduced to regularity and rule, then the random is unknowable. To be outside the realm of regularity and rule is to be outside that of knowledge itself: "A random process is one which cannot be simulated by any mechanism, nor described by any formalism."[3] Such phenomena are of no interest to the scientist. Thom goes further, however, and makes a stronger claim, which becomes an essential credo for a scientist in his mold. Not only is science not interested in what may escape its purview, the scientist from the outset assumes what Thom calls an optimistic stance and operates under the presumption that nothing in nature fits into the category of the unknowable. The philosopher may leave the question of whether or not an essential chance exists in suspense, but as for the scholar-scientist, Thom maintains, "it is for him an obligation of principle—under pain of internal contradiction—to adopt an optimistic position and to postulate that nothing, in nature, is unknowable *a priori*" (p.12).

Without going into detail about Thom's attempt to demonstrate how the deterministic explanation of phenomena is always the best one, I must say that the implications of his strongest claim, namely, to be a scientist one must be a determinist, are rather far-reaching. Not the least of those implications is that he sets himself up as a high priest of the scientific church, with the power to excommunicate on the basis of a single litmus test. He leaves himself an easy way of disqualifying anyone who does not pass the test and thus of refusing to grant serious attention to the arguments of those who, by formation, are not a part of the scientific establishment. The more fundamental question lies elsewhere, however, for by maintaining that scientists must postulate a nature constructed in a deterministic fashion, Thom engages in an act of faith as much as his adversaries do. To maintain that randomness exists is to believe in unknowable and thus unprovable phenomena. But the opposite position is no more logically tenable, for there can be no more definitive proof of the deterministic organization of nature than of the contrary, and, consequently, the determinists' ultimate speculation plunges as much into the unknown as the indeterminists' beliefs. Thom accuses indeterminists of appealing to chance as "a secular substitute for divine finality" (p.12), while he conveniently forgets a point made by Karl Popper, who reminds readers of *The Open Universe* that "the idea of determinism is of religious origin . . . connected with ideas of divine omnipotence" (p.5).

In this vein, it is more than a little ironic to find Thom firing a parting shot against French epistemology in the last paragraph of his essay by lamenting the absence of a French Karl Popper. He launches into a criticism of the present scene in French epistemology and attempts to suggest why things are in such a sad state. The culprit must be Edmund Husserl, Martin Heidegger, or Gaston Bachelard, but, in any case, the true inspiration in such studies has been lost. The next step in the argument is to cite Kuhn and Popper as examples without peer in France. The reference to Popper is self-defeating for Thom, nonetheless, because however rigorous Popper's thought may seem (to Thom) when compared with the French epistemologists' efforts, Popper remains one modern thinker who has addressed the Laplacean deterministic claim directly and carefully—and found it wanting. The most fundamental argument Popper brings to bear against the Laplacean formulation is "that the burden of proof [for scientific determinism] rests upon the shoulders of the determinist" (p.27). The reasons furnished for this assertion are worth considering for a moment. There are four: (1) "unsophisticated common sense favours the view that there are . . . events which are more predictable, and events which are less predictable"; (2) "there is a *prima facie* case for the view that organisms are less predetermined and predictable than at least some simpler systems"; (3) "if determinism is true, it should in principle be possible for a physicist or a physiologist who knows nothing of music to predict, by study-ing Mozart's brain, the spots on the paper where he will put down his pen. . . . [This appears] to me intuitively absurd"; and, finally, (4) "indeterminism, which asserts that there exists *at least one* event that is not predetermined, or predictable, is clearly a weaker asser-tion than 'scientific' determinism, which asserts that all events are in principle predictable" (pp.28–29). The point of the first three rea-sons is that common sense lobbies against the strongest form of the determinists' claim, and if indeed scientists want to go against com-mon sense, it is up to them to provide sufficiently convincing proof for taking such a step. The operational success of science in a gen-eral way cannot qualify as sufficient proof. The fourth argument for maintaining that determinists must first prove their case to indeter-minists is logical in nature: the stronger claim always requires the strongest proof, a proof whose force exceeds what is required if one is content to assert a weaker claim. It is thus determinists' respon-sibility to convince us that we must take the step toward their strong formulation. Contrary to Popper, Thom presents his case as if the determinist belief were a matter of common sense and the eas-iest to accept, in other words, as if indeterminists were incapable of proving their case. This is surely an un-Popperian way of present-ing the problem—Thom can find little solace in Popper against the "artistic fuzziness" of French epistemology.

Thom's assertions, presented in a polemical manner, are calcu-lated to provoke polemical responses. One of the most measured and, I think, most direct comes from Henri Atlan.[4] Atlan imme-diately addresses the question of belief in an *essential* chance, agree-ing with Thom that such a belief can only be metaphysical. In prin-ciple, science must not proceed on the assumption that there are things unknowable in the universe. This shared perspective does not, however, lead necessarily to Thom's conclusion, namely, that the universe must be understood as fully deterministic. Atlan asks, "Why must one believe *a priori* in an essential determinism? Such a belief, no less than the other, poses problems for the possibilities of knowledge" (p.43). Not the least of the problems at stake is that the assertion of absolute determinism amounts to a denial of the potential for the *new* in nature. It is no doubt true that positing essential chance poses immediate difficulties for any epistemology, but the reduction of chance to ignorance ("an illusory effect of our ignorance of a hidden determinism" [p.44]) is not a better solution, for it has the effect of transforming the universe into "an immense tautology" (p.44).[5] Not only epistemologically and metaphysically, but also operationally, one solution does not seem better than the other, if the aim of researchers is, in fact, to be as open as possible to what the universe offers in the absence of complete knowledge on our part. What Atlan ultimately proposes is that scientists should not opt a priori for either position but should instead espouse the richest operational position in each specific experimental situation: "On the one hand to posit, whenever possible, an *a priori* infinite possibility for knowledge as implied by the postulate of chance through ignorance. . . . On the other hand and at the same time, to take time, the unexpected, and the new seriously each time that we experience them. . . . This attitude thus amounts to refusing a choice between such postulates insofar as they imply closure" (p.44). Certain recent advances in chaos theory provide pertinent examples of cases where the intermingling of chance and order is so fine that any attempt to eliminate noise and disorder from the experimental structure leads to eliminating the possibility of perceiving and revealing those interactions.[6] Scientists will always be condemned to live in the space between these two positions, unless they believe, of course, that human beings are ultimately capable of discovering the full secret of the structure of the universe (provided they first believe there is such a secret).

Edgar Morin's response to Thom's contentions takes a different tack.[7] Not trained in the scientific laboratory, Morin, supposedly lacking the proper tools for formalization, is precisely the type of thinker who seems to be anathema for Thom. Morin, however, formulates the problem at issue in terms that Thom refuses to consider. Unlike the deterministic point of view, he argues, an attempt to deal with chance raises a question that is more or less ignored if one accepts the Laplacean postulate, namely, the question of the relation between the human mind and the universe: "The problem is this: does the impossibility of eliminating chance derive from a weakness in the means and resources of the human mind, from its ignorance, which prevent it from recognizing the determinism masquerading behind apparent happenstance? . . . Or instead does it not convey the inadequacy of algorithmicization, of formalization, of logic faced with the complex richness of what is real? Perhaps . . . it is fundamentally impossible to totally idealize and rationalize the universe. *It just might be richer than the mind*" (p.28). The first part of Morin's question is classical in this context, but the suggestive formulation of the second part furnishes the outlines of an approach to the universe that would perhaps be less autocratic and dominating than the deterministic attitude. For it is clear that there is a moral issue involved in the deterministic approach which is masked by the affected ethical tone employed by Thom in his arguments. I recall here the manner in which Thom couches the imperative of the deterministic postulate: "it is an obligation of principle." But the moral problem at stake lies elsewhere: to believe that the world is deterministic in nature is to postulate that it is a system in principle fully knowable, and our eventual knowledge of it will allow the human mind to dominate the universe down to its most secret recesses. This approach assumes that nature is a kind of stupid machine, as Prigogine and Stengers claim in *La Nouvelle Alliance*: "One could even say that [classical science] was constituted against nature, since it denied complexity and becoming in the name of an eternal and knowable world ruled by a small number of simple and immutable laws. . . . A large number of phenomena obey simple, mathematical laws. But given this situation, science seemed *to show* that nature is only a subservient automaton" (pp.14–15). The deterministic approach leads to an ideology of domination, Morin remarks in "Beyond Determinism," "and one winds up with a form of diaphor-rhetic idealism: whatever cannot be formalized does not have the right to exist" (p.29).

It must be said here that Thom does not totally ignore the political and sociological problem of domination that the present technocratic establishment entails. In a suggestive observation concerning the existence of experts, he argues that they are able to become influential not because they possess a certain knowledge but because they are called upon to negotiate with conditions of randomness. To those who would look for relief from the power of technocrats by appealing to chance as a means of undermining it, Thom responds, "The effective power of experts is founded on the existence of risk, of randomness, rather than on its absence. All theoretical progress which eliminates or diminishes this 'aura of random risk' is of a nature to restrict the power of experts, since the domain of competence of individual expertise is by just that much diminished. Determinism, when it is scientific, that is to say accessible to all, and theoretically intelligible in theory to all, is then an instrument of reason."[8] The argument is seductive, but it flies in the face of historical analyses of the rise of "expertise" in political and social affairs. The first self-proclaimed governmental experts, the fledgling statisticians of the nineteenth century, believed that they had identified regularities, better yet, that they had discovered immutable certainties, and therefore that they could intervene in the social arena to manipulate situations by appealing to those certainties. Population eugenics, for example, was born of this faith.[9] Technocrats may not be the same thing as these early statisticians, but their intervention is not without relation to a belief in the certainty of the knowledge they possess. If they succeed, it would seem that they could only enhance their power, not diminish it; that is, if they prove the regularities they claim, they would seem to appear even more invincible. Perhaps more important, Thom sidesteps the issue of humankind's relationship with nature in these remarks and overlooks the fact that the very ideology of domination which fuels the bureaucratic-technocratic phenomenon may well be modeled upon the autocratic manner in which classical science approached natural phenomena. For technocrats, society functions like an automaton just as nature supposedly does.

A science that does not proceed from the dogma of determinism is a science that does not position the observer as a distant overseer of a stark, lunar landscape, where everything is white or black, geometrically laid out in monotonously straight lines, but produces instead an observer attentive to the multiple, complex, and fragmentary nature of phenomena. This approach demands a new kind of relation of man to nature, a relation Prigogine and Stengers have termed the "new alliance." Morin gives his own description of what this alliance might entail:

Thought is not only knowledge/detection of constancies, regularities, "laws" present and acting in nature. It is also strategy, and as with any strategy, it must not only make maximum use of its knowledge of order, but also confront uncertainty, randomness, that is, the zones of indeterminability and unpredictability that it encounters in reality; it must work in spite of uncertainty, capitalize on it, utilize randomness, use ruse on adversity. In this sense, it is uncertainty and ambiguity, not certainty and univocality, that stimulate the development of intelligence. (p.34)

The reader can recognize in Morin's description what, following de Certeau, I have consistently called tactic throughout this study. To be attentive to those moments when knowledge is lacking, whether it be in an essential or simply in a temporary way, to meet circumstances and to be capable of making something of them, such would be the type of attitude which would grant a modicum of respect to the richness of the world.

Morin's approach to the problem has the advantage of drawing attention to the real complexities of the universe: these cannot be located definitively either on the side of order or on the side of disorder and the random. Instead, the intricacy of natural phenomena is composed of an interaction between the two, and their points of juncture lead to the occurrence of the new, to fluctuations, to bifurcations. At the limits between order and disorder the truly interesting phenomena, those that are thought provoking and rich in potential knowledge, reveal themselves: "There is no hierarchy in either direction between the 'underlying deterministic dynamism' that models the statistics of fluctuations and the 'triggering fluctuation.' It is a question of the indispensable complementarity of two realities of different order indispensable for conceptualizing the appearance of new forms, organizations, structures" (p.30). No doubt this formulation is somewhat vague and lacks the necessary formalization to make it operationally useful, but it brings home an important point not to be overlooked by the reader who has followed my argument in this study or by me. The title of this book, *Circumstances: Chance in the Literary Text,* establishes an apparent bias from the very inception of the argument deployed therein. My analysis was and is meant to be a meditation on certain phenomena which appear in the most orderly of moments to disrupt, trouble, at times even destroy, the methodical, rational, all-too-tidy description of the unfurling of worldly events proposed by the novelist. Each time aleatory elements appear, they do so in some combination with orderly elements, such that the chance event would be imperceptible in itself without order. But the opposite could and must also be said: order itself is imperceptible in the absence of the aleatory, the nonordered. This is the case for Fabrice on the road to Parma, for Gina as she plays her commedia dell'arte role, for Auguste de Maulincourt as he strolls down the streets of Paris, for Raphaël de Valentin as he throws down his bet on the roulette table. My purpose was to draw attention to events that call order into question and therefore suggest complexity beyond the apparent controlled and formal structures of the realist text. It has become clear in the course of my argument that such events occur at limits, frontiers, and intermediate spaces where order and disorder are inextricably intermingled. The claim that there is an essential chance should probably be tempered in favor of a formulation more like Morin's, namely, that the universe is composed of a combination of orderly and disorderly phenomena and that the place where such phenomena meet is something like the moment of contingency which is the present. In a new article appearing in the 1990 reissue of the texts published by *Le Débat* concerning the question of determinism, Ivar Ekeland reminds the reader of the significance of the first sentence of Wittgenstein's *Tractatus*: "Die Welt ist alles, was der Fall ist."[10] This statement may be translated something like the following: the world is everything which is the case. On the condition, of course, that the resonances of the noun *Fall* not be forgotten, namely, its fundamental connection with the notion of chance. The interface between "a *model* functioning according to its own internal logic, deterministic in nature, [and] the *world* [which] maintains an irreducible portion of contingence" is where complexities linked to chance can be located, Ekeland maintains (p.170; my emphasis). The realist novel as written by Balzac and Stendhal, in its struggle to formalize lived experience, offers something like an image of such a complexity, one that should under no circumstances be ignored.

Notes

INTRODUCTION

1. Cornelius Castoriadis, *L'Institution imaginaire de la société* (Paris: Seuil, 1975), p.59. This and all other translations from the French are my own, unless otherwise indicated.

2. Honoré de Balzac, *La Comédie humaine,* ed. Pierre-George Castex, 12 vols. (Paris: Gallimard, 1976–81), 1:11–12. Subsequent references to Balzac's work will be to this edition unless otherwise stated.

3. This statement occurs in a justification of fortune-telling and thus links causal explanation to superstition. I take up this problem in my discussion of Stendhal's *Lucien Leuwen* in chapter 2.

4. This ease is solely methodological, of course, because knowledge always remains incomplete, and the historian or novelist can never pretend to synthesize the totality of the events he or she is studying.

5. Castoriadis, *L'Institution,* p.61.

6. Anatol Rapoport, Introduction to *On War,* by Carl von Clausewitz, ed. Anatol Rapoport (London: Penguin Books, 1968), p.13.

7. Carl von Clausewitz, *On War,* ed. and trans. Michael Howard and Peter Paret (Princeton: Princeton University Press, 1976), p.128. Quotations from Clausewitz's text come from this edition.

8. Michel Serres, *Feux et signaux de brume: Zola* (Paris: Grasset, 1975), p.16.

9. For a recent thorough and very suggestive discussion of the relation between science and literature—and a plea for a more complex and realistic definition of scientific activity—see Paisley Livingston, *Literary Knowledge: Humanistic Inquiry and the Philosophy of Science* (Ithaca: Cornell University Press, 1988).

10. James Gleick, *Chaos: Making a New Science* (New York: Viking, 1987). See also Katherine Hayles, *Chaos Bound: Orderly Disorder in Contemporary Literature and Science* (Ithaca: Cornell University Press, 1990), for an argument relating the development of chaos theory to certain developments in literature.

11. Marcel Détienne and Jean-Pierre Vernant, *Les Ruses de l'intelligence: La Mètis des Grecs* (Paris: Flammarion, 1974).

12. See Lorraine Daston, *Classical Probability in the Enlightenment* (Princeton: Princeton University Press, 1988), for an interesting discussion of these matters from the perspective of intellectual history.

CHAPTER ONE: Tactics For Auspicious Occasions

1. Stendhal, *La Chartreuse de Parme,* in *Romans et nouvelles,* ed. Henri Martineau, 2 vols. (Paris: Gallimard, 1952), 2:181. Further references will be to this edition.

2. Much attention has regularly been called to Fabrice's near-fetishistic attachment to his genealogy, most recently in an article by Kurt Ringger entitled " 'Chronique Valserra' et 'Commedia dell'arte' dans *La Chartreuse de Parme,*" in *Stendhal: L'écrivain, la société, le pouvoir,* ed. Philippe Berthier (Presses Universitaires de Grenoble, 1984), pp.303–11.

3. These two categories of action are fundamental to Clausewitz's analysis in *On War* also, as I maintained earlier.

4. Michel de Certeau, *L'Invention du quotidien I: Arts de faire* (Paris: Union Générale d'Editions, 1980), p.85.

5. Baltasar Gracián y Morales, *L'Homme de cour,* trans. Amelot de la Houssaie (Paris: Editions Champ Libre, 1980), pp.32, 23.

6. Clément Rosset, *Logique du pire* (Paris: PUF, 1971), pp.87–88.

7. Sarah Kofman, *Comment s'en sortir?* (Paris: Galilée, 1983), pp.19–20. See also Détienne and Vernant, *Les Ruses de l'intelligence,* pp.201ff.

Kofman's work takes as its starting point the detailed and intelligent study by Détienne and Vernant.

8. Plato, *Theaetetus,* trans. Benjamin Jowett, *Great Books of the Western World* (Chicago: Encyclopedia Britannica, 1952), 7:544.

9. Although Fabrice does not specify the Greek text alluded to here, as my discussion shows, the Bellerophon story is a persuasive choice. See Homer, *The Iliad,* 6.160 ff. Briefly stated, the story of Bellerophon goes as follows: After murdering his own brother, Bellerophon, son of Glaucus, flees to the kingdom of Proetus. Proetus's wife, Anteia, falls in love with him. When he does not return her advances, she goes to her husband and accuses Bellerophon of having tried to seduce her. Afraid of provoking the vengeance of the Furies if he kills Bellerophon (who is a suppliant), Proetus sends him to Anteia's father, Iobates, with a sealed letter requesting that Iobates do away with him. When Iobates reads the letter, he too is unwilling to risk the vengeance of the Furies and decides to send Bellerophon out on a series of risky undertakings, believing he will be killed. The confrontation with the Chimaera is the first of those undertakings.

10. In fact, before taking on the Chimaera, Bellerophon must tame Pegasus and can do so only with the help of Athena's technical prowess and ruse (*metis*)—she invents and gives him the first bit in order to bridle the high-spirited animal. See Détienne and Vernant, *Les Ruses de l'intelligence,* pp.178–92. More generally, in the theft scene analyzed earlier, Fabrice, like Bellerophon, is involved in a horse story. I would recall here that Fabrice's theft of the horse on the road back to Parma begins when he seizes its bridle, thereby immobilizing the animal and the valet charged with leading it.

11. On the semantic network bringing together the concepts of falling and throwing in their relationship with chance, see the suggestive lecture by Jacques Derrida entitled "Mes Chances," in *Taking Chances: Derrida, Psychoanalysis, and Literature,* ed. Joseph A. Smith and William Kerrigan (Baltimore: Johns Hopkins University Press, 1984), pp.1–32, as well as my next chapter.

12. Kofman, *Comment s'en sortir?* p.46.

13. Louis Marin, *Le Récit est un piège* (Paris: Minuit, 1978), pp.61–62.

14. See, for example, Jacques Donzelot, *The Policing of Families,* trans. Robert Hurley (New York: Pantheon Books, 1979).

15. It is interesting to recall here that Fabrice meets Giletti by accident,

i.e., by chance, on a road near a frontier in much the same way he crossed paths with the valet in the episode discussed earlier—and that this encounter is what leads to Giletti's death and a fateful turn in Fabrice's destiny. But, then again, fortunate (or unfortunate) encounters on roads are a specialty of his—he meets Clélia in much the same way at the beginning of the novel and the helpful vivandière at Waterloo as well. I shall return to this subject later.

16. The expression "struck by lightning," normally rather trite in such contexts, takes on a certain nonhabitual significance here, given the chance nature of the sudden potential for action Gina discovers. Just where and when lightning is going to strike is perhaps the most aleatory problem of all.

17. Jacques Lacan, "Le Séminaire sur 'La Lettre volée,' " in *Ecrits,* Collection Points (Paris: Seuil, 1966), 1:19–75. Indeed, as Laplace and his contemporaries marveled around the time when Stendhal was writing, very nearly the same number of letters were lost in Paris every year. This fact suggested regularity in a phenomenon that appeared superficially to be the result of many random causes and was something that pushed probability thinkers during the first half of the nineteenth century toward the notion of stability in large numbers: "In Paris, the number of births every year is nearly the same; and I have heard that in the post office, in ordinary times, the number of letters ending up in the dead letter box because of faulty addresses changes little each year" (Pierre Simon de Laplace, *Essai philosophique sur les probabilités* [Paris: Courcier, 1814], p.42).

18. In the following discussion, I shall be using both the French text and the English translation of de Certeau's critique of *Surveiller et punir,* because the two do not always correspond exactly. The texts in question are the fourth chapter of *L'Invention du quotidien,* pp.101–23 (also devoted to a discussion of Pierre Bourdieu), and the chapter entitled "Micro-techniques and Panoptic Discourse: A Quid pro Quo," in Michel de Certeau, *Heterologies: Discourse on the Other,* trans. Brian Massumi (Minneapolis: University of Minnesota Press, 1986), pp.185–92.

19. De Certeau, *L'Invention du quotidien,* p.101.

20. De Certeau, *Heterologies,* p.186.

21. De Certeau, *L'Invention du quotidien,* p.103.

22. De Certeau, *Heterologies,* p.188.

23. De Certeau, *L'Invention du quotidien,* p.127–28.

24. De Certeau, *Heterologies,* p.189–90.

25. Ibid., p.191. De Certeau is not the only reader of Foucault to have targeted Foucault's style. See Jean Baudrillard, *Oublier Foucault* (Paris: Galilée, 1977). Baudrillard is considerably less positive in his evaluation of the effects of that style.

26. De Certeau, *Heterologies,* p.192.

27. Michel Serres, *Hermès I: La Communication* (Paris: Minuit, 1968), pp.11–20.

28. Ferdinand de Saussure, *Cours de linguistique générale,* ed. Tullio de Mauro (Paris: Payot, 1975), pp.125–27.

29. The strategic clash at stake here was simply not pertinent in Saussure's treatment of the game.

CHAPTER TWO: The Encounter, the Fall, and Superstition

1. Maurice Blanchot, *L'Entretien infini* (Paris: Gallimard, 1969), p.608.

2. The fact that Fabrice is looking at him down the barrel of a cocked pistol is not without significance. The sword equals the pen in this instance.

3. Fabrice's affinity with Gina is clear in this context. He also excels in situations in which he must improvise within the context of the social and political comedy of Parma. Witness his first encounter with the prince, during which he deftly sidesteps all the traps laid for him and leaves the prince comparing his perspicacity to Gina's: "Zounds! . . . This is a shrewd character, he has Sanseverina's wit" (2:146).

4. See, for example, Michel Crouzet, "Jeu de la vérité et vérité du jeu dans *Lucien Leuwen,*" in *Quatre études sur* Lucien Leuwen (Paris: SEDES, 1985), pp.5–26, or John West Sooby, "La société et le jeu dans *Le Rouge et le noir,*" in *Stendhal: L'Écrivain, la société, le pouvoir,* ed. Philippe Berthier (Grenoble: Presses Universitaires de Grenoble, 1984), pp.99–116.

5. J. Bonitzer, *Philosophie du hasard* (Paris: Editions Sociales, 1984), p.56, n.19.

6. Détienne and Vernant, *Les Ruses de l'intelligence.*

7. Geneviève Even-Granboulan, *Action et raison* (Paris: Klincksieck, 1986), p.74.

8. Roger Caillois, *Les Jeux et les hommes* (Paris: Gallimard, 1967), pp.14–16.

9. Just as the governor of the fortress to whom Vespasien del Dongo

presents himself reads the duke's letter as something other than what was intended.

10. Our own first meeting with Fabrice on the road back to Parma already made this fact abundantly clear.

11. Henri Bergson, *Les Deux Sources de la morale et de la religion,* in *Oeuvres* (Paris: PUF, 1970), p.1100. Bergson uses the story to argue for a subjective interpretation of chance. A variation of the story appears in Jacques Monod, *Le Hasard et la nécessité* (Paris: Seuil, 1970), p.149, as an argument in favor of an objective interpretation of chance. Although neither Bergson nor Monod refers to Cournot, it is not impossible that the story might be a variation on similar situations outlined by Cournot. See J. Bonitzer, *La Philosophie du hasard,* (Paris: Editions Sociales, 1984), p.66, n.1. In any case, even though neither of our two authors makes mention of Cournot, the incident they construct is based implicitly on Cournot's theory of chance. Two of Antoine Auguste Cournot's works in particular deal with questions of chance: *Exposition de la théorie des chances et des probabilités* (Paris: Librairie Hachette, 1843), and *An Essay on the Foundations of Our Knowledge,* trans. Merritt H. Moore (New York: Liberal Arts Press, 1956). The latter work dates originally from 1851.

12. Luc Ferry and Alain Renaut, *Système et Critique: Essais sur la critique de la raison dans la philosophie contemporaine* (Brussels: Ousia, 1984), p.137.

13. Blanchot, *L'Entretien infini,* pp.608–609.

14. Chance meetings always seem to conjure up images of bloody accidents. One of Cournot's examples in *An Essay on the Foundations of Our Knowledge* involves a train accident.

15. Mme de Lafayette, *La Princesse de Montpensier,* in *Romans et nouvelles,* ed. Emile Magne (Paris: Garnier, 1961), p.10.

16. Quoted in Roland Barthes, *Michelet* (Paris: Seuil, 1975), p.61.

17. See Michel Guérin, *La Politique de Stendhal* (Paris: PUF, 1982).

18. The various negotiations concerning horses which segment the whole Waterloo episode in an almost rhythmic manner (Fabrice buys three different horses and steals or buys a fourth before his adventure concludes) already prepare the reader for the "negotiation" which takes place on the road to Parma and which is so central to the last sections of the novel's first book.

19. Michel Serres, "Vie, information, deuxième principe," in *Hermès III: La Traduction* (Paris: Minuit, 1974), p.65.

20. We have, in fact, already seen that the chess board can be a vehicle

for the description of a network whose complexity defies any attempt to reduce it to easy geometry.

21. Let us not forget here that the description of the ride on the battlefield explicitly invokes the clouds of smoke which screen off visual perception.

22. Michel Serres, *La Naissance de la physique dans le texte de Lucrèce: Fleuves et turbulences* (Paris: Minuit, 1977), p.64.

23. Serres, *Hermès III,* pp.69–70.

24. If not in this case, later in the novel Julien will have a chance to fall from his horse repeatedly, and this act will be one of the reasons for his ability to fascinate Mathilde de la Mole.

25. Rosset, *Logique du pire,* p.75.

26. Derrida, "Mes Chances," p.8.

27. Rosset, *Logique du pire,* p.21.

28. Sigmund Freud, *The Psychopathology of Everyday Life,* trans. Alan Tyson, ed. James Strachey (New York: Norton, 1965), p.2.

29. Derrida makes much of the linguistic constellation containing the words "address," the French *adresse* and *maladresse,* and the German *Schiksal* as they play off against each other in the passage in question ("Mes Chances," pp.21–25). All of this to remind the reader that "Mes Chances" is a continuation of the debate with Lacan and psychoanalysis in general concerning destinations, a discussion which began with Derrida's criticism of Lacan's reading of Poe's "The Purloined Letter." See *La Carte postale* (Paris: Flammarion, 1980), pp.441–524.

30. Derrida, "Mes Chances," pp.22–23.

31. One should keep in mind that the notion of projection is an extremely problematic one, as Derrida's reflections on the question of the direction of the atomic flux in the texts of the Greek atomists show. "To project" means to throw out in front of one, well within one's field of vision, and therefore to avoid the fall, the arrival from above of something unexpected.

32. François Roustang, ... *Elle ne le lâche plus* (Paris: Minuit, 1980), pp.71–101.

33. Sigmund Freud, "The 'Uncanny,' " in *Studies in Parapsychology,* (New York: Collier Books, 1963), p.39.

34. See, for example, Frank J. Sulloway, *Freud, Biologist of the Mind: Beyond the Psychoanalytic Legend* (New York: Basic Books, 1979), pp.73–75.

35. Here one must recall the tight bond of understanding existing between Fabrice and Blanès through their belief in astrological and superstitious signs: they communicate almost without speaking in a unity not unrelated to mental telepathy.

CHAPTER THREE: The Demon, the Police, and Cacophony

1. Ilya Prigogine and Isabelle Stengers, *La Nouvelle Alliance: Métamorphose de la science* (Paris: Gallimard, 1979), pp.76–77.

2. In *La Nouvelle Alliance* Prigogine and Stengers have argued persuasively that the new science of the nineteenth century, the science of heat (thermodynamics), got its start in technological circles rather than in scientific circles as a result of the stultifying officialization of the French scientific establishment.

3. The effect of the *grandes écoles* is certainly debatable. In *La Nouvelle Alliance* Prigogine and Stengers suggest that the new organization of higher education in France had stifling consequences for scientific invention and creativity. Michel Serres agrees: "As soon as the so-called French School triumphed at the beginning of the last century, at Polytechnique and elsewhere, as soon as its results and methods began to be taught to a percentage of people chosen by those in power, its fecundity was finished and decadence followed swiftly" (*Hermès V: Le Passage du nord-ouest* [Paris: Minuit, 1980], p.142).

4. Serres, *Hermes III*, p.163.

5. "In contrast to the so-called Baconian sciences—including the early investigations of chemical reactions, electricity and magnetism, of life, and of the earth—the Newtonian tradition of mechanics, astronomy, optics, and, later, theories of heat, electricity and magnetism did not rely predominantly on an extended qualitative study of the phenomena, but rather on mathematical theory and experiment or observation that was informed by that theory" (Gerd Gigerenzer, Zeno Swijtink, Theodore Porter, Lorraine Daston, John Beatty, and Lorenz Krüger, *The Empire of Chance: How Probability Changed Science and Everyday Life* [Cambridge: Cambridge University Press, 1989], p.169).

6. Pierre Simon de Laplace, *Essai philosophique sur les probabilités* (Paris: Courcier, 1814), p.2.

7. The phrase "in theory" is necessary here, for Laplace never believed that anyone could, in fact, know all there is to know about the universe.

8. Laplace, *Essai philosophique,* p.2. In his reference to the atomic level here, Laplace indirectly recalls the sustained quarrel between the Newtonians and the French atomists of the eighteenth century. Only when atomistic theories were effectively repressed was Newtonian theory able to triumph in France. Unlike the situation existing within Newtonian circles, chance was a fundamental element in the thought of the atomists, as it had been ever since the invention of atomistic theories in ancient philosophy. The defeat of the atomists was another expression of the denial of the place and importance of chance within scientific theory.

9. The argument proposing the demon is striking and rigorous enough to have provided the terms in which numerous later discussions of causality and chance have been couched: "The defenders as well as the attackers of the causality principle of classical physics seem to be agreed at least in this respect, that this picture may be taken as an adequate expression of the problem," maintains Ernst Cassirer in *Determinism and Indeterminism in Modern Physics: Historical and Systematic Studies of the Problem of Causality* (New Haven: Yale University Press, 1956), p.3. When Karl Popper sets out to discredit determinism, it is Laplace's formulation which he knows he must combat: "I regard such Laplacean determinism—confirmed as it may seem to be by the *prima facie* deterministic theories of physics, and by their marvellous success—as the most solid and serious difficulty in the way of an account of, and a defence of, human freedom, creativity, and responsibility. Certainly Laplace's strong clear statement of determinism, which goes beyond common sense and which also is deeply intertwined with the history of western science, is far superior to the loose formulation" (*The Open Universe: An Argument of Indeterminism* [Totowa, N.J.: Rowman and Littlefield, 1956], p.xx).

10. What has been loosely called chaos theory is specifically the study of *nonlinear* phenomena, which an approach based on continuity cannot properly conceptualize. See N. Katherine Hayles, *Chaos Bound: Orderly Disorder in Contemporary Literature and Science* (Ithaca: Cornell University Press, 1990), pp.11–15.

11. Antoine Augustin Cournot, *Exposition de la théorie des chances et des probabilités* (Paris: Librairie Hachette, 1843).

12. Antoine Augustin Cournot, *An Essay on the Foundations of Our Knowledge,* trans. Merritt H. Moore (New York: Liberal Arts Press, 1956), p.41. Originally published in French in 1851.

13. It should be remarked that Cournot's effort to redefine a space for chance occurrences is both a new and a very old gesture, for it is clearly related to the Aristotelian definition of chance. A glance at one of the best-known illustrations of a chance occurrence provided by Aristotle in the *Physics* reveals the affinities at stake: "Example: A man is engaged in collecting subscriptions for a feast. He would have gone to such and such a place for the purpose of getting the money, if he had known. He actually went there for another purpose, and it was only incidentally that he got his money by going there" (2.5.196b33–34). This ministory sounds almost like the opening scene of a narrative by Balzac; more specifically, it nearly reproduces the beginning of *Ferragus,* as we shall soon see.

14. See Peter Brooks, *The Melodramatic Imagination: Balzac, Henry James, Melodrama, and the Mode of Excess* (New Haven: Yale University Press, 1976), and Christopher Prendergast, *Balzac: Fiction and Melodrama* (New York: Holmes and Meier, 1978).

15. Prigogine and Stengers, *La Nouvelle Alliance,* p.90.

16. Present under various forms in texts by Foucault, Lacan, and Gilles Deleuze, and a central textual figure in the writing of Alain Robbe-Grillet and Michel Butor, the labyrinth represents the modern taste for playing with meaning and the law—without ever calling meaning fully into question, maintains Clément Rosset (*Le Réel: Traité de l'idiotie* [Paris: Minuit, 1977], p.14). Although meaning circulates in unexpected and very improbable ways within the labyrinth, provoking as it goes encounters one might never have envisioned, and although meaning becomes more or less impossible to locate under such conditions, its ultimate existence is not finally questioned. It is out there somewhere even though reaching it has become infinitely more problematic. Those who toy with the notion of the labyrinth have yet to face the radical experience of chance, an experience which demonstrates not that meaning is deferred, but that it is not there at all.

17. See chapter 4 for a discussion of the relation between *hasard* and *sort* in the French semantic field covering the notion of chance and for more detailed analysis of the relation between providence and chance.

18. For the reader unfamiliar with *Ferragus,* that mystery consists of several elements. Ferragus (alias Bourignard, alias Funcal) is an escaped criminal and the father of Mme Jules (and, one might add, a prototype of Balzac's famous Vautrin). Mme Jules's husband, Jules Desmarets, knows

nothing of this paternity nor does anyone else in his wife's entourage, and Mme Jules is attempting to conceal her relationship to her father until he can assume a false identity which will hide his criminal background and allow him to acknowledge and spend time with his daughter. Hence the danger created by Maulincourt's glimpse of her on a visit to her father.

19. Michel Serres, "The Origin of Language: Biology, Information Theory, and Thermodynamics," in Michel Serres, *Hermes: Literature, Philosophy, Science,* ed. Josué V. Harari and David F. Bell (Baltimore: Johns Hopkins Unversity Press, 1982), pp.77–78.

20. Serres draws a further conclusion in his argument which is unwarranted by information theory, namely, that living beings are structured such that as one moves from one level to a more englobing level in biological structures, the change that occurs at the border between levels functions as a rectifier which regularly transforms noise into information. One thus eventually reaches a level where the cumulative effect of these transformations is the creation of something like structures of signification. See Katherine Hayles, *Chaos Bound: Orderly Disorder in Contemporary Literature and Science* (Ithaca: Cornell University Press, 1990), pp.205–6, for a criticism of this conclusion.

21. One could easily read a novel like *Le Lys dans la vallée* in a similar manner. It need only be recalled that the story recounted by Félix de Vandenesse, for all its naive beauty, simple tone, and extolling of the virtues of untouched natural virginity, is nonetheless the result of a contract entered into with a correspondent who is to be checkmated by the effects of that very story. It is, in other words, just one more tactic in a sexual confrontation between Félix and Natalie de Manerville. Natalie brings Félix brutally back to the reality of the artifice in the final letter with which the story closes.

22. See Michel Serres, *La Naissance de la physique dans le texte de Lucrèce,* and *Hermès IV: La Distribution* (Paris: Minuit, 1977). It is worthwhile recalling that Sadi Carnot, the first in a line of theoreticians who would formulate the thermodynamic theory which was to contest classical mechanics, was Balzac's contemporary.

23. Henri Mitterand rightly calls attention to the fact that the narrator compares Ferragus's trajectory to the path of a small wooden ball (*le cochonnet*) used in a lawn bowling game in France: "This figure was walking in harmony with the *cochonnet,* a small ball which serves as a target and con-

stitutes the center of interest in the game. . . . One might have mistaken him for the fantastic genie of the *cochonnet*" (5:902). Comments Mitterand: "The trajectory of the *cochonnet* is the last of those which crisscross Paris and the narrative itself. It corresponds to nothing if not chance" ("Formes et fonctions de l'espace dans le récit: *Ferragus* de Balzac," in *Le Roman de Balzac: Recherches critiques, méthodes, lectures,* ed. Roland le Huenen and Paul Perron [Montreal: Marcel Didier, 1980], p.16). Mitterand's analysis of space in the novella is extremely valuable to anyone reflecting on such matters.

24. Cournot, *Exposition,* p.70.

25. Rosset, *Logique du pire*, p.72.

26. Prigogine's position on the question of chance has been roundly criticized by René Thom, the inventor of mathematical disaster theory. Moreover, Jacques Monod's *Chance and Necessity,* a popularized explanation of molecular biology in which a prominent position is given to chance in biological processes, was not well received by many scientists. See, for example, the collection of articles about this debate gathered in *SubStance* 12, no.3 (1983), to which I shall return in my conclusion.

27. Michel Serres, "Musique et bruit de fond," in *Hermès II: L'Interférence* (Paris: Minuit, 1972), pp.181–94.

28. The agitation of the body marvelously reproduces the motion of the cloud of notes that is at the origin of Gambara's music.

29. But didn't Fabrice del Dongo himself encounter a stochastic Lucretian state when he also had drunk too much?

30. An analysis of Balzac's *Le Chef d'oeuvre inconnu* along similar lines would be possible. One could well say that what Frenhofer is attempting to reproduce on canvas is the fluctuating cloud from which all color and line proceed. Thus Poussin and Porbus could not be more mistaken when they view the canvas and react in the same dumbfounded surprise which marked Marcosini's reaction to Gambara's *Mohamet* and when they decide that *nothing* is on the canvas. On the contrary, the potential for *everything* is there. For suggestions about the lines such an argument would follow, see Michel Serres, *Genèse* (Paris: Grasset, 1982).

CHAPTER FOUR: Balzac's Gamblers

1. Samuel Weber's *Unwrapping Balzac: A Reading of* La Peau de chagrin (Toronto: University of Toronto Press, 1979) contains a well-developed

reading of the scene in question and offers an explanation of the fascination it holds for the modern reader. Weber touches on the question of chance and its implications, however, only in passing.

2. See Gigerenzer et al., *The Empire of Chance,* p. 1, for example.

3. See ibid. and see Daston, *Classical Probability in the Enlightenment,* for recent discussion of these matters.

4. Rosset quotes from the Old French translation of the passage found in *Histoire générale des croisades: Guillaume de Tyr et ses continuateurs,* ed. M. Paulin (Paris: Didot, 1879), 1:229.

5. See my "Epigrams and Ministerial Eloquence: The War of Words in Balzac's *La Peau de chagrin, Nineteenth-Century French Studies* 15 (Spring, 1987): 252–64.

6. Unless the strategy outlined by the dealer is interpreted as one which aspires to prolong and multiply the experience of perdition.

7. The distinction Raphaël later expounds on between gambling in social gatherings and gambling in gaming houses is rather pharisaical, to say the least: "I threw myself into a whirlwind of pleasures, both empty and real at the same time. I gambled, won and lost, one after the other, enormous sums of money, but always at soirees, at friends' houses, never in gambling houses, for which I kept my saintly and original horror" (10:195). The least this remark proves is that he has given a lot of thought to the question of gambling. It hardly exonerates him from what appears more and more to be a repetitive habit.

8. Content with Raphaël's behavior during the evening at the duke of Navarreins's house, his father (unaware that Raphaël gambled) tells him with unintentional irony, "Now you are a man, *my child*" (10:125, Balzac's emphasis).

9. Weber, *Unwrapping Balzac,* p. 21.

10. In order to express the difference between biological need and cultural need, Lacan will invent the categories of need and desire. Marx (and Balzac also) use the category of need in a broader sense, encompassing parts of both Lacanian categories.

11. Weber, *Unwrapping Balzac,* p. 23.

12. André Orléan, "Hétérodoxie et incertitude," *Les Cahiers du CREA* 5 (September 1986): 247.

13. Emile Durkheim, *The Division of Labor in Society,* trans. George Simpson (New York: Free Press, 1933), p. 193.

14. Orléan, "Hétérodoxie et incertitude," pp.257–58.

15. J. M. Keynes, one of the fathers of orthodox liberal theory, is himself less inclined than his epigones to ignore the importance of such phenomena, as the following remarks concerning long-term expectation in investment markets attest: "The outstanding fact is the extreme precariousness of the basis of knowledge on which our estimates of prospective yield have to be made. Our knowledge of the factors which will govern the yield of an investment some years hence is usually very slight and often negligible. If we speak frankly, we have to admit that our basis of knowledge for estimating the yield ten years hence of the railway, a copper mine, a textile factory, the goodwill of a patent medicine, an Atlantic liner, a building in the City of London amounts to little and sometimes to nothing; or even five years hence. In fact, those who seriously attempt to make any such estimate are often so much in the minority that their behaviour does not govern the market" (*The General Theory of Employment, Interest, and Money,* in *The Collected Writings of John Maynard Keynes* [London: Macmillan, 1973], 7:149–50). Keynes, unlike too many theoreticians of classical liberal orthodoxy, would not exclude a discussion of such matters from economic theory.

16. Orléan, "Hétérodoxie et incertitude," pp.266.

17. That Orléan's analysis rests on the mimetic theory developed by René Girard since *Deceit, Desire, and the Novel* (Baltimore: Johns Hopkins University Press, 1965) and *Violence and the Sacred* (Baltimore: Johns Hopkins University Press, 1977) goes almost without saying.

18. The mimetic hypothesis has inhabited orthodox liberal economic theory from the beginning for anyone willing to read carefully enough. Reference need only be made to the chapter of Keynes's *General Theory* from which I quoted above. In that chapter Keynes distinguishes between what he terms *speculation* and what he terms *enterprise* in the following manner: "If I may be allowed to appropriate the term *speculation* for the activity of forecasting the psychology of the market, and the term *enterprise* for the activity of forecasting the prospective yield of assets over their whole life, it is by no means always the case that speculation predominates over enterprise. As the organisation of investment markets improves, the risk of the predominance of speculation does, however, increase" (7:158). By "forecasting the psychology of the market" Keynes means quite simply the capacity to predict what the other will do in given situations, so that

one can foresee what types of mimetic crystallizations will occur.

19. The Italian's reasoning would go something like this: the young man looks desperate enough to want to lose. He must therefore know something about how to do it. I should thus bet the opposite way if I want to win. And in any case, even if the young man has no idea what he's doing, I won't be any worse off by giving it a try, because I have no other surer knowledge upon which to base my wager.

20. The conversation takes up ten pages in the text of the Pléiade edition.

21. Which is possible in piquet, to which Vautrin is alluding here.

22. I would remind the reader of the demise of the del Dongo family in *La Chartreuse de Parme* in the person of Fabrice's father, who inherits a fortress gained by someone else's ruse and is content to hide within its walls.

23. Later on during the scene, the *pas indécis* will be described as an *allure d'insouciance,* an insouciant gait, that is, without forethought or care.

24. See my remarks on Clausewitz in the Introduction and my commentary on military scenes in *La Chartreuse de Parme* and *Lucien Leuwen* in chapter 2.

25. See Serres, "Discours et parcours," in *Hermès IV,* pp.197–210.

26. See my *"La Chandelle verte* and the *fait divers,"* L'Esprit créateur, 24 (Winter 1984): 48–56, for a discussion of the significance of the *fait divers* as a modern journalistic phenomenon.

27. When Ida Gruget in *Ferragus* plans her own suicide by jumping in the river, she is careful to go beyond Saint-Cloud so that her body will not end up back in the morgue in Paris, just another number in the city's record keeping.

28. The confusion is due to the fact that the Arabic version of the inscription was an afterthought added to a later edition of the novel by Balzac, who asked a friend to provide the Arabic text. Balzac simply neglected to correct the word "Sanskrit" once the Arabic transcription was added.

29. That form was already present in the earliest edition of the novel. The Arabic text added later conforms with some difficulty to the typographical convention of the French original. I simply want to underline here the crucial nature of the typographical decision made by Balzac.

30. Diogenes Laertius, *Lives of the Philosophers,* trans. A. Robert Caponigri (Chicago: Henry Regnery, 1969), p.19.

31. I am thinking here of the series of consultations Raphaël arranges with the representatives of the most advanced scientific theories of his day.

1. René Thom, "Halte au hasard, silence au bruit," *Le Débat* 3 (1980). Thom's article and the ensuing responses by certain of the researchers targeted by "Halte au hasard" were gathered together under the title "Stop Chance! Silence Noise!" in *SubStance* 40 (1983). Since the *SubStance* issue is not only conveniently available but reproduces the debate in English translation, I will use it in the following discussion. The discussions appearing in *Le Débat* in 1980 have now been reissued in a volume which also contains new essays by the participants involved in the debate and which is entitled *La Querelle du déterminisme: Philosophie de la science aujourd'hui,* ed. Krzysztof Pomian (Paris: Gallimard, 1990).

2. Those publishing responses to Thom included Edgar Morin, Ilya Prigogine, Henri Atlan, Michel Serres, Antoine Danchin, Jean Largeault, and Claude Richard.

3. Thom, "Stop Chance! Silence Noise!," p.11.

4. Henri Atlan, "Metaphysical Postulates and Methods of Research," *SubStance* 40 (1983): 43–47.

5. The phrase was used as well by Prigogine and Stengers, *La Nouvelle Alliance.* See my reference to their work in chapter 3 above.

6. See Gleick, *Chaos: Making a New Science,* for some fascinating examples.

7. Edgar Morin, "Beyond Determinism: The Dialogue of Order and Disorder," *SubStance* 40 (1983): 22–35.

8. René Thom, "By Way of Conclusion," *SubStance* 40 (1983): 82–83.

9. See Gigerenzer et al., *The Empire of Chance,* and Ian Hacking, *The Taming of Chance* (Cambridge: Cambridge University Press, 1990).

10. Ivar Ekeland, "Le Roi Olav lançant les dés," in *La Querelle du déterminisme,* p.169.

Selected Bibliography

Aristotle. *Physics*. Trans. R. P. Hardie and R. K. Gaye. In *Great Books of the Western World*. Vol. 8. Chicago: Encyclopedia Britannica, 1952.

Atlan, Henri. "Metaphysical Postulates and Methods of Research." *SubStance* 40 (1983): 43–47.

Balzac, Honoré de. *La Comédie humaine*. Ed. Pierre-George Castex. 12 vols. Paris: Gallimard, 1976–81.

Barthes, Roland. *Michelet*. Paris: Seuil, 1975.

Baudrillard, Jean. *Oublier Foucault*. Paris: Galilée, 1977.

Bell, David. "*La Chandelle verte* and the *fait divers*." *L'Esprit créateur* 24 (Winter, 1984): 48–56.

———. "Epigrams and Ministerial Eloquence: The War of Words in Balzac's *La Peau de Chagrin*." *Nineteenth-Century French Studies* 15 (Spring, 1987): 252–64.

Bergson, Henri. *Les Deux Sources de la morale et de la religion*. In *Oeuvres*. Paris: PUF, 1970.

Blanchot, Maurice. *L'Entretien infini*. Paris: Gallimard, 1969.

Bonitzer, J. *La Philosophie du hasard*. Paris: Editions Sociales, 1984.

Brooks, Peter. *The Melodramatic Imagination: Balzac, Henry James, Melodrama, and the Mode of Excess*. New Haven: Yale University Press, 1976.

Callois, Roger. *Les Jeux et les hommes*. Paris: Gallimard, 1967.

Cassirer, Ernst. *Determinism and Indeterminism in Modern Physics: Historical and Systematic Studies of the Problem of Causality*. New Haven: Yale University Press, 1956.

Castoriadis, Cornelius. *L'Institution imaginaire de la société*. Paris: Seuil, 1975.

Certeau, Michel de. *Heterologies: Discourse on the Other*. Trans. Brian Massumi. Minneapolis: University of Minnesota Press, 1986.

———. *L'Invention du quotidien I: Arts de faire*. Paris: Union Générale d'Editions, 1980.

Clausewitz, Carl von. *On War*. Ed. and trans. Michael Howard and Peter Paret. Princeton: Princeton University Press, 1976.

Cournot, Antoine Auguste. *An Essay on the Foundations of Our Knowledge*. Trans. Merritt H. Moore. New York: Liberal Arts Press, 1956.

———. *Exposition de la théorie des chances et des probabilités*. Paris: Librairie Hachette, 1843.

Crouzet, Michel. *Stendhal: Quatre Études sur* Lucien Leuwen: *Le Jeu, l'or, l'orvietan, l'absolu*. Paris: SEDES/CDU, 1985.

Daston, Lorraine. *Classical Probability in the Enlightenment*. Princeton: Princeton University Press, 1988.

Derrida, Jacques. *La Carte postale*. Paris: Flammarion, 1980.

———. "Mes Chances." In *Taking Chances: Derrida, Psychoanalysis, and Literature*, ed. Joseph A. Smith and William Kerrigan. Baltimore: Johns Hopkins University Press, 1984.

Détienne, Marcel, and Jean-Pierre Vernant. *Les Ruses de l'intelligence: La Mètis des Grecs*. Paris: Flammarion, 1974.

Donzelot, Jacques. *The Policing of Families*. Trans. Robert Hurley. New York: Pantheon Books, 1979.

Durkheim, Emile. *The Division of Labor in Society*. Trans. George Simpson. New York: Free Press, 1933.

Ekeland, Ivar. "Le Roi Olav lançant les dés." In *La Querelle du déterminisme*. Ed. Krzysztof Pomian. Paris: Gallimard, 1990.

Evan-Granboulan, Geneviève. *Action et raison*. Paris: Klincksieck, 1986.

Ferry, Luc, and Alain Renaut. *Système et Critique: Essais sur la critique de la raison dans la philosophie contemporaine*. Brussels: Ousia, 1984.

Freud, Sigmund. *The Psychopathology of Everyday Life*. Trans. Alan Tyson. Ed. James Strachey. New York: Norton, 1965.

———. *Studies in Parapsychology*. New York: Collier Books, 1963.

Gigerenzer, Gerd, Zeno Swijtink, Theodore Porter, Lorraine Daston,

John Beatty, and Lorenz Krüger. *The Empire of Chance: How Probability Changed Science and Everyday Life*. Cambridge: Cambridge University Press, 1989.

Girard, René. *Deceit, Desire, and the Novel*. Trans. Yvonne Freccero. Baltimore: Johns Hopkins University Press, 1965.

————. *Violence and the Sacred*. Trans. Patrick Gregory. Baltimore: Johns Hopkins University Press, 1977.

Gleick, James. *Chaos: Making a New Science*. New York: Viking, 1987.

Gracián y Morales, Baltasar. *L'Homme de cour*. Trans. Amelot de la Houssaie. Paris: Editions Champ Libre, 1980.

Guérin, Michel. *La Politique de Stendhal*. Paris: PUF, 1982.

Hacking, Ian. *The Taming of Chance*. Cambridge: Cambridge University Press, 1990.

Hayles, Katherine. *Chaos Bound: Orderly Disorder in Contemporary Literature and Science*. Ithaca: Cornell University Press, 1990.

Keynes, J. M. *The General Theory of Employment, Interest, and Money*. In *The Collected Writings of John Maynard Keynes*. London: Macmillan, 1973.

Kofman, Sarah. *Comment s'en sortir?* Paris: Gallimard, 1983.

Lacan, Jacques. *Ecrits*. Paris: Seuil, 1966.

Laertius, Diogenes. *Lives of the Philosophers*. Trans. A. Robert Caponigri. Chicago: Henry Regnery, 1969.

Lafayette, Madame de. *La Princesse de Montpensier*. In *Romans et nouvelles*, ed. Emile Magne. Paris: Garnier, 1961.

Laplace, Pierre Simon de. *Essai philosophique sur les probabilités*. Paris: Courcier, 1814.

Livingston, Paisley. *Literary Knowledge: Humanistic Inquiry and the Philosophy of Science*. Ithaca: Cornell University Press, 1988.

Marin, Louis. *Le Récit est un piège*. Paris: Minuit, 1978.

Mitterand, Henri. "Formes et fonctions de l'espace dans le récit: *Ferragus* de Balzac." In *Le Roman de Balzac: Recherches critiques, méthodes, lectures*, ed. Roland le Huenen and Paul Perron. Montreal: Marcel Didier, 1980.

Monod, Jacques. *Le Hasard et la nécessité*. Paris: Seuil, 1970.

Morin, Edgar. "Beyond Determinism: The Dialogue of Order and Disorder." *SubStance* 40 (1983): 22–35.

————. *La Méthode*. 3 vols. Paris: Seuil, 1976–86.

Orléan, André. "Hétérodoxie et incertitude." In *Les Cahiers du* CREA 5 (September 1986): 247–75.

Paulin, M., ed. *Histoire générale des croisades: Guillaume de Tyr et ses continuateurs*. Paris: Didot, 1879.

Plato, *Theatetus*. Trans. Benjamin Jowett. In *Great Books of the Western World*, Vol. 7. Chicago: Encyclopedia Britannica, 1952.

Pomian, Krzysztof, ed. *La Querelle du déterminisme: Philosophie de la science aujourd'hui*. Paris: Gallimard, 1990.

Popper, Karl. *The Open Universe: An Argument for Indeterminism*. Totowa, N.J.: Rowman and Littlefield, 1956.

Prendergast, Christopher. *Balzac: Fiction and Melodrama*. New York: Holmes and Meier, 1978.

Prigogine, Ilya, and Isabelle Stengers. *La Nouvelle Alliance: Métamorphose de la science*. Paris: Gallimard, 1979.

Rapoport, Anatol. Introduction to *On War,* by Carl von Clausewitz, ed. Anatol Rapoport. London: Penguin Books, 1968.

Ringger, Kurt. " 'Chronique Valserra' et 'Comedia dell'arte' dans *La Chartreuse de Parme*." In *Stendhal: L'Écrivain, la société, le pouvoir,* ed. Philippe Berthier. Grenoble: Presses Universitaires de Grenoble, 1984.

Rosset, Clément. *Logique du pire: Eléments pour une philosophie tragique*. Paris: PUF, 1971.

———. *Le Réel: Traité de l'idiotie*. Paris: Minuit, 1977.

Roustang, François. . . .*Elle ne le lâche plus*. Paris: Minuit, 1980.

Salloway, Frank J. *Freud, Biologist of the Mind: Beyond the Psychoanalytic Legend*. New York: Basic Books, 1979.

Saussure, Ferdinand de. *Cours de linguistique générale*. Ed. Tullio de Mauro. Paris: Payot, 1975.

Serres, Michel. *Feux et Signaux de brume: Zola*. Paris: Grasset, 1975.

———. *Hermes: Literature, Philosophy, Science*. Ed. Josué V. Harari and David F. Bell. Baltimore: Johns Hopkins University Press, 1982.

———. *Genèse*. Paris: Grasset, 1982.

———. *Hermès I: La Communication*. Paris: Minuit, 1968.

———. *Hermès II: L'Interférence*. Paris: Minuit, 1972.

———. *Hermès III: La Traduction*. Paris: Minuit, 1974.

———. *Hermès IV: La Distribution*. Paris: Minuit, 1977.

———. *Hermès V: Le Passage du nord-ouest*. Paris: Minuit, 1980.

———. *La Naissance de la physique dans le texte de Lucrèce: Fleuves et turbulences*. Paris: Minuit, 1977.

Sooby, John West. "La Société et le jeu dans *Le Rouge et le noir*." In

Stendhal: l'écrivain, la société, le pouvoir, ed. Philippe Berthier. Grenoble: Presses Universitaires de Grenoble, 1984.

Stendhal. *Romans et nouvelles,* ed. Henri Martineau. Paris: Gallimard, 1952.

Thom, René. "By Way of Conclusion." In *SubStance* 40 (1983): 78–83.

———. "Halte au hasard, silence au bruit." In *La Querelle du déterminisme: Philosophie de la science aujourd'hui,* ed. Krzysztof Pomian. Paris: Gallimard, 1990.

———. "Stop Chance! Silence Noise!" *SubStance* 40 (1983): 11–21.

Weber, Samuel. *Unwrapping Balzac: A Reading of* La Peau de Chagrin. Toronto: University of Toronto Press, 1979.

Index

Fall, the: and clinamen, 95; in Derrida, 95; as equestrian event in Stendhal, 90. *See also* Clinamen; Epicurus; Lucretius

Fermat, Pierre de, 156

Ferry, Luc, 77

Flâneur: artist as, in Balzac, 137; definition of, in Balzac, 118–19; in *Gambara*, 143

Foucault, Michel, 50–54, 56, 58, 88

Freud, Sigmund, 100–108

Gambler: and mimetic behavior, 174; as speculator, 168; and worker in Marx, 168. *See also* Gambling

Gambling: and economic structures, 167; as speculation, 169. *See also* Gambler

Game: in *La Chartreuse de Parme*, 69–70; theory of, 71

Gleick, James, 11

Gracián y Morales, Baltasar, 24

Hasard: definition of, 156; and disorder, 158; etymology of, 157; relation of, to games of chance, 157; and silence, 159. *See also* Chance

Hegel, Georg Wilhelm Friedrich, 3, 77

Heidegger, Martin, 197

Husserl, Edmund, 197

Incipit, in Balzac, 118, 142

Influence, literary, 9–10

Information theory, in Balzacian narrative, 126

Interpretation: and mental telepathy in psychoanalysis, 106–7; relation of, to chance, 12, 99

Kairos: and encounter, 120; opposed to duration, 36; as tactical occasion, 24, 34. *See also* Circumstance; Encounter; Occasion

Kofman, Sarah, 31

Kuhn, Thomas, 14, 197

Labyrinth: in contemporary theory, 214n.16; structure of, in *Ferragus*, 121, 138

Lafayette, Madame de, 80

Laplace, Pierre Simon de, 8–9, 112–16, 139–41, 155, 186

Law, opposed to chance, 25, 94

Literature, and science, 11–12

Lucretius, 134–35, 140

Machiavelli, Nicolò, 24

Marin, Louis, 36

Marx, Karl, 167, 174

Melodrama, in Balzac, 117

Memory: relation of, to chance, 27; relation of, to tactic, 62

Mental telepathy, in psychoanalysis, 105–8

Metis, 13; in agonistic struggle, 72

Meyerbeer, Giacomo, 150

Michelet, Jules, 81

Mimetic behavior, in economic domain, 170, 173

Mimetic hypothesis, in orthodox liberal economic theory, 218n.18

Mimetic phenomena, unpredictability of, 173

Mimetic polarization: as agent of social cohesion, 172; in exchange economy, 172

Monod, Jacques, 85

Morgenstern, Oskar, 71

Morin, Edgar, 199–200, 202, 204

Mozart, Wolfgang Amadeus, 198

Music: as aleatory fluctuation, 148; and interpretation in *Gambara*, 147, 150; and noise, 147–48

Narrative: in *La Chartreuse de Parme*, 54; in *Lucien Leuwen*, 54; relation of, to tactics, 19, 55, 68; as theoretical tool, 54

Narrator: as *flâneur* in Balzac, 119;